ENVIRONMENT, DEVELOPMENT AND POLITICS IN INDIA

RENU KHATOR

UNIVERSITY
PRESS OF
AMERICA

Lanham • New York • London

Copyright © 1991 by

University Press of America®, Inc.
4720 Boston Way
Lanham, Maryland 20706

3 Henrietta Street
London WC2E 8LU England

Library of Congress Cataloging-in-Publication Data

Khator, Renu.
Environment, development, and politics in India / Renu Khator.
p.   cm.
Includes bibliographical references and index.
1. Environmental policy—India.   2. Environmental policy—
India—Citizen participation.   3. Pressure groups—India.
4. India—Economic policy—1966-   I. Title.
HC440.E5K43 1991
363.7'056'0954—dc20   90–29898 CIP

ISBN 0–8191–8189–7 (alk. paper)

The paper used in this publication meets the minimum requirements of
American National Standard for Information Sciences—Permanence
of Paper for Printed Library Materials, ANSI Z39.48–1984.

To Suresh
for helping me
realize my dreams.

Preface

Undoubtedly, the issue of environmental preservation is a timely topic for a book. Although volumes of technical reports and news articles appear every year on the distressing condition of the physical environment in the Third World, very little attempt is being made to put the crisis in a larger perspective. More is known about environmental problems than about how these problems can be solved. What seems to be lacking is the overall picture of the issue as it relates to the social, economic and political setting of a country. This book does not claim to offer any solutions to the environmental crisis, but it is hoped that it can help us in understanding the context in which this crisis needs to be solved.

Although I have made a sincere attempt to shed light on a variety of topics, several dark patches must remain. But that should only educate us about the complexity of the issue in question. Perhaps it is because of my training as a political scientist or perhaps it is because of my fascination with political power in general that I choose to view the environmental issue as a political question mark. Even if there is a solution, can it be implemented? This analysis, therefore, is primarily about the political capacity of the Indian government to undertake the environmental challenge.

I have enjoyed working on this manuscript. The work took me to several parts of India and gave me the opportunity to experience the love and affection of the people. My visits at the Ministry of Environment and Forests were also well-received. My request to visit Mrs. Maneka Gandhi, the Minister of State for Environment, was also accommodated, even on an extremely short notice. On occasions, I had to face bureaucratic tantrums, but these were far too few to have discouraged me. My special thanks are due to the officials of the Ministry of Environment for their patience in answering my queries year after year.

I express my gratitude to all the people, who, in one way or another, have provided me with guidance and encouragement. I am particularly indebted to Dr. Lester Ross for helping me find my focus. In addition, I am unable to forget the panelists, discussants and the members of the audiences in several conferences. Their comments and challenges have kept me on track. I am thankful to the anonymous reviewers of this manuscript for their constructive criticism and insightful suggestions.

My heart fills with emotions as I express my thanks to my family on their cheerleading role. My two little daughters, Pooja and Parul, refused to be deterred by the closed doors of my study. They always barged in with "coffee, care and company," as they called their team, and managed to rescue me from those tense moments of mental block. Indeed, my deepest appreciation is due to my husband, Suresh, for his loving guidance throughout the preparation of this manuscript.

Renu Khator

Table of Contents

List of Tables

List of Figures

CHAPTER 1

Introduction

E nvironmental protection started to emerge as a policy issue only in the late 1960s. Three decades later, in the 1990s, the issue has already become one of the top priority items on the international agenda, and is also accepted by the governments of most countries. Some observers even believe that the issue, after reaching its zenith in the late 1970s, has started to lose its zeal in many developed countries. In the developing world, however, there is no indication that the concern for environment is withering away.[1] Despite economic setbacks and instances of political instability, most Third World countries are welcoming the environmental issue. New environmental laws are being passed and new enforcing networks are being established[2]. It is too early to assess the impact of these arrangements; nevertheless, the enthusiasm in the Third World is worthy of scholarly attention. What is it that attracts (or perhaps, forces) the Third World countries toward the environmental issue? What motivates them to take political and legal actions? How does the issue fit into their prevailing political and economic ideologies? What are the policy choices and what are the limitations faced by developmental planners? These and other similar questions are the bases for the study of environmental politics in India.

This study focuses on India's environmental policy. The context of analysis is, however, quite different from similar studies in the past, for the issue of environmental protection is viewed as one among many pressing issues on the nation's agenda. The agenda of any society is necessarily full of issues, but for developing countries, such as India, the most important issue must be the issue of society's development. Development, in this context, is defined not as a goal, but instead as a process that aims at improving the quality of life for the people. Thus, issues of modernization, infrastructure-building, social justice and equality all are considered as developmental issues. Since the issue of environment is one among many issues demanding and, therefore, competing for society's resources, the role of political processes in managing the competition becomes a crucial element in the analysis. In an effort to examine the priorities and programs related to the preservation of the environment, this study covers the entire policy cycle beginning with problem identification and issue creation to policy formulation, policy implementation and finally, policy impact. It is hoped that this endeavor will unfold not only the environmental priorities of India but also of developing nations in general. More importantly, the study should also uncover the challenges and predicaments that the developing nations must face in their effort to search for an equilibrium among various pressing needs.

Politics of Environmental Issue

Environmental issue is undoubtedly a modern and a recent issue. The issue is universal; therefore, all societies are faced with the situation where they must find a solution without any historical directions and through trial and error. Environmental issue is also unique in the sense that it arouses a sense of fearfulness and panic. The true nature and scope of the environmental crisis is unknown; yet, its solution must immediately be sought.

Environmental issue is also adversarial. It challenges not only the status quo, but also the basic philosophy of the modern society. The modern society or the post-Industrial Revolution society, thrives for progress, growth and development in order to improve the quality of the life of its citizens. Political agendas of societies are crowded with issues that enhance the ability of a society to obtain this basic objective. The issues of social security, family welfare, employment guarantees, mass education and universal suffrage, in one way or another, contribute to this goal-attaining process. Nevertheless, environmental issue is different from other social welfare related issues because it challenges this goal and evokes a new thinking of no-growth or even reverse-growth. Thus, environmental issue is not an extension of the overall objective of the modern society; instead it is a challenge to it. Any emerging environmental policy must, therefore, be an effort of reconciliation between the established goals of development and the newly-found goals of environmental preservation.

Based on the environmental experiences of industrialized nations, a number of possible means of reconciliation (which I shall later refer to as models of reconciliation) can be identified. The most obvious, and perhaps the most desirable, means of reconciliation in a democratic polity is the electoral politics itself. Under the electoral political model, it is assumed that the support for the environmental issue comes naturally through democratic processes. In a usual scenario, according to Anthony Downs[3], the environmental issue first appears on the social (or the informal) agenda because of the realization of the problem by society.[4] The issue stays as one of the many competing issues on the social agenda, until it gathers an adequate level of political support from the society. Often, as Downs concedes, catastrophes and tragedies may help build the desired support base for the issue. The issue, then, is elevated to the status of a political issue, and is placed on the institutional (or the formal) agenda. At any given time, there may exist more than one institutional agenda, the number depending on the number of institutions involved in the process of policy formulation. The placement of the issue on the institutional agenda, then, leads to governmental deliberation on alternatives to resolve the issue and, consequently, to the adoption of a policy choice.

An excellent example of the electoral politics model is the environmental politics of the United States, where the public's concern for the environment in the late 1960s led to some of the most stringent environmental laws in the world. The government of the United States, for instance, found itself compelled to pass amendments to the Clean Water Act, which according to Charles Jones were nothing more than a case of "speculative augmentation."[5] The government, under public pressure, committed itself to a policy that it was not capable of implementing.

While the pressure of electoral politics may force a quick reconciliation between the conflicting goals of a society, such a reconciliation is always heavily dependent on public's support, as is clearly revealed by the American case. If the interest of the public recedes, the issue starts to lose its vitality. And as Downs argues, the interest of the public in environment withers away once the cost of environmental protection on individual lives in the form of high prices, industrial shut downs and tax increases is realized. The realization affects the policy process directly, since the government corresponds to the lack of public pressure by reducing the fervor of its enforcement efforts.

The characteristics of the electoral politics model, thus, are (1) the fast and quick process of issue-creation, (2) over-ambitious policies, (3) uneven implementation, and finally (4) a visible and active role of the public.

To some extent, electoral politics affects the environmental policy process of every nation. But in some nations, particularly in Sweden, Great Britain, Japan and Germany, the reconciliation is being achieved primarily through organizational initiatives. Organizational initiative is identified here as the second means of reconciliation. Under this organizational initiative model, the environmental issue is stressed within the echelon of the permanent state organization, i.e., the bureaucracy. It is assumed that structural and behavioral changes within the bureaucracy eventually result in a permanent change of priorities in the favor of the environment. Changes in bureaucratic behavior create the least amount of confusion and, yet, because of their non-electoral nature the changes are long-lasting albeit slow. Leonard Lundqvist's comparative study of the American and Swedish environmental protection laws led him to appropriately label the two as "the hare and the tortoise."[6] Similarly, several studies on the British pollution control laws have also acknowledged the performance of the British Alkali Inspectorate, which has achieved extraordinary success in reducing the air pollution level in major urban areas.[7] Furthermore, the environmental policy history of Japan indicates that the emphasis on economic growth did not permit the emergence of the environmental issue through electoral process, but local municipal authorities were able to initiate the issue without the national government's support. City governments in Japan, for instance, opted to strike independent deals with individual polluters.[8]

The organizational initiative model allows a unique flexibility to mold and change a policy according to its changing goals. Since the reconciliation is sought within the government and, therefore, away from the public's surveillant eye, the government can experiment and can also absorb initial policy failures. The British Alkali Inspectors, for instance, have the liberty to implement different standards for different industries within the same geographical area depending on an industry's ability to absorb the cost of emission treatment.[9] This has allowed the British government to undertake the air pollution control program without causing major industrial lockouts. Under the electoral politics model, however, such leniency is treated as inefficiency and such subjectivity is labeled as unfairness on the part of the government. Moreover, the bureaucracy, under the electoral politics model, becomes easily over-stressed as it is continuously pressured by the public for quick and visible results.

The organizational initiative model has been possible only in the countries where bureaucracy enjoys a certain amount of credibility and autonomy. In many Third World countries, where the organizational initiative model is the most promising model considering the relatively weak position of their elected institutions, bureaucracy has failed to obtain a reconciliation. The prime reason for this failure is the corrupt, unwilling and non-cooperative nature of the bureaucracy itself. The experiences of communist countries, especially China and the Soviet Union, also indicate that the organizational initiative model may fail if there is lack of serious political commitment for the issue. Despite a powerful position of the state, both nations have failed to integrate the environmental concern into their overall planning strategy. The production quotas set for each ministry in the Soviet Union and for each local unit in China have undermined the urgency of environmental protection.[10] The reward system in both nations is biased in the favor of short-term economic production goals, rather than long-term investments in the quality of the physical environment.

The characteristics of the organizational initiative model, nevertheless, appear to be (1) the quiescent role of the public, (2) the closed policy process, (3) incremental and cautious policies, and finally (4) a slow albeit steady implementation.

The third means of reconciliation is provided by international forces in the model that I label as the issue diffusion model.[11] Under this particular mode of reconciliation, it is assumed that agendas are altered through vertical or horizontal pressures. Unlike the previous two models, it is believed that the pressures are generated outside of the system and are adopted by the system at some point in time as its own pressures. National agendas, thus, are influenced by international agendas (vertical pressure) or by the agendas of other nations (horizontal pressure).

In the context of the environmental issue, it can be said that the issue arrived on the global agenda in the early 1970s, and since then it has influenced the environmental agendas of various nations. The most obvious influence has come in the form of the 1972 United Nation's Conference on the Human Environment, which requested all participating nations to prepare a report on the state of their environment for submission to the Conference. In many Third World countries, including India, this was the first time that the environmental issue received any serious governmental attention. Some form of issue diffusion from the international environmental agenda to national policy agendas was obvious, as most developing nations adopted their environmental policies shortly after the Conference. Furthermore, the United Nation's Environmental Program (UNEP), established as a result of the Conference, has also influenced environmental choices of individual countries by making cross-national information and technology available to them. Moreover, other international agencies, such as the World Bank and the International Monetary Fund, have also contributed to the process of issue diffusion by designing the terms of their aid and loans in such a way that recipient nations were forced to incorporate environmental concerns in their developmental planning.

Issue diffusion also occurs horizontally, i.e., from one nation to another.

Several donor agencies from developed countries offer program-specific loans to developing nations for environmental programs. The most notable of these programs is social forestry which has received enormous support from Canada, Sweden, the United States, and Great Britain. The aid offered for environmental programs may provide the aid-receiving nations with an impetus for agenda change and may foster the process of issue-creation.

Under the issue diffusion model, the issue of environmental protection directly arrives at the institutional agenda of a society, and is readily accepted by its government as an important issue. Contrary to the electoral politics model, the issue does not wait for public support and neither does it compete with other social issues. Consequently, despite its appearance on the institutional agenda, the issue does not become a political issue.[12] Since the policy process is closed and the change is artificially induced by international forces, the role of the public and non-governmental institutions, in this context, is minimal. Moreover, policies are adopted without much deliberation, for the knowledge of local environmental conditions is not available. Further, the successful implementation of environmental policies, under the issue diffusion model, depends on one of two factors: the continuing support from the international community and/or the ability of the government to take the environmental issue to its social (or the informal) agenda, where the issue may be redefined according to the society's needs.

The characteristics of the issue diffusion model are (1) the quiescent or follow-up role of the public, (2) the absence of the issue from the social agenda, (3) general and vague policies, and finally (4) sporadic and unwilling implementation.

While the three models cover a wide variety of variables that instigate environmental activism in a nation, nevertheless, the treatment given by the three models to the "political dimension" is less than adequate. Politics in the electoral political model, for instance, has only a limited place. It is a vehicle that can be used to promote environmental activism provided that sufficient demand for their use exists. The use of politics is also meant exclusively for electoral purposes. Thus, the model cannot explain why environmental issue may emerge in authoritarian societies where leaders are not necessarily concerned about their electoral victory.

Similarly, politics receives only a secondary treatment in the organization initiative model. Organizational culture and bureaucratic initiatives emerge as critical elements in shaping environmental movements. While the first model emphasizes the electoral political aspect, this model emphasizes the organizational political aspect. Both are complimentary, but not complete. It is essential to learn, for example, why a state bureaucracy undertakes one issue and not the other, and why one bureaucracy champions the issue while another bureaucracy under the similar circumstances fails to do so. The third model, the issue diffusion model, is the most faulty in this respect. The role of politics is mostly avoided since the assumption is that the pressure comes from outside sources.

The role of politics, however, is more real than envisioned by any of the models. While politics may serve as a vehicle (as in the electoral political model) or as a supplement (as in the organizational initiative model) or as a passive observer (as in the issue diffusion model), the possibility of politics playing a central role cannot be denied. One way in which politics may play this role is through transforming an environmental issue into a political issue and then exploiting it for political purposes. The environmental issue, for instance, may become readily acceptable to leaders who may wish to use it to acquire political benefits (beyond electoral victory). The environmental issue itself may become a tool for obtaining political objectives, rather than the politics becoming a tool to obtain environmental objectives.

The assumption of politics playing a central role, and not just any role, leads us to an investigation of the environmental policy process from a political perspective. Policy process, under the political perspective, is viewed as a process that involves political calculations behind every action. In other words, for every public policy action, there must exist some political purpose. For the study of the environmental policy process in India, I look at this political purpose from two different angles: the system angle and the individual angle. The system angle provides an external explanation and asks the question: how does environmental issue fit in with other issues and priorities at the time? The issue, thus, is viewed as a part of the overall policy system. The external "environment" of the issue is recognized as an important force in designing and shaping the survival of the issue. The receptivity and tolerance of the system depends on a set of political calculations based on the expected costs and benefits from the issue for the system. The individual angle, on the other hand, focuses on the internal aspect and asks the question: why do policy actors support the environmental issue? Their support is indeed a result of their political calculations regarding the costs and benefits of the issue for them. Any answer to the question of an individual's support is bound to be perceptive and subjective. But in developing countries, where personalities play dominant roles in the control of the political system, one cannot afford to ignore them as determining policy variables.

Political purposes and calculations behind policy actions are the major focus of attention under the model of reconciliation that I refer to as the political perspective model. Under this model, the policy process must display the following characteristics: (1) the process of policy formation has a zig-zag pattern marked by sudden shifts and changes; (2) policies reflect an inherent bias for the system and individuals involved, in the sense that they provide direct or indirect political benefits to the system and/or its supporters; (3) the implementation process is dependent on the system's tolerance for the issue and, therefore, is unpredictable; and finally (4) the role of the public is negligible.

This study attempts to analyze the environmental policy process of India through the framework of these arguments. A substantial treatment is given to the political dimension of the environmental policy process. The selection of the environmental policy area as a field of study is particularly due to the policy's "newness" which offers us an opportunity to examine the process of issue-creation and, consequently, to establish a link between issue creation and policy directions. The study necessarily begins with some assumptions. First, it is assumed that the primary objective of the Indian government is to promote growth and development and to improve the quality of the life of its citizens. (Although it is an assumption, I have provided enough evidence to support this argument in the following section.) Second, it is assumed that there is a conflict between the pure goal of economic development and the pure goal of environmental preservation. Thus, any effort to seek a balance between the two is a reconciliatory act. The third and the most inherent assumption of the study is that political processes, and political processes alone, can provide a means for reconciliation.

The explicit objective of the study is to gain a better understanding of the nature and scope of the environmental issue and policy in India, but there are two other subtle goals that this study attempts to achieve. First, an in-depth look into any individual policy process is expected to lead to some insights to the basic questions frequently raised in the public policy discipline: why issues emerge on agenda, why policies are adopted, and why and how policies are implemented. Although several studies exist in this field, nevertheless, a need to examine them in the particular context of the Third World still remains. A large number of the existing studies fall into the category of "test-and-then-reject-Western-models"; therefore, they make little contribution beyond the revelation that Western models are unsuitable for Third World countries. This study, circling around the various stages of the policy cycle, is expected to bring some new variables into the picture.

Second, it is also expected that an analysis of the Indian environmental policy from a political perspective will expose the nature of politics in India.

The research strategy used in the study is primarily historical, covering a time frame from 1960 to 1988. If a policy can be defined as an authoritative decision to act or not to act on an issue, then the post-1960 time frame for the syudy is fully justifiable. Prior to this period, the inactivity on the part of the Indian government was not deliberate; it was merely a reflection of a no-issue situation. Even though environmental problems existed, the issue of environmental protection was still in the pre-stage of the issue-creation process. The historical description of the environmental policy process is substantiated through the liberal use of interviews and side studies undertaken in India. Formal and informal interviews were conducted at four different stages during the study: first, during October-January in 1983-84; second, during December-January in 1985-86; third, during June-July in 1988; and finally, during July-August in 1990. Formal interviews were arranged for those government officials that were directly associated with the designing and interpretation of the environmental policy. These interviewees included the Directors of the Department of Environment, Chairman of the National Committee on Environmental Planning and Coordination, Director of the Central Board for the Prevention and Control of Water Pollution (CBPCWP), Chairmen of State Water Pollution Control Boards, and the representatives of some selected environmental groups.

Informal interviews were conducted in a number of villages and cities in Northern India. An attempt to conduct a more systematic mass survey failed, because in 1983 (when I started my study) people were not aware of the environmental problem as an issue. I was able to gather more information through informal interviews where people were not asked to give their opinion on environmental problems per se, but their opinions came naturally through the discussions on more general topics. No particular sampling method was followed to select the subjects for interviews. Nevertheless, over 350 people from a variety of sectors—rural and urban, educated and uneducated, women and men, young and old—were interviewed. The non-rigorous style of the interviews is justifiable, for the interviews are not the basis for this study and are not being used for any statistical analysis. The purpose of these interviews was to get a better grip at the cultural and social aspect of the issue.

The scope of the study is further tightened through an explicit focus on policy developments at the national level. This focus is necessary since state governments in post-independent India are highly dependent on the national government for policy directions. Moreover, states are not natural political entities: they are the results of a deliberate plan in the 1960s to divide the nation into manageable administrative units. The political philosophy of the nation still presupposes that policy priorities must be set by the national government (through Five-Year Plans) and policy implementation must be kept under the domain of state governments.

The study follows through four basic policy stages: (1) issue-creation, where the emphasis is placed on the identification of the problem and its interpretation by policy makers; (2) policy institutionalization, where the examination of bureaucratic developments is pursued; (3) mass participation, in which the role of the public through individual and group efforts is analyzed; and finally (4) policy evaluation, where a specific policy program is evaluated for its effectiveness.

In the following section I undertake to build the context for the environmental policy process in India first by establishing the developmental priorities of the government and then by highlighting the characteristics of the political system as they relate to the environmental policy process.

The Developmental Challenge

India is a poor country with a per capita income of only $290.[13] Despite its large industrial base, India is predominantly an agrarian society, where agriculture accounts for more than one-third of the real gross domestic product and two-thirds of the employment. Even though only one-third of the nation's income derives from the business and industrial sector, India ranks as the world's 17th most industrialized country. Its nuclear capabilities and space programs are clearly impressive. Yet, according to the 1981 census, nearly 40 percent of the people are classified as living below the poverty line. This irony of being rich yet poor stems, to some extent, from the rapidly increasing population: India has grown from 360 million in 1947 (at the time of the nation's independence) to almost 850 million today. Given this large base, even though the population growth rate is only 2.2 percent, it translates into adding nearly 16 million people—more than the population of the continent of Australia—every year. Despite this hardship, India has been successful in improving the rate of its national income from 0.7 percent under the British to almost 3.5 percent in the 1980s. Its efforts to make basic education and primary medical care accessible to the people are also statistically impressive, but have had a little real impact on the society: even though the number of schools and hospitals have grown by four to five times in the past, the demand for them (due to population increase) has grown even more sharply. Among other issues, the issue of family planning and population control remains as a priority issue for planners. The management of the economy also occupies more than sufficient space on the nation's agenda. India, following the Soviet model of long-term centralized planning, adopted a system of Five-Year Plans. These plans, drafted by the Planning Commission, provided an impetus for "guided development," in which the government, and not the self-adjusting market mechanism, was to play the major role. The Plans, therefore, provide an excellent source of information on policy priorities of the government.

In its Five-Year Plans, the Indian government has been very forthright in declaring its preference for fast and accelerated growth. In 1952, the Planning Commission declared that "the central objective of planning in India is to raise the standard of living of the people and to open out to them opportunities for a richer and more varied life."[14] To fulfill this objective, the government was expected to manage the economy by building infrastructure and by offering economic incentives. This economic strategy led to a system of limited capitalism, where infrastructure-building commodities, such as steel, roads, transportation, energy, etc., were controlled by the government, while a competitive market existed for other goods. The objective of central planning remained unchanged in decades; nevertheless, the strategy to achieve this objective kept swaying between industrial growth and agricultural growth in each planning period. Once the nation's economy showed the signs of stability, new issues started to appear on the agenda. Particularly, the issues of fair and equitable distribution of resources came to the forefront following the spectacular success of the 1965 Green Revolution. Consequently, along with growth, the government was forced to devote significant attention to social reforms. From 1969 to 1973, sweeping constitutional, legal and structural changes affecting property rights and individual privileges were made by the Indira Gandhi government to restructure the economy.

Needless to say, the national agenda was too crowded to have accommodated the environmental issue, even though serious environment-related problems involving direct threat to human lives were beginning to appear as early as the 1950s. It was only in the Fourth Five-Year Plan (1969-1974) that for the first time the issue of environmental protection was given official recognition. The recognition was minimal and non-committal; nevertheless, it was sufficient to pave the way for more serious considerations in the future.

The Plan stressed that environmental aspect should be made an integral part of the overall developmental planning.

> Planning for harmonious development recognizes the unity of nature and man. Such planning is possible only on the basis of a comprehensive appraisal of environmental issues. There are instances on which timely, specialized advice on environmental aspects could have helped in project design and in averting subsequent adverse effects on the environment leading to loss of invested resources. It is necessary, therefore, to introduce the environmental aspect into our planning and development.[15]

Even though the pleas of "harmony with nature" appeared frequently in the following Five-Year Plans, it would be misleading to assume that the overall development strategy was altered in any significant way. In fact, the government's commitment to developmental and distributional issues became even more obvious during the Fifth and the Sixth Five-Year Plans. An allocation of Rs 40 billion (from the total outlay of Rs 975 billion) was made to initiate new programs on family planning, rural development, slum rehabilitation and rural electrification. The on-going Seventh Five-Year Plan also declares the "fair and equal development" to be the central objective of government planning. In short, the government continues to show its preference for fast economic growth and also its commitment to the welfare state ideology. Translating this preference into policy terminology, one may say that the development, and not the environment, continues to be the top priority of the Indian government. The issue of environment, thus, is identified within the broader parameter of the development issue. The environmental issue, in this context, must either adapt to the developmental needs or it must piggy-back ride with the development issue.

Other than the implicit preference for fast development in the nation's planning, the mediocre performance of the Indian economy has also affected the ability of the government to accept the environmental issue. The performance of the Indian economy during the last four decades has been noteworthy, yet it has been far from being satisfactory. Figure 1.1 indicates that the growth rate of the economy has varied between 2.2 percent and 5.3 percent, although the targets have always been set much higher.[16] The economy did fairly well, to the surprise of planners, during the late 1950s and the early 1960s. The achievements were, however, soon over-shadowed by the sluggish performance of the economy that lasted for more than a decade. The situation became particularly acute in the early 1970s, when the major

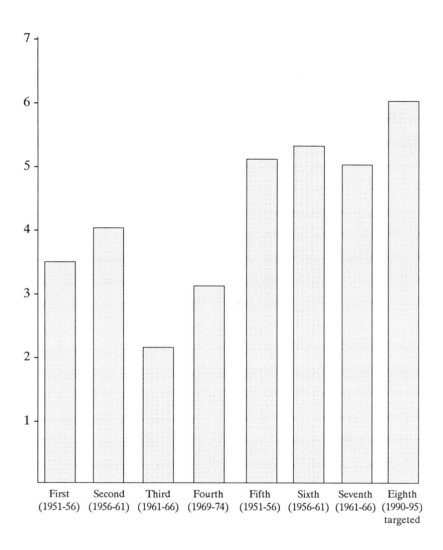

Five Year-Plans

Figure 1.1 Growth Rate of the Indian Economy During Five Year Plans

devaluation of rupee (over 55 percent) in 1966 and the oil crisis in 1973 left India with a large balance of payment deficit. In an effort to save the economy, the government opted to take several concessional and non-concessional loans from international sources to offset the rising deficit. By the mid-1970s, the nation was, however, facing one of the worst economic crises in its history.

The reform strategy that followed the 1970 crisis focused on the strengthening of market forces by making the public sector more competitive, improving industrial output and encouraging exports. The emphasis on development continued and most of the development planning needs were met by an unusually high rate of savings by the people and by international borrowing. The Indian savings rate of 21 percent of the gross domestic product is a text book example. Among democratic nations, the level is exceeded only by countries with three or four times India's per capita income. Most of the economic success, however, is offset by a rapid increase in the population. Compared to the per capita GNP of 1.76 for the non-African nations excluding China during the twenty-year period from 1963 to 1983, India's per capita rate was only 1.5 percent. The rate for the lower middle-income developing countries for the same period was almost double: 2.9 percent.[17]

The less-than-expected economic performance of the Indian economy puts an stress on the nation's policy agenda. A slow growth rate leaves few options for the planners for other emerging issues. Moreover, economic issues continue to occupy large space on the agenda, thus, making it less likely for social issues to gain prominence. Economic issues have been, and will continue to be, a major challenge for the government, since the achievements of the on-going Seventh Five-Year-Plan (1985-1989) are far from being spectacular. The targeted growth rate of 5 percent may not be achieved, for it has been 4.9 percent in 1985, 4.1 in 1986, and only 1 to 2 percent in 1987. The government has been running a huge foreign deficit of an estimated $25.3 billion. In general, during the six-year period between 1981-82 to 1986-87, government revenue has grown at an average rate of 17.2 percent, while the outlay has soared by 18.3 percent.[18]

The evidence indicates that the government will continue to stress developmental needs in coming years: the forthcoming Eighth Five-Year-Plan envisions a higher growth rate (6 percent as opposed to 5 percent in the Seventh Plan), and seeks for the further liberalization of the economy by allowing a greater role of the open-market forces and thus attracting foreign investments.[19] Exports are to be increased substantially, and incentives are to be provided to push the domestic savings rate at a 23 percent level. The over-ambitious targets set in the Eighth Five-Year Plan will certainly demand a solid political and financial commitment from the government, the result of which could very well be adverse on other emerging issues, such as the environment. Developmental needs will also pose serious challenge for the government, particularly because the resource base to finance the development is still fragile. So far these needs have been financed primarily through three sources: high domestic savings, international borrowing and money deposited by Indian emigrants.[20] Today, many economists concede that the government may find it difficult to depend on these sources in the future. The savings rate has already been pushed to its peak; and further, the evidence suggests that the Indian consumer is starting to get attracted to luxuries, such as televisions, scooters and vacations. Both of these trends may lead to a decline in the nation's savings rate. Similarly, it is expected that in coming years, the ability of the Indian government to secure foreign loans and assistance is likely to be sharply reduced as other nations, particularly China, enter the group of borrowers. The pressure to finance the development will, then, fall upon domestic savings which are already squeezed to their near maximum. In addition, the contribution of remittance of Indian emigrants, which accounted for more than 18 percent of the increase in currency and bank deposits during the late 1970s, is also bound to shrink due to the changing profile of the oil-producing nations.

While India's abilities to finance the development remain scarce, its developmental needs continue to accelerate; and considering the high rate of population growth, the trend is more than likely to continue in the future. In comparison to other low-income economies, India already fares poorly on the indicators of economic development. Despite impressive progress in various areas of development, India's ability to cope with the developmental stress remains lower than average. For an easy comparison, I have presented comparative data on various attributes of needs, ability, and priority of non-industrialized economies in Table 1.1. Need indicators include the most commonly used economic indicators; ability indicators measure the resource base; and priority indicators reflect the spending patterns in selected nations. The categories are neither exhaustive, nor are they meant to provide a systematic index of the variables. The comparison, nevertheless, is helpful in establishing the critical nature of India's developmental needs. According to Table 1.1, with the exception of the health variable (population per physician), India faces a higher-than-average developmental challenge even among the low-income economies. In terms of the government's ability (per

Table 1.1
Selected Development Indicators for India and Other Countries

	India	Low Income Economies	Industrial Market Economies
NEED INDICATORS			
Population growth (1980-86)	2.2	1.9	0.6
Population per physian	3,700	6,050	550
Percent of secondary age population in school	35	34	93
Daily calorie supply per capita	2,126	2,329	3,357
Percent of populaiton in urban areas	25	22	75
Life expectancy at birth	57	61	76
Infant mortality per 1,000 live births	86	69	9
Percent of labor force in agriculture	70	72	7
Percent of labor force in industry	13	13	35
ABILITY INDICATORS			
GNP per capita (US$)	290	270	12,960
Average annual growth rate (%) (1965-86)	1.8	3.1	2.3
Average annual rate of inflation (%) (1980-86)	7.8	8.1	5.3
Average annual growth rate in agriculture (%) (1980-86)	1.9	4.9	2.5
Gross domestic savings (%)	21	25	21
PRIORITY INDICATORS (Percentage of total expenditure on)			
Defense	18.4	-	16.4
Education	2.1	-	4.5
Health	2.1	-	12.9
Housing, amenities, social security etc.	5.6	-	39.0
Economic services	23.4	-	9.5

Source: *World Development Report, 1988* (World Bank, 1988)

Table 1.2
Distribution of the Central Government Expenditures in
Selected Low-Income Economies

Percentage of Total Expenditure	Low Income Economies	India	Uganda	Tanzani	Kenya	Pakistan
Defense	17.7	18.4	26.3	13.8	8.7	33.9
Education	9.8	2.1	15.0	7.2	19.7	3.2
Health	3.6	2.1	2.4	4.9	6.4	1.0
Housing/welfare	6.2	5.6	0.8	1.4	0.5	10.5
Economic services*	23.8	23.4	14.8	24.0	27.6	25.8
Administrative cost	38.9	48.5	40.7	48.6	37.0	25.6

* include expenditure associated with the regulation, support and more efficient operation of business; economic development, redress of regional imbalances; employement, research, trade promotion; and inspection and regulation of industry.

Source: *World Development Report, 1988* (World Bank), 266-67.

capita gross national product, annual growth rate, domestic savings rate and inflation rate), it is evident that India possesses a lower-than-average ability. And according to the priority indicators (expenditure on defense, education, health, housing and welfare) the Indian government, despite its centralized planning, spends a minimal share of its total expenditure on social needs. The greatest expenditure comes in the form of economic services, such as developmental projects, inspection and regulation of industry etc. (Table 1.2)

In addition, Table 1.3 provides comparative data on selected per capita expenditures in India and compares the figures for India with the aggregated figures for "developed" and "developing" countries. If expenditure trends of developed countries may be treated as the "desirable goals," then the comparison presents a gloomy picture for India. Compared to developed countries, India spends very little on health, education and welfare. One may argue that the cost of living in India is much lower than the similar cost in any of the developed countries, and thus, the expenditure figures are bound to be lower for India. Nevertheless, the high rates of illiteracy and infant mortality themselves indicate that a serious challenge is faced by the Indian government to fulfill the basic education and health needs of its citizens.

Environment, Development and Politics in India

Table 1.3
Development and Expenditure Indicators for Selected Countries

Country	GNP (PC)	(PC) Expend. on Educ.	Literacy Rate	% Pop. with Safe Water	(PC) Expend. on Health	Life Expectancy	(PC) Calories Supply	(PC) Foreign Aid Rec'd.
Developed	9,795	497	99	97	469	73	3,383	—
Developing	752	28	62	53	11	59	2,439	7.30
India	266	8	44	54	2	54	2,161	2.20
Brazil	1,449	57	78	75	23	64	2,629	1.20
Mexico	3,027	79	90	74	11	66	3,147	1.10
France	10,152	537	99	99	676	75	3,337	—
Greece	4,273	102	92	95	156	74	3,660	1.20
Italy	6,901	319	97	99	406	74	3,486	—
Spain	4,808	120	94	95	224	75	3,335	—
U.K.	8,616	447	99	100	470	74	3,130	—
USSR	7,095	332	99	100	227	70	3,403	—
Egypt	718	31	44	75	9	58	3,262	37.40
Israel	5,915	500	95	98	208	74	3,049	313.50
Pakistan	385	7	30	44	2	51	2,186	7.50
Japan	10,300	529	99	98	474	77	2,804	—
S. Korea	2,126	101	94	83	5	66	2,822	- 0.90
USA	15,541	771	99	100	674	75	3,652	—
China	307	8	69	NA	4	67	2,564	0.80

Source: Sivard, Ruth L., *World Military and Social Expenditures, 1987-88*
(Leesburg: WMSE Publications, 1988).

Moreover, India's public expenditure figures are also lower than the average figures for developing countries.

While developmental needs remain critical, statistics on environmental needs are also shocking. Not much comparative data are available on environmental protection needs and efforts across nations; however, one indicator presented in Table 1.3 (the percentage of total population with safe drinking water) reveals that India faces a pressing challenge in this aspect as well. Nearly half the population in the nation remains without any access to safe drinking water. In fact, according to estimates, 70 percent of the available water in India is polluted. Nevertheless, it must be realized that out of the 46 percent population that lives without safe water, a large percentage does not have easy access to water—polluted or unpolluted— at all. For thousands of people living in the states of Rajasthan and Bihar, the closest water source may be more than ten miles away. Therefore, while the quality of drinking water is a challenge for policy planners, the availability of water is even a greater challenge.

The Political Challenge

Since policies are designed and implemented within a political framework, it is essential to understand the inherent characteristics of the Indian political system. The present system has evolved through a number of changes induced by the nation's social, economic and cultural developments during the last four decades. Political arrangements in India can be studied through three predominant themes: (1) the semi-democratic mode of rule, (2) the emergence of new state-society relations, and finally (3) the politicization of the masses. These three characteristics define and shape the political context within which the environmental policy is likely to develop.

Democratic arrangements form an important political framework within which every policy proposal must proceed. These arrangements define the boundary for policy actions. Therefore, it is essential to identify the challenges posed by the scope and nature of the Indian-style democracy. In contrast to the evolution of the democratic system in the West, democracy in India did not grow naturally as a result of any gradual revolution. India inherited its democratic system from the British, who superficially implanted it before granting the nation its freedom. The Indian democracy also did not coexist with capitalism. The essence of Western democracy, scholars argue, is the limit imposed on the state power by the independent power of capitalist forces. Since capitalism allows the idea of private property and economic rights, the elite may gain enough power to off-set the power traditionally held by the king and the aristocratic class. The emergence of capitalism prior to democracy in practically all of the countries of Europe and North America have even led Barrington Moore and many other scholars to conclude that "No bourgeois, no democracy."[21]

Neither democracy nor capitalism grew naturally in India. Both concepts were discussed and agreed upon after the nation's independence. While there was no dispute regarding the mode of popular democracy which was based on the principles of universal suffrage and freedom of speech and organization, serious disagreements existed regarding the appropriate mode of economic development. Hardgrave has identified at least three different visions for the nation's economic system: Gandhi's fully decentralized model; Nehru's controlled liberalism; and finally, Patel's Western capitalism. After much deliberation, the Nehru's vision prevailed. A unique type of social-liberalism was introduced in which most infrastructural commodities remained under the government's tight control while consumption-related commodities were freed to be handled through Western-style capitalism. Thus, while political democracy was allowed to develop fully in the nation, capitalistic growth was artificially monitored and restricted.

The second source of influence on the political system comes from the existing relationship between the state and the society. Complex state-society relations have evolved in the nation since its independence in 1947. These relations are based on two other developments: first, the emergence of several new "free floating"[22] political classes; and second, the establishment of the patronage-based alliance system between the state and the privileged classes. Prior to the nation's independence, the fruits of economic progress were distributed among a restricted number of privileged classes. These benefitting classes included civil servants employed by Her Majesty's government, big industrialists engaged in industrial activity outside of India, foreign-returnees utilizing their professional skills, traditional feudal lords controlling the utilization of land and the royalty enjoying their ancestral wealth.

After the independence, however, the scope of these privileged classes expanded significantly. Small-scale industrialists, supported by the state's aggressive industrial policy, mushroomed. Professionals, such as lawyers, doctors, and engineers, were able to accumulate social status. Also, even though the feudal system was theoretically extracted, the inability of the government to penetrate the rural side still allowed feudal lords to maintain their control over farm lands. Moreover, with the expansion of the education system, a technically oriented, educated middle class also emerged. While the economic system adapted to these new classes, the political system failed to socialize them into any particular political ideology. The political allegiance and loyalty of these new classes was not restricted to any political platform. Thus, they became the "free-floaters."

The emergence of the new privileged classes has a significant implication for the political system. It eventually allows the state to function more independently. The essence of India's democracy is argued to be the fierce competition that exists between various privileged classes, such as rich farmers, small-scale industrialists, white-collar workers, and professionals.[23] The competition insures that no single class possesses the ability to dominate the state, although each aspires to do so. Because no one class ultimately dominates, the state remains over and above the competition and is able to bargain its resources through a complex system of patronage distribution. Since the state retains its control over the society's resources, any class desiring to obtain them must trade them for their allegiance to the state. Thus, the state, through its hold over resources, is able to undermine the independent power base of the elite. With the help of this patronage-based alliance, the state can, and does, pursue policies independent of the wishes of any class.

Other than the emergence of the Indian-style democracy and the new state-society relations, the Indian political system is also influenced by an unusually high degree of mass politicization, especially the politicization of the rural and urban poor. Mass politicization tends to threaten the stability of a society when it is not matched by a similarly high degree of institutionalization. Over the last four decades, the poor classes in India have realized the potential of their political rights and are demanding their political share in the state system. However, while mass groups are ready to enter the political scene, the political arena is not ready to face their entry. According to James Manor, political institutions are continuously loosing their ability to adjust to this expanded demand.

The process of politicization is posing a double challenge: on one side, it is accelerating pressure on the state to accommodate the newly politicized public groups; on the other side, it is being forced to open up new and even non-traditional (such as violent protests and strikes) avenues of participation for the masses. When traditional avenues of participation, such as political parties and interest groups, fail to accommodate the new groups, they resort to non-traditional and often violent methods. The politicization of new mass groups, and the close competition within the privileged classes has led to what

Robert Hardgrave labels as "the revolution of rising frustrations."[24]

The political system of India is thus characterized by (1) the lack of institutionalization, (2) rapid politicization, (3) high degree of demands and (4) a fierce competition between privileged classes. While competition and state autonomy may ensure democratic treatment to an issue, lack of institutionalization creates confusion, unpredictability and inconsistency in the development of the issue.

Environmental Response: Politics of Reconciliation

The developmental agenda does not overshadow the environmental agenda of the Indian government. India is one of the leading countries in the Third World to have institutionalized its environmental concern. During the last 15 years, India has adopted a number of environmental laws at the national and state levels. A full-fledged Ministry of Environment and Forests with its budget exceeding that of many previously existing ministries has been established. Moreover, the government has launched a massive campaign to educate the public about the causes and consequences of environmental degradation. While travelling by car in the northern part of India during the summer of 1987, I was overwhelmed to see the streets practically covered with colorful posters stating the importance of environmental protection. I noticed the similar enthusiasm in and around the building which the Ministry of Environment and Forests occupies. A newer and larger space was available to the occupants, the furnishings were clearly modern. While comparing it with the first office of the Department of Environment which I visited in 1982, I realized that the issue of environment had certainly been favored and had been well-bureaucratized. The public has responded in a significant and positive way as well. More than 500 non-governmental organizations are dealing with the environmental issue today. In addition, court battles involving environmental assault are mushrooming. Over a thousand cases were filed against violating organizations and individuals in the last decade alone.

Environmental politics in India can be viewed only as the politics of reconciliation, since a conflict between the two issues—development and environment—is obvious in the early history of the environmental policy. Mrs. Gandhi, while speaking at the opening session of the 1972 United Nation's Conference on Human Environment at Stockholm, identified this conflict very clearly.

The environmental problems of developing countries are not the side effects of excessive industrialization but reflect the inadequacy of development. The rich countries may look upon development as the cause of environmental destruction, but to us it is one of the primary means of improving the environment for living, or providing food, water, sanitation and shelter; of making the deserts green and the mountains habitable...On one hand the rich look askance at our continuing poverty—on the other, they warn us against their own methods. We do not wish to impoverish the environment any further and yet we cannot for a moment forget the grim poverty of large numbers of people. Are not poverty and need the greatest polluters?[25]

Despite the strong rejection of the environmental issue in favor of the development issue, Mrs. Gandhi found herself engaged in formulating environmental legislation just a few months after her return from Stockholm.[26] The Water (Prevention and Control of Pollution) Act was passed in 1974, followed by the Air (Prevention and Control of Pollution) Act in 1981 and then, by a more explicit Environment (Protection) Act in 1986. The National Committee on Environmental Planning was established in 1972, followed by the Central Board for the Prevention and Control of Water Pollution in 1974, Department of Environment in 1980, and the Ministry for Environment and Forests in 1985. Mrs. Gandhi herself crusaded for the environmental cause.

Surprisingly, the process of reconciliation has been extremely smooth and swift in India. Significant environmental laws have been passed unopposed and new ministries have been established without much debate. The response from industry, to the surprise of many scholars, has been equally unchallenging. The smoothness of the Indian environmental policy process is puzzling; nevertheless, it offers an interesting area of investigation for social scientists. Clearly several factors have contributed to the swift and smooth process of reconciliation. The reconciliation in India did not follow any of the three models identified earlier in the text, even though all of them—electoral politics, organizational initiative and issue diffusion—may explain the process partially. The politics of environmental protection in India, at best, is the politics of opportunism. An unequivocal role has been played by national leaders who used the impetus provided to them by international forces to come up with policy choices that could establish their commitment to the cause without challenging the status quo in any significant way. The central argument of this study is that the social and political fabric of India throughout the 1970s provided an excellent opportunity for reconciliatory actions—actions that required minimum financial and political resources, but still rendered significant political benefits. The reconciliation became feasible because of (1) the pro-environment social and religious culture of the nation; (2) the severity of the environmental deterioration; and (3) the potential of the environmental issue to become a political resource. It is this third characteristic that separates the Indian policy context from the similar policy contexts available in other Third World countries; therefore, it may explain the dominating and the enthusiastic role played by the Indian government in bringing about the environmental movement. In the following section, I highlight some of the grounds on which the environmental issue was found to be compatible to the general social, economic and political philosophy of the ruling party.

The government of India followed a specific pattern in the evolution of the environmental policy. The policy, to begin with, emphasized the extension of the legal and bureaucratic support to the environmental cause. Several new laws were created, and numerous state and federal level agencies were established in a short span of twelve years (from 1974 to 1986). Laws were adopted in an incremental fashion. Such an approach allowed the government to keep the issue of environment away from visibility, and consequently, away from potential conflict. The laws that were passed were non-specific in nature; ample room was left for bureaucratic discretion in the implementation process. The anti-pollution laws of India, for example, were strikingly different from the similar laws in the United States which, according to Jones, were the case of "speculative augmentation."[27] In contrast to the American laws, the Indian laws were designed under a no-pressure situation. The laws, similar to the environmental-related laws of Great Britain, relied on voluntary compliance and established no time schedules or emission standards, and left no scope for litigation.[28] Since the government was operating under little or no pressure, it adopted a policy strategy that was incremental, non-specific and broad in scope but modest in its impact.

Even though the Indian anti-pollution laws were similar to the British laws in nature, they failed to match their counterparts in terms of their effectiveness. Considering the near limitless influence of the business sector on the economy and the existence of the feudalistic structures at the local level, the concepts of bureaucratic discretion and voluntary compliance turned out to be the biggest shortcomings of the Indian laws. Interestingly, the establishment of a new environmental enforcement network also proved to be nothing more than a ritual. Enforcement officers were given the scope to use their discretion, but were equipped with no power to actually exercise it.[29]

Despite its symbolic appeal, the environmental issue provided sufficient political benefit to the government. First, it corresponded well with the protectionist and interventionist style of Mrs. Gandhi's leadership. The political scene throughout the early and mid-1970s was dominated by the policies that glorified the role of the central government at the expense of state governments. The power, under Mrs. Gandhi's rule, flowed toward the center of the pyramid.[30] The environmental issue became yet another tool in the hands of the central government to centralize its power. By undertaking the responsibility of protecting the environment, the central government expanded its domain to the previously restricted areas, such as forests, energy and development-related projects in the states. With the newly available power of requiring environmental impact assessment (EIA) on public projects, the center obtained fresh opportunities to use its discretion in distributing resources to the states. Even though the scope of these assessments was limited, it would be misleading to assume that the leadership did not view them as tools for seeking loyalty and compliance from state governments. Several projects, such as the Silent Valley Project in Kerala, the Tehri Dam in Uttar Pradesh, the Sardar Sarovar Project in Gujarat, and Narmada Development Scheme in Madhya Pradesh involved millions of dollars of federal aid and created several hundred jobs in the states.

The environmental policy was also in agreement with the pattern of democratic development in India. The environmental issue served, and still serves, a very important political purpose: working as a safety valve, the issue made the venting of the mass frustration possible without disturbing the base of the system. While it gave the people an opportunity to raise their voices against the existing system, it also gave the state an opportunity to distract the people's attention from other, perhaps more threatening, issues. It is not surprising, therefore, that most of the protests which emerged in rural areas in favor of environmental protection, in fact, mirrored the mass dissatisfaction toward the practices of the local elite (local industry or contractors). What makes the case more interesting is the fact that the government also ignored the appeal for changing the basic economic structure; it, instead, opted for quick solutions to the more visible environmental problems. The Chipko Aandolan, the most famous mass movement to protect the forests, was a good example of this hide-and-go-seek game. Even though the Chipko Aandolan came to be known for its fight against the massive felling of the trees by contractors, a closer look at the origin of the movement would reveal that the villagers were also dissatisfied with the proportion of their share from tree-felling.[31] Before launching a mass level movement, several attempts had already been made to secure a more equitable distribution of forest resources. (A more substantial treatment to the Chipko Aandolan is given in the section dealing with mass participation in the environmental policy area.)

The environmental movement in India provided to the people, especially the newly politicized groups, an opportunity to assert themselves in political processes. Indeed, often the movement served as a forum for the people to display their general dissatisfaction with the system itself. The movement also served an important purpose for the state. By adopting policies and creating enforcing networks, the government reinforced its neutral and people-oriented image. The environmental policy provided the state with yet another opportunity to manipulate dominant classes and, subsequently, to enforce its power over the society. As discussed earlier, the state in India makes a deliberate attempt to buy patronage from dominant classes in return for letting them use society's resources. Since the pot of rewards is shrinking, while the number of reward-seekers is increasing, the state must generate new rewards to buy loyalty from the dominant classes. Needless to say, the environmental regulation area with its licenses to start new industry, permissions to build major power plants, classification of protected areas, and establishment of emission standards, etc., offers an enormous potential in this regard.

In addition, the environmental policy area opened up new horizons for reshaping the relationship between the people and the government. In a situation where traditional channels of communication (through political parties and interest groups) between the two were breaking, politicians were opting for direct mass appeal and a more personalized style of leadership. The environmental issue certainly offered the potential to establish this appeal, and Mrs. Gandhi, despite her emphasis on fast economic growth, was quick to realize it. The protection of environment became an important part of her populist policies that were meant to separate her from the villainous industrialists, traders and feudal lords.

Interestingly, the reconciliatory efforts that were later shaped into the environmental policy posed no significant threat to the status quo. The policy to protect the physical environment, as designed, blended well with the policy to achieve fast economic growth. Unfortunately, the smoothness of the process also meant that the priorities were not shifted, and the alternatives were not carefully considered. Consequently, despite its commitment to protect the environment, the government was unable to pursue any environmental program that threatened either the goal of political stability or the process of economic development. Today, the constant increase in the size of the population demands that the sturdy growth of the economy be maintained, while the rise in the level of political awareness of the previously quiescent groups requires that the game of patronage-trading be continued.

Plan of Study

The study follows the four major areas of investigation highlighted by the four models of reconciliation: (1) the process of policy formation, (2) the selection of policies, (3) the process of implementation, and finally (4) the role of the public. However, before embarking on the policy process, Chapter Two makes an attempt to identify major environmental problems and to relate these problems with the nation's environmental culture. It is an analysis of the magnitude of the environmental crisis. Since the idea is not to present a technical report on the state of the nation's environment but simply to get an understanding of the issue boundaries, the section covers only the general degrading sources, and reveals their overall impact on the society. I have also tried to build a cultural context for the environmental policy process in this chapter. It is often argued that it is not the problem itself, but how the problem is perceived in a society, that eventually defines the boundaries of a policy process. India harbors a pro-environment culture- —a culture in which the teachings of love and respect for natural resources is an integral part of the socialization process. Nevertheless, as Chapter Two reveals, two paradoxical situations exist: one, in which cultural beliefs are not put to practice in the day-to-day life-style; and second, in which the government ignores the importance of cultural harmony and is reluctant to transform this into a mass support for environmental activism.

Chapter Three presents the evolution of the environmental policy. Major laws, such as the Water Act of 1974, the Air Act of 1981, the Forest Act of 1927, and the Environment Act of 1986, are assessed for their strengths and weaknesses. The focus of the chapter is the national policy, and the process with which the important environmental decisions have been taken over during the last two decades. Even though the method is descriptive and provides only a historical account of the developments in the environmental policy field, nevertheless, the account is presented in a wider context of the nation's overall priorities during that time period. Two analytical frameworks are used to analyze the emergence of the environmental issue. The first is the holistic look at the nation's agenda. The focus is on the numerous political and economic issues that were present at the nation's agenda at that time and were likely to have given a challenge to the environmental issue. The second is the use of personalities to explain policy shifts. The analysis of Mrs. Gandhi's personality traits, her style of ruling and her perception of the world reveals the importance of the linkage between personalities and issues—an area which has not received much attention from scholars in the policy science discipline.

The analysis of the implementation of major environmental laws is further developed in Chapter Four. The powers and limitations of the environmental bureaucracy, especially the newly created water boards and environmental departments, are discussed. The objective is not merely to demonstrate that implementation inefficiencies and bureaucratic inadequacies exist; instead, the objective is to reveal why these inefficiencies exist. I examine the implementation process from the varying perspectives of grass-roots regulators, regulatees, and politicians. The combined effect of these three perspectives is the development of a unique policy culture—a culture in which non-implementation, rather than implementation, becomes the safest political move.

Chapter Five offers a micro look at the non-regulatory functions of the environmental bureaucracy. More often than not, environmental bureaucracy in the Third World is asked to perform a large number of non-regulatory functions, such as the promotion of mass awareness, collection and dissemination of information and distribution of natural resources. Consequently, any evaluation of environmental bureaucracy based solely on its regulatory performance is unjust. Moreover, since the policy thinking in developing countries is more toward "eco-development" rather than toward "no-growth" or "zero-growth," governments find themselves increasingly involved with environmental programs that are distributive in nature. The objective of these programs is to distribute or redistribute social resources in such a way so as to reduce any unnecessary stress on physical resources. In this context, environmental bureaucracy is forced to perform the functions of a distributive bureaucracy.

In order to assess the nature and scope of the non-regulatory functions of the environmental bureaucracy in India, I turn to the government's social forestry program which is a model example of the eco-developmental strategy. This examination takes us to the grass-roots politics in India. The chapter starts with a discussion of the relationship between forest-related needs and forest management objectives. The program of social forestry is then evaluated for its assumptions and its incompability with local politics.

Chapter Six attempts to assess the form and nature of public participation in environmental policy process. The study examines four major channels of public participation: direct protests, interest group lobbying, political party support, and finally, the media. While analyzing the public's direct response to the environmental crisis, the chapter offers insights to many environmental protest cases, especially the Chipko Aandolan. In addition, major environmental movements and organizations are examined. In order to examine the role of the media, which is assumed to have played a paramount role in the formation of environmental movements in developed countries, I offer a content analysis of an English newspaper. The findings reveal that even though the scope of public participation is limited in India, the localized awareness of environmental issues is not non-existent. Admittedly, the use of indigenous methods by the people to express their preferences makes it hard for a foreign observer to detect the true nature and scope of public participation in the nation.

Finally, in Chapter Seven, I highlight the findings of the study and make an attempt to tie them with some broader issues in the discipline. Particularly, implications for three areas are discussed: the agenda-setting process, the question of administrative capabilities and the role of the state in policy process.

Notes

1. Anthony Downs raised this concern as early as 1972 in his article "Up and Down with Ecology: The Issue-attention Cycle," in *Public Interest* 28 (1972): 28-50. His claim was that once the cost of solving a problem becomes clear, the enthusiasm toward it also withers away, until there is again a revival for some reason. The thesis was supported by various other scholars in many developed countries.

2. According to the International Center for Science and Technology, Washington, DC, there were only 11 developing countries that reported having some administrative body in charge of environmental administration. In 1982, the number had increased by ten times to 111.

3. Downs, "Up and Down with Ecology," 29-30

4. For the discussion of policy agendas, refer to R. Cobb, J.K. Ross and M.H. Ross, "Agenda-building as a Comparative Political Process," *American Political Science Review* 76 (1976): 126-138.

5. Charles C. Jones, *Clean Air: The Policies and Politics of Pollution Control* (Pittsburgh: University of Pittsburgh Press, 1975).

6. L.J. Lundqvist, *The Hare and the Tortoise: Clean Air Policies in the*

United States and Sweden (Ann Arbor: University of Michigan Press, 1980).

7. Michael Hill, "The role of the British Alkali and Clean Air Inspectorate in Air Pollution Control," in *International Comparisons in Implementing Pollution Control*, by Paul Downing and Kenneth Hanf (Boston: Kluwer-Nijhoff, 1983).

8. Steven Reed, *Japanese Prefectures and Policymaking* (Pittsburgh: University of Pittsburgh Press, 1986), Ch.4.

9. According to the 1973 Annual Report of the Alkali Inspectorate, "The Chief Inspectorate, with the help of his deputies lays down the broad national policies and provided they within their broad lines, inspectors in the field have plenty of flexibility to take into account local circumstances and make suitable decisions. They are given plenty of autonomy and are trained as decision-makers with as much responsibility and authority as possible." (quoted in Michael Hill, "Role of British Alkali Inspectorate," 90-91).

10. T. Gustafson, *Reform in Soviet Politics: Lessons of Recent Policies on Land and Water* (Cambridge: Cambridge University Press, 1981); M.I. Goldman, *The Spoils of Progress: Environmental Pollution in Soviet Union* (Cambridge: Cambridge University Press, 1972); Lester Ross, *Environmental Policy in China* (Bloomington: Indiana University Press, 1988). Ross's study concludes that market mechanisms, and not the state-initiated mass campaign or other policy reforms, are successful in controlling the deterioration of environment in China.

11. Initial discussion on policy diffusion is provided in J. Walker, "The Diffusion of Innovation Among the American States," *American Political Science Review* 63 (1969): 880-899; Virginia Gray, "Innovation in the States: A Diffusion Study," *American Political Science Review* 67 (1973): 1174-1185.

12. I have discussed this possibility earlier in "Environment as a Political Issue in Developing Countries: A Study of Environmental Pollution in India, "*International Journal of Environmental Studies* 23: 105-112.

13. The World Bank report puts India in the bottom 25 percent of the nations. *World Development Report 1988* (The World Bank, Oxford University Press) 222-23.

14. The Planning Commission, *The First Five Year Plan: A summary* (New Delhi: Government of India, 1952), 1.

15. The Planning Commission, *The Fourth Five Year Plan*, 1969-74, (New Delhi: Government of India), Ch. 2, Par. 2.46.

16. Mohan Ram, "8th Plan Aims at 6% Growth Rate," *India Abroad*, 4 November 1988, 16.

17. Richard S. Eckaus, "Prospects for Development Finance in India," in *Financing Asian Development 2: China and India* by Robert F. Dernberger and Richard S. Eckaus, ed. (Lanham: The Asia Society, 1988).

18. "Eighth Plan: A Time for Austerity," *India Today*, 31 October 1988, 90-93.

19. Ibid., 91

20. For a detailed discussion of these trends, see Eckaus, "Prospects for Development."

21. Barrington Moore, Jr., *Social Origin of Dictatorship and Democracy* (Boston: Beacon, 1966), 418. The logistic connection between capitalism and democracy has also been supported by Charles Lindblom, *Politics and Markets: The World's Political-Economic Systems* (New York: Basic, 1977); and Samuel Huntington, "Will More Countries Become Democratic?" *Political Science Quarterly* 99:2. In addition, Seymore Martin Lipset has also provided the most convincing argument on the connection between economic development and democracy ("Some Social Requisites of Democracy: Economic Development and Political Legitimacy," *American Political Science Review* 53: 69-105).

22. "Free-floating" is a term used to refer to those groups that have no historical pattern of alliance with any of the political groups or parties.

23. For a lively discussion, refer to Atul Kohli, *India's Democracy* (Princton: Princeton University Press, 1988).

24. Robert L. Hardgrave and Stanley A. Kochanek, *India: Government and Politics in a Developing Nation* (San Diego: Harcourt Brace Jovanovich, 1986).

25. Indira Gandhi, "Man and his Environment," (address by Mrs. Gandhi at the plenary session of the United Nations Conference on Human Environment at Stockholm, Sweden, 14 June 1972).

26. O.P. Dwivedi and B. Kishore, "Protecting the Environment from Pollution: A Review of India's Legal and Institutional Mechanisms," *Asian Survey* 22:9 (1982): 894-911.

27. Charles C. Jones (in *Clean Air*) presented the thesis on speculative augmentation--a situation where government designs a policy on hasty speculations under tremendous pressure.

28. David Vogel, *National Styles of Regulation: Environmental Policy in Great Britain and the United States* (Ithaca, Cornell University Press, 1986), Ch. 4.

29. Upendra Baxi, "Environmental Law: Limitation and Potential for Liberation," in *India's Environment: Crises and Responses* ed. by J. Bandyopadhyay et al. (Dehradun: Natraj, 1985).

30. Robert Hardgrave, Jr. *India Under Pressure: Prospects for Stability and Change* (Boulder: Westview Press, 1984); Mary C. Carras, *Indira Gandhi in the Crucible of Leadership: A Political Biography* (Boston: Beacon Press, 1979); Zarrer Masani, *Indira Gandhi: A Biography* (New York: Crowell, 1976).

31. S.L. Bahuguna, "People's Response to Ecological Crises in the Hill Areas," in J. Bandyopadhyay, et al., *India's Environment*.

CHAPTER 2

Environmental Crisis

I ndia faces two types of environmental problems: those emerging due to underdevelopment, such as unhygienic surroundings, poverty, non-availability of water, and poisonous smoke from wood-burning stoves, etc.; and those emerging from the development itself, such as chemical pollution, acid rain, noise pollution, pesticide pollution, loss of usable land, deforestation, and air pollution. The problems in the first category fall under the developmental agenda, while the problems in the second category fall under the specific environmental agenda.

Before the 1970s, the developmental agenda enjoyed the focal position in the nation's agenda. The decade of the 1970s, however, witnessed a frantic search for a combination of the two agendas—environmental and developmental. During this time, programs labelled as "eco-development" or ecologically sound development and "sustainable growth" attracted the attention of the policy planners. In the post-1980 years, however, policy planners are looking at the environmental agenda as an entity in itself. This policy shift has resulted from the realization that the environmental crisis poses a serious challenge and must be dealt with as an entity and not as a subset of the overall developmental agenda. For the purpose of this study, I treat environmental issues as those issues that are on the environmental agenda. In the following section, I discuss some of the major issues on the environmental agenda of the nation today.

Water Pollution

The pollution of water is said to be one of the two most severe environmental problems faced by the nation today. According to the scientists at the National Engineering and Research Institute (NEERI), a staggering 70 percent of the available water in India is polluted, and an estimated 73 million workdays costing the society Rs 60 million are lost every year because of pollution-related health problems.[1] The management and disposal of water poses two different types of problems: (1) the inefficient use of water resources, which results in the shortage of water supply; and (2) the neglect of waste water disposal system, which is responsible for pollution. According to the estimates[2]:

— India uses only a tenth of the rainfall it receives annually. If current policy to maximize the use of rain water is implemented properly, India will still be using not more than one-fourth of its rainfall in the year 2025.

— The groundwater resources in the nation are ten times more than the rainfall. But during the 1970s, nearly 170,000 tubewells were added each year. More and more such wells are constructed each year, thus putting a continuous burden on the groundwater resources.

— Each year, the people of India suffer either from drought or from floods. In 1987, all but three states faced severe drought (said to be the worst in one hundred years). The three remaining states experienced major floods.

— All but two of the high-altitude lakes are steadily dying because of pollution.

— Only 3 percent of the total population has access to a sewage treatment system. Even in the metropolitan cities with a population of one million or more, only 57 percent of the wastewater is treated. The percentage of treated water declines sharply to 5 percent for cities with a population between 50,000 and 100,000 (see Figure 2.1).

— Only 27 percent of the large and medium-sized industries have full or partial treatment facilities. Table 2.1[3] provides a distribution of water polluting industries and their treatment facilities across states.

Three primary sources of water pollution have been identified by scientists: the discharging of industrial effluent, the dumping of untreated sewage (which is responsible for the 90 percent of the pollution by volume), and finally, the contamination of the underground water from pesticides. Because of inadequate treatment facilities in residential and industrial areas,

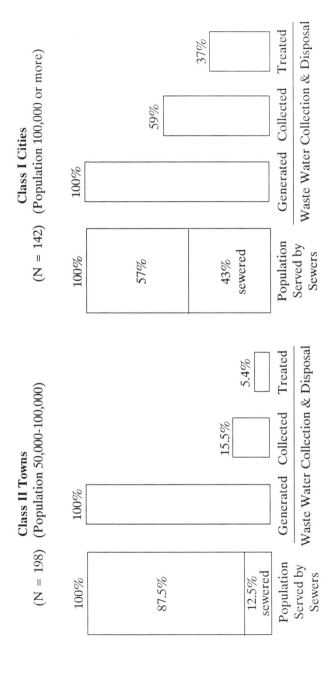

Figure 2.1. Waste Water Treatment and Sewerage Condition in Major Urban Settlements

Source: Based on CBPCWP (New Delhi, India) Publication Nos. CUPS/61/1978-79 and CUPS/6/1979-80

Table 2.1
Distribution of Major Water Polluting Industries
and Their Water Treatment Facilities in States

Name of State	Total Water Polluting Industries	Industries with Full or Partial Facilities
Andhra Pradesh	114	54
Assam	30	4
Bihar	95	8
Gujarat	389	68
Haryana	110	6
Himachal Pradesh	20	—
Jammu & Kashmir	3	1
Karnataka	166	79
Kerala	130	39
Madhya Pradesh	119	30
Punjab	68	13
Rajasthan	108	62
Uttar Pradesh	102	32
West Bengal	120	37
Central Board for Union Territories	136	27
TOTAL	1700	460

Source: *The Directory of Non-Governmental Organizations in Environment* (New Delhi: Government of India, Department of Environment, 1985).

stream pollution has also reached a point of crisis.[4] For long stretches, water from the two holy rivers, the Ganga and the Yamuna, is unfit for drinking or even bathing. Even though the Indian standard for inland surface water requires MPN (coliform organism) content not to exceed 5000 per 100 ml., the Yamuna River below Delhi at Okhala contains an MPN of 24 million parts per 100 ml. of water.[5] Similarly, the Ganga water, after receiving sewage from the city and wastes from textile mills in Kanpur, is unfit for bathing and even for fish culture. The water in other rivers, lakes, and streams used for drinking has also been reported to contain harmful metallic and organic substances.

Water pollution, thus, is a serious crisis; nevertheless, one cannot ignore the fact that the supply of water is also an equally alarming problem. In rural areas, people walk up to ten or fifteen miles in search of water for their daily needs. The life of city dwellers is by no means any easier, for they may receive water for only two to three hours a day in their water taps. People in small towns as well as in major cities are forced to store water in in-house tanks for their daily needs. During my frequent trips to India, I realized that the availability of water was not only unpredictable, it was often at an inconvenient time. Moreover, the color of the tap water, especially during the monsoon, was light yellow or light brown.

Water, thus, is a two-sided issue. One cannot speak of the quality of water if the water is not made available in the first place. The twin problems of water supply and of water quality pose a policy problem in India that is quite different from problems faced by policy makers in the West. Considering its limited resources, the government in India is forced to search for a reconciliation—reconciliation which may not be the most desirable solution from either the environmentalist or the developmentalist point of view, but nonetheless, may be the only viable political solution available to policy planners. While formulating a policy to deal with the pollution of water, the government cannot afford to ignore the need to invest in policies related to the supply of water. India ranks 84th in the world in terms of the percentage of population that has access to safe water. This is remarkable considering India's large population and low GNP, which is 128th in the world.[6] Nevertheless, it still means that over 350 million people in the nation are without any access to safe water.

The control of water polluting sources also requires a multi-dimensional approach. The easiest and the safest approach that the government finds is the setting of emission standards for effluent discharge. In cases where pollution is caused by industry, the primary responsibility of action lies with the industry, and not with the government. The government only needs to provide the surveillance. However, in cases where pollution is caused by residential sources, the government finds itself in a political dilemma. Since no one person or group can be held responsible for this pollution, the responsibility falls upon the government itself, which has to provide treatment facilities from its limited resources. The environmental issue, now, becomes a political issue and competes against other developmental issues, such as the supply of water. This is the reason why the government is more successful in establishing emission standards than it is in building treatment facilities.

Air Pollution

Air pollution, although apparently very serious, remains a little-studied problem. It first became a national issue in the late 1970s when the Indian government decided to build an oil refinery near Mathura in the state of Uttar Pradesh. The Taj Mahal, just 40 kilometers away from the proposed refinery, was seen by environmentalists as the prime victim of air pollution at the time of the refinery site selection in the early 1970s.[7] Since then, many studies have focused on the dimensions of the air pollution problem, and its implications for human lives and historic monuments.[8] Some of the findings are shocking:

— While cooking, women alone inhale 40 times the volume of suspended particles considered safe by the World Health Organization (WHO). In three hours, they may inhale an amount of carcinogenic benzo(a) pyrene that equals 20 packs of cigarettes.

— In a mountain village, researchers found an unusually high infant mortality rate of 490 per thousand. Two of the three deaths were attributed to respiratory diseases arising from smoke pollution.

— In 15 years, the quality of sulphur dioxide released into the air in major cities has tripled.

— Out of 48 thermal power stations surveyed in 1984, 31 had taken no pollution control measures at all.

— Traces of acid rain have already been found in major Indian cities, and no steps have been taken to deal with them.

Table 2.2 provides a comparative overview of the extent of air pollution in major Indian cities. There is a distinct feature about the air pollution problem: in urban areas, it is highly localized; and in rural areas, it is greatly subtle. The main contributing factors of the air pollution in cities are "thermal power generation plants, iron and steel mills, petrochemical and fertilizer complexes, synthetic fiber factories, metallurgical works, and chemical, ceramic, and pharmaceutical industries."[9] Auto emission is another significant source of air pollution in major cities.[10] According to the government's

Table 2.2
Comparable Data on Air Quality in Selected Cities

Name of City	Suspended Particulate Matter (in microgram per cubic meter)*
(IN INDIA)	
Ahmedabad	243
Bombay	275
Calcutta	578
Delhi	481
Hyderabad	295
Jaipur	379
Kanpur	344
Nagpur	386
(OUTSIDE INDIA)	
Brussels	170
London City	250
Los Angeles	70
Milan	600
New York	110
Paris	110
Toronto City	170

* The accepted level of Suspended Particulate Matter (SPM) set by the World Health Organization is 150.

Source: *Air Quality Control in Selected Cities of India* (Nagpur, India: National Environmental Research Institute, 1979).

survey of 1,633 gasoline-driven vehicles in Delhi, 42 percent of the vehicles did not comply with the emission standards set by the government under the Air Act. According to another report, air pollution in all metropolitan cities of India exceeds the limit set by the World Health Organization at least two to four times.[11] The result of this heavy pollution is the increase in respiratory diseases, which have gone up nearly 100 to 200 percent in the last decade.

Air pollution in developing countries, however, is not limited to highly urbanized and modernized areas. Rural areas, because of the use of wood-burning stoves, are inflicted with a far more serious atmospheric pollution problem. In India, the use of stoves, called *chullahs*, threatens the quality of the environment by producing harmful smoke, as well as by causing stress on the nation's already limited forests. The elimination of smoke *chullahs*, however, is not an environmental issue; but instead, it is a developmental issue. With more than half of the villages being without a single road or a single electrical connection, the use of cooking gas or electrical stoves remains only a dream. Another alternative, solar stove, is expensive, and is unfit for the hot humid weather. The level of rural poverty makes the use of other high-priced stoves consuming refined fuel an unrealistic solution.

Land and Forests

According to the estimates by the Delhi-based Society for Promotion of Wastelands Development (SPWD), nearly one-third of India's land is suffering from serious environmental degradation.[12] As Figure 2.2 points out, almost 160 million hectares of land is classified as degraded or as endangered. The estimates of degraded lands vary from 17.6 million hectares to 37.5 million hectares, and the total extent of wastelands ranges from at least 111 million to a maximum of 131 million hectares.[13] Despite a variation between the government's low figures and the high figures quoted by independent sources, it is generally agreed that the land suffers from forest cutting, soil erosion, wind erosion, mining, and development-related activities. Surprisingly, the land is also under stress due to extensive cropping. The Green Revolution of the 1960s, which had made India self-sufficient in food is showing its environmental side-effects now.

> Is the green revolution killing the goose that lays the golden egg? Is it draining the very soil where the high-yielding varieties are planted? It would seem so. Scientists are discovering to their dismay that extensive cropping is removing the crucial micronutrient elements—zinc, iron, copper, manganese, magnesium, molybdenum, boron—which form only one percent of the weight of a plant but control various aspects of a plant's processes. For instance, Ludhiana district of Punjab records the highest yields of many crop but it also records the most alarming deficiency of micronutrient.[14]

According to estimates, the nation is loosing over 8,000 hectares of productive land to ravines each year. These ravines result from the loss of vegetation cover due to excessive cropping, extended cultivation and reckless tilling of the land. The government both at the central and state level

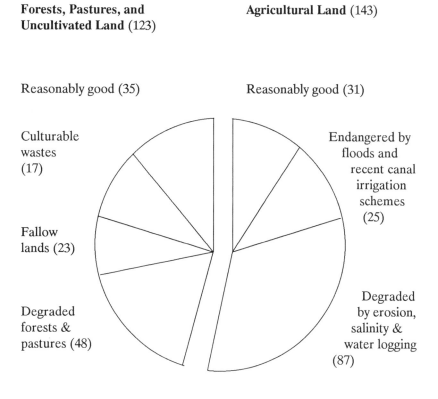

Forests, Pastures, and   **Agricultural Land** (143)
Uncultivated Land (123)

Reasonably good (35)   Reasonably good (31)

Culturable wastes (17)

Endangered by floods and recent canal irrigation schemes (25)

Fallow lands (23)

Degraded forests & pastures (48)

Degraded by erosion, salinity & water logging (87)

Figure 2.2.   Land Estimates of Degraded and Endangered Areas*
(in million of hectares)

* The total area relevant to environmental management is estimated to be 266 million hectares (81% of India's total geographical area).

Source: Anil Agarwal, Ravi Chopra and Kalpana Sharma, *The State of India's Environment: A Citizens's Report* (New Delhi: Centre for Science and Environment, 1982)

recognized the problem as serious as early as the 1960s. The government of Madhya Pradesh, for instance, established a commission to study the feasibility of reclaiming ravines in 1954. Based on the commission's report, a regional plan was introduced and more than 3,000 hectares of ravine land was reclaimed in the following 25 years. The central government also offered a massive plan operated by the Home Ministry in 1971 to reclaim land in Uttar Pradesh, Madhya Pradesh and Rajasthan, but the plan failed because of the lack of support from the local people.

Mining activity in India adds further stress to the available land. The mining production in the country has grown fifty times in the last three decades. Fossil fuels, iron ore, limestone and coal are the chief mining resources distributed unevenly throughout the nation. Other than coal, the nation's mineral reservoirs are short in supply. Nevertheless, mining is pursued vigorously through open cast mining as well as through underground mining. Since the mines are located in selected areas and since transport is expensive, most of the mineral-based industries, such as steel plants, power plants and cement factories, are concentrated in selected regions. These regions are heavily stressed because other than the direct mining activity, they also loose their productive land to infrastructural buildings, such as railroads, roads and establishments. The Bhilai-Bokaro-Durgapur region is particularly affected by mining because most steel plants are situated in this region. Similarly, over 40 percent of the forest area of Goa is leased out for mining activity. Several mining-based companies, such as Bharat Aluminium Company and Hindustan Aluminium Company in Amarkantak, are also the source of water pollution in major rivers of Narmada and Damodar. Thus, the mining activity destroys the land directly, but it also produces several environmental side-effects such as water pollution, air pollution, desertification, deforestation and nutrient drain.

The land is further threatened by an unusually high rate of deforestation. The statistics on the nation's forests are alarming: the latest satellite data provided by the National Remote Sensing Agency confirm that the nation is losing 1.3 million hectares of forests each year.[15] Though the government claims that 23 percent of the total land area is under the control of the forest departments and, therefore, is forest area, satellite pictures reveal that not more than 14 percent of the area actually has tree cover. During a period of six years between 1975 and 1981, it is estimated that a sixth of the forest area was lost. Table 2.3 provides the data on the loss of forest land. Surprisingly, this was the time when the government was most active in the adoption of new policies and programs to protect the nation's natural

Table 2.3
Loss of Forest Land in Indian States

Name of State	State forest area lost in 1972-1982 (million hectares)	Percent of forest area lost since 1972
Andhra Pradesh	0.86	17.6
Assam	0.13	6.2
Bihar	0.26	11.5
Gujarat	0.44	46.3
Haryana	0.04	50.0
Himachal Pradesh	0.60	39.7
Jammu & Kashmir	0.79	35.4
Karnataka	0.38	12.9
Kerala	0.12	14.0
Madhya Pradesh	1.84	16.9
Maharashtra	1.03	25.3
Manipur	0.13	8.6
Meghalaya	0.19	13.2
Nagaland	0.01	1.2
Orissa	0.90	18.6
Punjab	0.06	54.5
Rajasthan	0.53	46.9
Sikkim	0.0	0.0
Tamilnadu	0.35	21.0
Tripura	0.12	19.0
Uttar Pradesh	0.49	18.9
West Bengal	0.18	21.7

Source: Based on the estimates given by the National Remote Sensing
         Agency, Hyderabad, India.

resources. The stress on the forests comes from industrialization, urbanization, increase in population; but interestingly, it also comes from the corrupt practices of the bureaucracy that is in charge of protecting them.[16] There are at least 40 million people classified as forest-dwellers, who depend on forests for their basic survival, and who, regardless of all the restrictions and regulations, continue to use forest material. The government has identified the forests-dwellers to be a major source of stress on forests.[17]

Large and small dams also contribute to the assault on the availability and quality of land. The need for dams is acute in India for two reasons: first, the rainfall is uneven ranging from very high in Cherapunji to almost negligible in the areas of Rajasthan; second, the rainfall is concentrated during the four months of monsoon leaving the rest of the year extremely dry. More than 700 dams for the collection of water are under operation storing about 16 million hectare meters of water. The government foresees a need to increase this number to 40 million hectare meters through the development of several medium and large irrigation projects. These irrigation projects are, however, criticized by environmentalists for their social and environmental costs that are borne by the people. Dams, it is argued, disturb the ecological balance and increase the threat of natural disasters. Also, dams involve the relocation of a large number of people who eventually face serious resettlement costs not borne by the government. Major dams that have come under popular attack in the last decade include the Silent Valley and Munnar in the state of Kerala, Bedthi in the state of Karnataka, Tehri and Vishnuprayag in the state of Uttar Pradesh, Doel-Karo in the state of Bihar, Lalpu in the state of Gujarat, and Narmada Valley in the states of Gujarat and Madhya Pradesh. The protest in these cases has ranged from social issues, such as better terms for rehabilitation, to environmental issues. The issue of the right of reclamation of land by the people disturbed from projects has even led to legislative battles. The state of Maharashtra granted this right in 1976; but in many other states, the lack of any such guarantee evokes frustration and panic.

Other than the visible problems of water, air and land deterioration, the physical environment in India also suffers from the more sophisticated yet less detected problems of noise pollution and acid rain. The focus of the governmental and public activity, however, remains on the above discussed environmental problems.

Environmental Issue and the Cultural Context

The environmental policy process, like any other policy process, begins with the realization of the problem by society. How, why, and in what context the problem is defined sets the tone of the remaining process. The pollution issue, for example, was first seen as a health issue by the governments of most industrialized societies and, therefore, was dealt with at the local level. It was not until the 1960s when several pollution crises, such as Minamata, London Fog, and Love Canal, emerged simultaneously in different countries that the universal and urgent nature of the problem was realized. In India, the pollution issue remained a sub-issue of the larger health and safety issue until the 1970s. This arrangement led to a policy of "quick-fixing," in which each time a problem occurred some immediate, but temporary, relief was provided to victims, but no effort was made to search for a long-lasting solution.

The severity of the environmental degradation today provides an important impetus for environmental decision-making. Since the degradation of the natural resources has already reached an alarming point, it is no longer possible for the society to ignore the pollution problem as being secondary to other developmental problems. Nevertheless, solutions available to the society, or to its government, are limited by various factors. These factors define the boundaries within which the process of arriving at decisions must take place. The culture of a society sets an important policy boundary. Most industrialized societies, for example, found the environmental issue unacceptable for a long period, simply because it conflicted with their consumption-oriented policy of development. It was realized that the acceptance of the issue meant a significant change in the society's behavior. But once accepted, the issue was quick to find political and economic support. In developing countries, on the other hand, the acceptance of the issue came effortlessly, because in most cases, the acceptance required moral, rather than real, support.

In India, the culture is an asset for environmental planners. Not only does the nation harbor a pro-environment culture, but it also supports an economic strategy based on conservation and non-materialism, and a political ideology based on non-violence and co-existence. The support for the environment is an integral part of the socialization process.

India is a secular country with at least seven major religions including Hinduism, Islam, Christianity, Buddhism, and Sikhism. Religious preachings almost always encourage love and respect for the physical environment. The

Hindu religion (which is practiced by 82 percent of the nation's population) emphasizes a harmonious relationship between people and their natural surroundings. The concern for natural resources is well engraved in the oldest writings of Indian philosophers. Surprisingly enough, it was noted two thousand years ago in *Atharva Veda* that the environment needed protection from the human need and greed. The following verses reflect not only the respect for the natural resources, but also a concern for their replenishment.

May Earth yield milk, this earth of many streams,
and shed on us her splendour copiously.

Impart to us those vitalizing forces
that come, O Earth, from deep within your body,
your central point, your navel; purify us wholly.
The Earth is mother, I am son of Earth.

Mother of plants and begetter of all things,
firm, far-flung Earth, sustained by heavenly Law,
kindly and pleasant is she. May we ever
dwell on her bosom, passing to and fro
Whatever I dig up of you, O Earth,
May you of that have quick replenishment;
O purifying one, may our thrust never
reach right into your vital points, your heart.[18]

Throughout my fieldwork in India, I was reminded of the strong respect that the society upholds for its natural resources. The underlying belief was stated clearly even by the illiterate people. While the people strongly believed that natural resources must be protected, they were equally unconvinced of the fact that any serious danger to their natural resources, especially the sacred rivers of Ganga and Yamuna, existed. Since my interviews were conducted in the northern parts of India, especially in the states of Uttar Pradesh, Madhya Pradesh, Himachal Pradesh and Haryana, I found that the Hindu philosophy was often quoted by the people to support their environment-related views. I summarize some these views in the section below. The focus on Hinduism does not in any way reflect that other religions do not adopt to a pro-environmental stand.

The Hindu religion provides support to the environment through its basic belief in the personification of natural resources.[19] Even though the objective here is not to establish a linkage between one's religious beliefs and environmental beliefs, I feel that some understanding of this linkage is essential to understand the policy preferences of the masses. The personification of natural resources is the cornerstone of the Hindu view of the environment; and various mythological stories continue to reinforce this belief. In Hinduism, rivers, forests, mountains, and trees all are considered to have some form of god in them and are, therefore, respected. The Ganga (also called Ganges), for example, is believed to be the daughter of Lord Brahma, the creator of the universe, and is believed to have been sent to the earth to help people find *moksha*, the ultimate freedom. She is a Goddess herself, and any disrespect to her is seen as a religious crime. Even today millions of people gather on the banks of the Ganga on designated days to take a dip in the river.

Other than personifying natural resources, the Hindu faith also establishes a heavenly connection for them. Ocean, forests, animals, and birds all emerge as angels in *Ramayana* and *Mahabharatha*, the two most widely read books in the society today. According to *Ramayana*, when Lord Rama was in search of his wife Sita, his path was led by trees and stones; his messages were given by birds; and his army consisted of only monkeys and bears. These and similar other stories have established a harmonious, friendly, yet mysterious relationship between the people and their natural surroundings.

The religious support to the environment is also reflected in society's customs and rituals. In the hill areas where tribal culture still prevails, rituals and superstitions play a significant role in defining the relationship between the people and their physical environment. Some of the natural resources are protected by superstitions. A good example is the belief that the *peepal* tree is housed by ghosts and wandering souls and, therefore, should not be chopped down. Also, it is widely believed that forests are protected by the *vandevi* and, therefore, cannot be destroyed. Similarly, Jainism and Buddhism rely almost exclusively on building a harmonious relationship between the people and their natural surroundings.

The cultural setting of the environmental protection policy in India is complex, for two cultures seem to exist within one dominant culture. While the respect for an abstract Mother Nature is well emphasized, the regard for natural surroundings is yet to find its place in the day to day behavior of the society. Several rituals that are tied to either the religion or social customs are insensitive, and often even harmful, for the natural resources. In addition, these rituals also limit the options available to policy planners in a society where social laws, and not governmental laws, dictate the society's behavior. India's policy history is full of examples where policies failed not because of their legal weakness, but because of their conflicting stand with social laws.

In an attempt to establish the importance of the cultural context for a policy process, I cite two examples of policy failures below.

Population growth, which is cited as one of the major factors behind the environmental stress, offers a serious policy challenge for planners. The government of India has made several attempts to check the rate of population growth; however, the allegiance to and the impact of these attempts have both been unsatisfactory. In fact, it was the boomerang effect of the population control policy that prompted Mrs. Gandhi's defeat in the 1977 general elections.[20] As designed under Sanjay Gandhi's guidance, the population control policy was based on providing incentives to people for voluntary sterilization through local governmental bodies. Quotas were set for each administrative unit, and local officials were given the flexibility to avail their own measures to reach the quota. In their zeal, implementors used harsh strategies, including non-payment of salaries to government employees and refusal to reissue permits. The policy brought immediate success by improving the statistics, but it eventually failed in the long run.[21]

The population control policy failed because of its incompatibility with the social culture. It ignored the cultural dimension of the problem. Factors, such as the religious need to have at least one son; the economic necessity of sons being the only form of old-age pension, social security, medical insurance, and life insurance; social reality of children being the primary source of identity were entirely overlooked. In addition, the policy also showed insensitivity to the high rates of urbanization and infant mortality, which have always been the important determining factors in peoples' decision to have more children.

With strong cultural beliefs favoring large families, it is not surprising that the population control programs that sought voluntary compliance failed, while the programs that imposed involuntary restrictions invited political instability and, thus, became undesirable. Today, while the governmental policy of population control still continues, the enthusiasm behind it has withered away. It is ironic that the street posters that I found filled with environmental slogans during my field-trip to India in 1987 had been pasted over the poster-boards that had carried the message of population control just a few months ago.

Another example of policy failure, where culture played a determining role, is the 1961 Prohibition of Dowry Act. The act abolished any form of dowry in the nation; however, the practice of dowry remained untouched. Once again, the act failed to relate to social perceptions which resulted from a variety of complex factors. The dependent status of women, an explicit preference for sons, marriages serving as vehicles for upward social mobility, and the emergence of consumption-oriented lifestyle are some of the contributing factors, and even in their combined explanatory power, they only touch the tip of the iceberg.

Having established the importance of the cultural context in determining policy outcomes, let's turn our attention to some specific aspects of environment-related programs of the past. Several such programs have failed in spite of explicit legal and bureaucratic support. A good example is the government's effort to stop shifting cultivation—called *Jhuming* by the people—in the northeast part of the nation. The practice of *Jhuming* is destructive to the forests, resulting in the destruction of nearly half of the forests in the state of Mizoram alone. *Jhuming* involves the simplest method of farming in the regions with not much fertile soil. A typical "Jhumia family clears a part of the forest, burns the wood and foliage, ploughs the land——mixing the ash with the top soil—and then sows the seeds. The poor soil does not sustain more than two or three crops and the family then moves on to another part of the forest, repeating the destructive process."[22]

Since nearly 50,000 *Jhumia* families relied on this form of shifting cultivation in Mizoram alone, the government evolved a program in the 1970s to stop the practice by helping the *Jhumias* to farm on a permanent land. For the *Jhumias*, the change from shifting cultivation to permanent farming was a style which did not suit their cultural belief. The whole life-style of the *Jhumias*, including their rituals, songs, and festivals, all revolved around the *Jhuming* cycle. In addition, they were non-settlers by nature, and numerous superstitions existed prohibiting them from settling at any one place.

Another example is the "cleaning of the Ganga" program. One of the significant sources of pollution is identified as the throwing of dead bodies in the river. The problem is particularly acute in the holy cities of Banaras and Haridwar. Cremation centers along the banks also add to the pollution, for ashes of human bodies after cremation are placed in the water. The belief is that a Hindu body, if purified with the Ganga water, attains immediate *moksha*. Attempts to provide electric cremation centers have failed, and programs to construct free cremation centers in the holy cities have had only partial success. The problem is serious enough, and has been raised several times in the national and state legislatures.

In urban areas, a significant level of pollution is caused by the careless attitude toward basic hygiene. Unhygienic surroundings are created because of general habits. It is a general practice to dump garbage near the front gates at any convenient time. Each municipal government has a system of garbage pick-up; however, the hours of pick-up are rarely observed. The garbage serves as a breeding ground for street animals, such as cows, donkeyes and even pigs. Similarly, in an effort to beautify cities, local governments have installed trash cans in public places, such as parks and railway stations. However, one only needs to travel in India to see the casual manner in which these trash cans are continuously ignored. Throwing off of plastic spoons, paper pieces, and fruit peels from a running train or a bus is a common sight as well.

While the nation harbors a strong pro-environment culture, very little is put to practice in reality. The ideals of simplicity, non-violence, and non-materialism, which are preached by every religion in the nation, are not reflected in the society's behavior. Over the years, Indians have learned to thrive for materialistic gains, and showing off of those gains, just as vigorously as any other people in the supposedly materialistic Western society.

Despite certain specific actions of the people that are alarming from an environmental point of view, India hosts a pro-environmental culture. The environmental policy is unlikely to run into the barriers that the population control policy and the anti-dowry policy had stumbled over during their implementation. For policy planners, this is an important asset. There is also a consensus that natural resources must be preserved at any cost. In addition, the general culture does not support a materialistic, consumer-oriented way of living. The threat to the environment, therefore, does not come from the mass culture, but it comes from the neglect of that culture by the elite. So far, very few attempts have been made by the government to emphasize the environmentally suited aspects of the culture; instead, the actions taken by the government have almost always undermined the harmonious relationship between the people and the environment, and have stressed the need for more and more regulation.

Notes

1. Anil Agarwal, Ravi Chopra and Kalpana Sharma, *The State of India's Environment, 1982: A Citizen's Report* (New Delhi: Centre for Science and Environment, 1982), 17.

2. The statistics have been compiled from various sources, but the most important are Anil Agarwal and Sunita Narain, *The State of India's Environ-*

ment (New Delhi: Centre for Science and Environment, 1985); and the reports of the Central Board for the Prevention and Control of Water Pollution.

3. Eight states--Maharashtra, Tamilnadu, Orissa, Manipur, Meghalaya, Nagaland, Sikkim and Tripura--are not in the table. Since the statistics are based on a survey conducted by the Central Water Pollution Control Board in April-May of 1981 when these states had not accepted the Water Act of 1974, these states could not be included in the survey. Since then, the states have adopted the law and have established their independent water boards. According to the officials in the Central Water Pollution Control Board, the numbers have only increased in the last few years.

4. A large volume of reports exist in this respect. More specifically, one may refer to D. Dixit, "Deadly Pollution of our Rivers," *Imprint* (August 1981), 15-17; S.D. Ray, "Pollution Spreads to India's Sacred River," *Earthwatch* 3 (1980); B.B. Vohra, "Needed--A Policy for Water," *The Hindustan Times*, 2 June 1981, 17 & 21; "Laws Needed to Prevent Sea, Water Pollution," *The Hindustan Times*, 4 January 1981, 7; Raj Gill, "Waste Water Hazard to Urbanization," *The Hindustan Times*, 23 April 1980, 1 & 8.

5. Agarwal, *The State of India's Environment*, 1982, 20.

6. Ruth Legar Sivard, *World Military and Social Expenditures 1987-88*, 12th ed. (Washington, DC: World Priorities, 1987).

7. "Plants Near Taj Must Go," *The Hindustan Times*, 25 August 1978, 1-2; "Ecologists Fast to Save Taj, *"The Hindustan Times*, 23 May 1977, 3; S.K. Gupta, "Pollution Threat to Taj, Dal Lake," *The Hindustan Times*, 19 November 1981, 17.

8. "Air Pollution Rate in Big Cities Alarming." *Overseas Hindustan Times*, 25 February 1982, 4; A. Balram, "Spector of Pollution," *The Hindustan Times*, 9 June 1981, 17 & 19; G.S. George & A. Abraham, "The Air We Breath, the Noise We Hear," *The Hindustan Times*, 16 October 1977, 1; R.S. Mehta, "Air Pollution Problem in India," *Asian Environment*, 1 (1978): 26-28.

9. O.P. Dwivedi and Brij Kishore, "Protecting the Environment from Pollution: A Review of India's Legal and Institutional Mechanisms," *Asian Survey*, 22:9 (1982): 904.

10. Nandita Sharma, "Foul Fumes," *India Today*, 31 March 1987, 55. Sharma estimates that more than half of the pollution in Delhi is caused by

auto-rikshwas that emit 250 tons of pollutants every day. There has been a ten-fold increase in the number of vehicles in the city. The situation is the same in Bombay and Calcutta.

11. "Heavy Air Pollution in Big Cities," *Indian Express*, 8 February 1982, 4.

12. Agarwal, *The State of India's Environment,* 1984-85, 1-26.

13. Ibid, 3-28.

14. Ibid, 20.

15. The agency is located in Hyderabad, and publishes periodic reports on the status of forests and land. The statistics collected by the agency are most often cited by the press and environmentalists, since there is a common feeling that the government figures do not reflect reality.

16. I have discussed this point in my earlier work, *Forests: The People and the Government* (New Delhi: National Book Organization, 1989).

17. *Report of the National Commission on Agriculture Part IX: Forestry,"* (New Delhi: Government of India Publications, Part 9, 1976) caused a major controversy by claiming that the forests need to be protected from the people. The report was criticized by environmentalists and social workers alike. Nevertheless, it provided an inspiration for the program of social forestry in the 1980s.

18. Translated version taken from Rev. Eric J. Lott, "India's Religious Resources for a Global Eco-theology," in J. Bandyopadhyay et. al., eds., *India's Environment: Crises and Responses* (Dehra Dun: Natraj, 1985), 178.

19. For a general discussion of Hindu religion through Vedas, one may refer to Eric. J. Lott, *Vedantic Approaches to God* (London: Macmillan, 1980). Several papers presented at the "Religious and Social Basis of Environmental Policies in India," in the meeting in Bangalore, India on December 4, 1984 also raised these three points.

20. Myron Weiner, *India at the Polls: The Parliamentary Elections of 1977* (Washington, D.C.: American Enterprise Institute, 1978) stressed this point.

21. Robert L. Hardgrave and Stanley A. Kochanek, *India: Government and Politics in a Developing Nation* (San Diego: Harcourt Brace, Jovanovich, 1986), 16-17.

22. Ramesh Menon, "A Brave Attempt," *India Today*, 15 January 1988, 93.

CHAPTER 3

Making of an Environmental Policy

T he issue of environment in India is neither new, nor is it insignifi-
cant. What is new is the bureaucratization of the issue. The evidence
suggests that the issue of environmental degradation had already
emerged under the British in the early twentieth century. After realizing the
immediate threat to the lavish forests of India, the British government passed
the Indian Forest Act in 1927—a legislation which provides guidelines for
managing the forests even today. Another major legislation forwarded was
the Indian Motor Vehicle Act of 1939, which conferred legal powers upon
state governments to make rules regarding emission of smoke, visible vapor,
and noise caused by motor vehicles.

The British-made legislation, especially the Forest Act, helped shape the
focus of environmental policy process in the nation. One of the major
characteristics of the legislation was its emphasis on the regulatory aspect
of the policy process. Bureaucracy was seen as a primary actor and was asked
to play a prominent role in the preservation of the environment. In addition,
the British-designed policies granted the government an uncontested right
over natural resources. The Forest Act, for example, was based on the
principle that the forests needed protection *from* the people, and not *for* the
people. The forests, according to the act, were divided into various categories, and forest departments at the state level were delegated the responsibility for supervising their protection in each of the categories. While the
forests in several categories were made inaccessible to the people, the
government continued to grant licenses to contractors to cut the trees. The
Forest Act, in fact, became an instrument of exploitation in the hands of the
government, especially the bureaucracy.

Soon after the nation established its independence in 1947, three environment-related laws were passed by the newly elected government under
the leadership of Jawaharlal Nehru (a Western-educated, liberal-minded
leader of India). The Mines and Minerals (Regulation and Development)

Act won approval in 1947, the Factories Act in 1949, and the Industries (Development and Regulation) Act in 1951; nevertheless, all of the acts dealt more with the safety and health issues than with the environmental issue per se. The issue of environment was, in fact, missing from the policy agenda, and so was an integrated approach to define the issue in a definite way. Even though several environment-related issues were beginning to appear on the surface, the inter-relationship among these sub-issues was not being recognized. This oversight led to a policy approach, which was piecemeal in nature. The government was attacking the problem of environmental degradation with a "fire-brigade" attitude, providing resources to emergency areas, instead of working in the direction of designing an integrated, comprehensive policy.

The environment received a low priority, if any, throughout the 1950s and 1960s. The lack of knowledge regarding the extent of destruction, and regarding its implications for the living beings became the primary hurdle. The evidence suggests that various health-related effects of pollution were noticed as early as in the 1950s[1]; nevertheless, the political and economic climate of the country did not favor the emergence of the pollution issue. Several other issues, such as secessionism, droughts, wars, and social welfare crowded the political and policy agenda for the first two decades after the independence in 1947. Jawaharlal Nehru's vision of "liberal democracy with socialist economy" guided the nation's policy process until the late 1960s. The emphasis on liberal democratic ideas brought new issues of mass mobilization, mass participation, political literacy, nation-building, and building of the political infrastructure to the agenda. The government took upon itself the responsibility of educating the people—people who had been, for centuries, ruled by kings and queens—in the art of running a nation.[2]

At the same time, the socialist model of economy demanded that a greater attention be paid by the government to the management of the economy. Stressing the welfare role of the state, the government embarked upon a massive effort to provide the people with basic necessities, such as schools, hospitals, transportation, communication, energy, and most importantly, employment. In order to fulfill this task, the government was forced to monopolize the key industries and bring them under the public sector. The policy agenda of the government, thus, was full of issues related to the management of the economy. Additionally, the nation faced two major national wars—with China in 1962 and with Pakistan in 1965—which made the national defense a top priority. The wars left India in need of foreign economic and military assistance.

The environment did not emerge as a policy issue until 1971, when the United Nations requested India to prepare a report on the nation's environment in preparation for the United Nation's Conference on Human Environment in Stockholm, Geneva (known as the Stockholm Conference). The ad hoc committee, headed by B.B. Vohra, prepared the document; and on the basis of this document, the government established a National Committee on Environmental Planning and Coordination (NCEPC) within the Department of Science and Technology in 1972.[3] The report pointed out the extent of the environmental destruction, which according to Vohra himself, was "shocking"; nevertheless, it is interesting to note that the government's attitude still remained pro-growth and anti-environment. The attitude was well-reflected in the remarks made by Mrs. Gandhi, who was so confident of her pro-development agenda that she, along with the leaders of other developing nations, refused even to participate in the United Nation's conference until the definition of the word "environment" was broadened to include the issues of poverty, hunger, and sanitation.[4] No question of reconciliation existed in Mrs. Gandhi's mind as she noted that:

On one hand the rich look askance at our continuing poverty—on the other, they warn us against their own methods. We do not wish to impoverish the environment any further and yet we cannot for a moment forget the grim poverty of the large numbers of people. Are not poverty and need the greatest polluters?[5]

Mrs. Gandhi's skepticism toward the issue of environmental protection existed because of the political situation that she faced at home and abroad. Having won the unexpected landslide victory in the 1971 parliamentary elections on the populist platform which revolved around the theme of Garibi Hatao (Remove Poverty), Mrs. Gandhi was committed toward a faster pace of growth to fulfill her campaign promises. Additionally, Mrs. Gandhi, during this time, was influenced by the agenda of the two Communist parties whose hands she had joined as an electoral strategy. In any case, she relied upon an impressive show by the nation's economy. Moreover, Mrs. Gandhi was riding a tide of high popularity both at the national and international fronts due to the Indian army's decisive victory over Pakistan in the 1971 war. The war became necessary as millions of refugees from East Pakistan (now Bangladesh) flooded the Indian bordering states, further stressing the already sluggish economy. The 1971 war portrayed Mrs. Gandhi as the crusader of the people. Mrs. Gandhi's people-oriented policy approach did not allow her, and consequently her government, to incorporate the issue of environmental protection in the nation's development strategy.

The tone of the government's argument, however, changed quickly in 1974, following Mrs. Gandhi's return from the Stockholm Conference. Environment-related issues started to appear on the national policy agenda. The speed and vigor with which they were handled was surprising. The following section covers the policy histories of major environmental laws passed during the last two decades.

Laws Against Pollution

The single most important law that launched the Indian government's environmental policy movement was the Water Act of 1974. The Water Act, a pioneering effort, was followed by the Air Act in 1981, and finally, the Environment Act in 1986. Until 1974, water pollution was definitely perceived as a local problem. Despite the fact that the pollution of water in one state affects the quality of water in other states, no laws were enacted at the national level to control the sources of water pollution. This inactivity was predominantly due to the fact that the Indian Constitution did not permit the central government to pass laws on water related issues. According to the distribution of legislative powers stated in the Constitution, "water" came under state governments' jurisdiction. During the 1950s and 1960s, several water pollution control laws were enacted by states.

(1) Orissa River Pollution Act of 1953

(2) Punjab State Tubewell Act of 1954

(3) West Bengal Notification No. 7 Regulation—Control of Water Pollution Act of 1957

(4) Jammu and Kashmir State Canal and Drainage Act of 1963

(5) Maharashtra Water Pollution Prevention Act of 1969

By 1960, however, the need for a nationwide policy for the control of water pollution was being realized. The impact of pollution on human lives was being questioned by scientists. Polluted water from the Yamuna River, for example, was reported to have affected 40,000 people in Delhi during 1955-56. In response to these findings, as well as several others, the then-Ministry of Health at the central level appointed an Expert Committee in October 1962, to study the problem and also to prepare a draft legislation to regulate water pollution from domestic and industrial sources. It was interesting, although not unique in India, that the problem was initially seen as a health problem rather than as an environmental problem with health-related effects. For example, the first Japanese governmental agency to deal with the environmental issue, the Environmental Pollution Division, was also established within the Ministry of Health and Welfare in 1964. Similarly, in 1977, the Government of the Republic of Korea created its environmental agency within the Ministry of Health and Social Welfare.

The Expert Committee, after examining all aspects of the question, recommended the enactment of both central and state laws. However, any central law was out of the question without first establishing the central government's right of jurisdiction over the subject matter. According to the Constitution, the areas of legislation have been divided in three primary categories: (1) the Central List on which the central government has the primary jurisdiction; (2) the State List, on which the right of jurisdiction goes to the state legislatures; and finally (3) the Concurrent List, on which the law can be considered at any level of the government, but in case of conflict, the laws passed by the central government persist.[6] The area of "water" fell under the State jurisdiction; therefore, the central government found itself unable to enact a nationwide law. Although several states had already initiated or passed such laws, nevertheless, the need for a uniform law still remained.

In order for the central government to take an initiative role in the pollution-related policy process, a constitutional reform was necessary. According to the Constitution, the parliament can pass legislation on subjects that fall within the state jurisdiction: (1) if the Council of States or Upper House in the national parliament passes a resolution to that effect by a two-thirds majority; (2) if a proclamation of emergency is in force, or (3) if two or more states request the passage of one single legislation by the parliament.[7] In the case of water pollution legislation, the third route was followed. The second route was not possible at that time, while the first route allowed only a temporary solution since the Constitution further states that legislation passed through this route is in effect for only one year. However, a significant characteristic of the third route is that the legislation passed is enforceable only in consenting states. The scope of the legislation is, thus, limited.

The recommendations made by the Expert Committee were considered by the Ministry of Health and in 1965 they were passed on to the Central Council of Local Government, whose responsibility was to ensure that no unwarranted encroachment was made upon state powers. Once the Committee accepted the recommendations unanimously, a draft bill was prepared by the central government and was circulated to all state governments in December of 1965 with the request to pass a resolution authorizing the parliament to enact a necessary law on their behalf.

The response to the request was apathetic. No significant pressure from the media existed at that time, and the support from the people was also negligible. In fact, the request was regarded more as a bureaucratic procedure rather than a substantive issue. The issue failed to gain serious attention primarily because the distribution of water, rather than its pollution, was considered a priority.

Despite the initial setback, within the next four years, six states—Gujarat, Haryana, Jammu & Kashmir, Kerala, Karnataka, and West Bengal—passed the needed resolution. Consequently, the central government introduced the Water (Prevention and Control of Pollution) Bill in the Upper House of the Parliament in 1969. The origination of the bill in the Upper House[8] may have been due to the fact that the subject under consideration was originally a "State List" issue; nevertheless, it raises several policy questions here. India's political system is parliamentary, where the government is controlled by the majority in the Lower House rather than in the Upper House or in both of the houses. In fact, the Upper House (known as Rajya Sabha), like in the United Kingdom, has a dignified, yet powerless, role to play in the system. The Upper House even lacks the power to ratify treaties and major governmental decisions, a function that makes the Senate in the United States a powerful body. It is argued that the Rajya Sabha, like the House of Lords in Great Britain, permits leisurely, extended, and non-partisan debates; nevertheless, studies have revealed that the Upper House in India has even failed to provide any such opportunity.[9]

The bill was later referred to the Joint Committee comprising the members of the two houses. The Joint Committee, after making several modifications, submitted its report to the Parliament in November, 1972. Even though the process of policy definition and formulation had already begun in 1971, it was revealed to me during my interviews in 1983-84 that the process was accelerated because of the pressure from Mrs. Gandhi herself which she increased tremendously after her return from the Stockholm Conference in 1972. The law was finally passed by the Parliament in 1974, about 14 years after it had first been proposed. Figure 3.1 describes the legislative procedure in greater detail. Meanwhile, six more states consented to the resolution; and on March 23, 1974, the Water (Prevention and Control of Water Pollution) Act became applicable to the states of

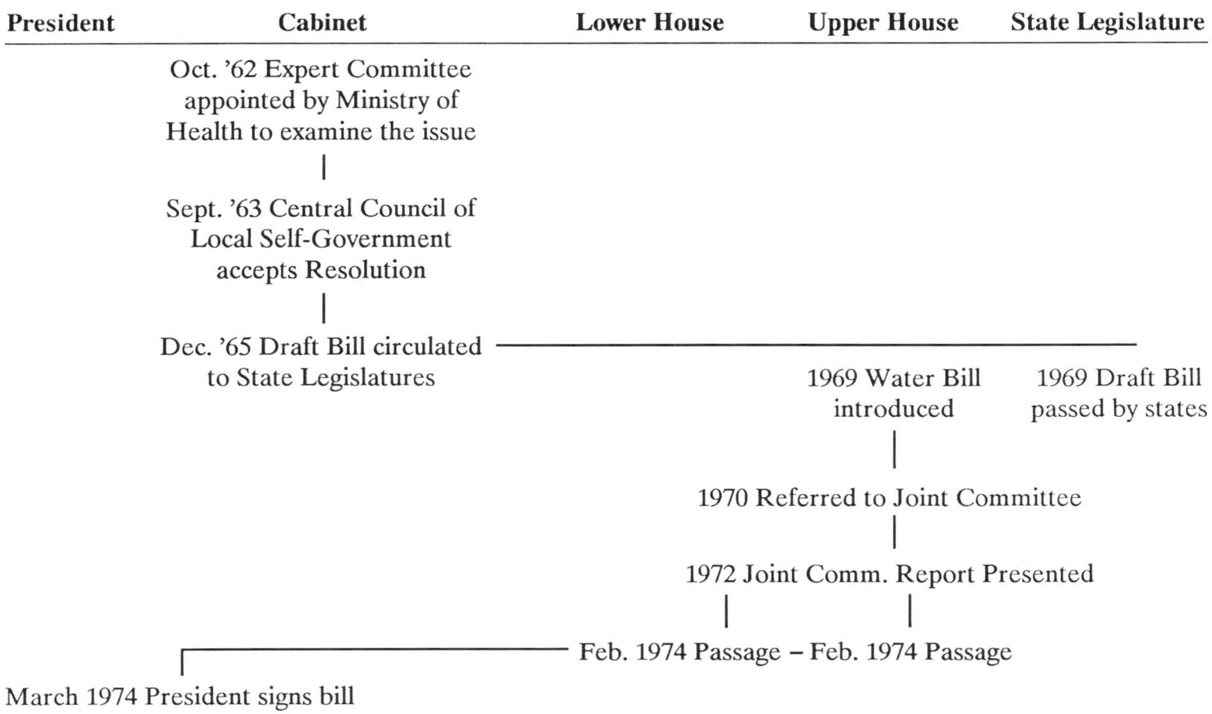

President	Cabinet	Lower House	Upper House	State Legislature
	Oct. '62 Expert Committee appointed by Ministry of Health to examine the issue			
	Sept. '63 Central Council of Local Self-Government accepts Resolution			
	Dec. '65 Draft Bill circulated to State Legislatures		1969 Water Bill introduced	1969 Draft Bill passed by states
			1970 Referred to Joint Committee	
			1972 Joint Comm. Report Presented	
		Feb. 1974 Passage – Feb. 1974 Passage		
March 1974 President signs bill				

Figure 3.1. Flow of Legislative Measures Leading to the Water Act of 1974

Assam, Bihar, Gujarat, Haryana, Himachal Pradesh, Jammu & Kashmir, Karnataka, Kerala, Madhya Pradesh, West Bengal, and all of the Union territories, which are independent units but are administered by the central government.[10]

Interestingly enough, most states, regardless of their level of advancement or their relationship with the central government, had granted the needed authorization and, thus, had accepted the central jurisdiction. It is surprising that the relatively poor states, such as Himachal Pradesh, Bihar, and Assam, that needed an industrial boom to boost their economies should have so willingly opted for policies that could be viewed as detrimental to their industrial growth. On the other hand, the already industrialized state of Maharashtra did not accept the intervention by the national government, despite a significant concern for the quality of water within the state. Similarly, the process fails to identify any strong political factor behind state responses as well. The governments of Kerala and West Bengal, despite their rule by opposition parties and their communist strongholds, cooperated with the central government, which was controlled by a centrist party.

A closer look at the Lok Sabha (the Lower House) debates during the period of 1969-1974 indicates that the legislation was passed without much political drama. The issue did not arouse much public interest, and it did not create a political battleground similar to the ones observed in developed countries. It is actually a difficult task to try to single out politicians who were actively pursuing the issue. Even if some names can be cited, it is again difficult to say whether their political career depended on the environmental issue.[11] The debate that preceded the formal passage of the law on February 21, 1974, raised several questions regarding the nature of the environmental issue. Saradish Roy, a member of the Parliament, felt that "because the government is reluctant in this regard, we have an apprehension that this will not be properly implemented."[12] Ram Gopal Reddy, another member, expressed his fear that "officials would take undue advantage of the bill because neither water will be purified nor pollution will be stopped but bribery and corruption will increase ten times."[13] During the same debate, the lack of public awareness was also raised as a matter of prime concern.

In fact, no parliamentary forum or caucus on environmental issues even existed. The first such forum was established in 1981, seven years after the major pollution law was passed by an over-whelming majority. Without any parliamentary forum, debates on environmental issues lacked not only political perspective; they also lacked substantive discussions. The following is an excerpt from one such debate.

K. Pradhani (Member of Parliament): Will the Minister of Works and Housing and Supply and Rehabilitation be pleased to state whether environmental factors are responsible for incidence of cancer to the extent of 90 percent; and if so, what preventive measures Government of India propses to take in this regard?

R. Kinkar (Minister of State of Works and Housing and Supply and Rehabilitation): Experiments have shown that large proportion of cancers are related to individual's personal environment and the environment around the person during work and rest. The percentage would vary in different regions of the country from 50 to 80. As a first step towards the control of environmental pollution the Water Act, 1974 was enacted. Under the Act, Water Pollution Control Boards have been set up in various states in the country to tackle the water pollution problem. To control air pollution, the Government has already introduced the Air Bill, 1978, in the Parliament, which is at present under the consideration of a Joint Committee of both the Houses.

K. Pradhani: May I know from the Hon. Minister whether all the States including Orissa have constituted the Water Pollution Control Boards; and if so, what action they have taken so far to prevent water pollution?

S. Bakht (Minister of Works and Housing and Supply and Rehabilitation): The reasons which cause water pollution are industrial effluents and domestic sewage. They happen practically in every State. The steps that we have taken are: we have already passed Water Pollution Act during 1974, and during December 1977, we passed the Cess Act too, so that these problems are provided with proper funds. Very recently, on Air Pollution also a new Bill has been introduced.

Mr. Speaker: His question is whether all the States have formed the Boards.

S. Bakht: Most of the States have formed the Board. The remaining States are being persuaded to adopt this Act. There are only three States remaining and they are also going to fall in line with others.

Mr. Speaker: He asked whether Orissa has formed the Board.

S. Bakht: No. Orissa has not yet formed the Board.

K. Halder (Member of Parliament): Sir, all of us know that in West Bengal both the Ganges and Damodar rivers are flowing and both the sides of these two rivers are the industrial belts. So the waters of both these rivers get polluted. I would like to know whether in co-ordination with the State Government, the Central Government has any scheme to prevent the water pollution of these two rivers in West Bengal.

S. Bakht: Sir, the State Board itself is looking after the control of water pollution in these two rivers.[14]

Until 1969, there was no indication that the issue of environmental protection received any attention from the base of the system, i.e. the public, or from outside of the system, i.e. international forces. The issue was already on the government's agenda, but the speed of the action, even within the governmental sphere, was lax. While the public interest in the issue remained negligible even during the 1970s, international influences were visible at the turn of the decade. The single most significant input came from the Stockholm Conference. The attitude that prevailed at that time was summarized by Thomas Mathews.

Around the time of the Stockholm Conference, there was very little awareness in India about development-related environmental hazards. The more well-read and knowledgeable among our educated classes considered all references to the environment in India to be merely fashionable that were borrowed from among the issues considered important by the advanced nations.[15]

The evolution of the water pollution policy, which is considered as the foundation stone of the modern environmental movement, reveals a significant finding: the environmental issue was initiated at the governmental (also called the institutional), and not at the social, agenda.[16] Here, the process differed significantly from the similar processes in developed countries. In Japan and the United States, for example, the issue emerged first on the social agenda—the agenda which is determined by the society—and then, after gaining significant support from political parties and/or mass organization, the issue was pushed on the institutional agenda. The issue of environmental protection, whether general or specific, had enough political weight before being considered for policy action. In the process, the resulting policy clearly reflected the preferences of the people and the urgency of the situation. The public interpretation of the issue figured of great importance; and as Anthony Downs and Steven Reed have pointed out, the intensity of the public interest became sufficient to undermine political or financial barriers.[17]

By contrast, in India, the issue was favored by policy-makers, and was directly brought onto the policy agenda of the government. As a result, while laws came into existence, the context for their implementation could not be established. The issue was defined by the government as based upon the perceptions of the people within the government. The strategies adopted to solve the issue were the ones that were preferred by the government itself. Assuming that the government acted in good faith and with a real intention to preserve the nation's natural resources, the policy implications of this pre-empted action still proved to be disastrous. To begin with, the pre-emption by the government left the issue of water pollution without any clear cut definition and boundaries. The time simply did not exist for the issue to mature.

> The more well-read and knowledgeable among our educated classes considered all references to the environment in India to be merely fashionable—conversation subjects at best, that were borrowed from among the issues considered important by the advanced nations. A significant number even believed that anyone who advocated spending money on environmental protection was a misguided stooge of the Western nations, who wanted to keep India backward by diverting attention from more important issues. The academics and professionals were of course fully aware of the environmental hazards, forestry, industrial hygiene, soil conservation, etc. What was not then perceived was the totality of the linkages between these problems. More importantly, the solutions to these problems were also conceived in narrow sectoral terms, with strict demarcation of administrative jurisdiction. Thus forests were the business of the Forest Department, irrigation that of the Irrigation Department, agriculture of Agriculture Department—and so on.[18]

Second, the environmental issue could not be politicized. The public, political parties, and interest groups lost the basis on which they could rally political support. Third, the implementation of the anti-water pollution law remained totally in the hands of the bureaucracy. Since the public consensus could not be built, it became clear that the public could play only a minimal role, if any at all, in the implementation of the law. Last, even though it can be argued that "something was better than nothing," the quick adoption of narrowly-focused laws, such as the water pollution law and later the air pollution law, undermined any immediate need to seek a comprehensive and integrated environmental policy.

The display of enthusiasm by the government for the water pollution issue was surprising, especially at the time when the country faced an unprecedented economic crunch due to the international oil crisis of 1973, which left the nation with a huge foreign deficit. In order to make up for the increased oil prices, it was suggested that India would need to expand its export market. The emphasis shifted clearly to the greater "technologization" of the Indian industry. The increases of productivity and efficiency were labelled as the major strategies of the 1970s. India clearly became unable to compete in the world market because of its high-cost economy.[19] It is surprising, then, that the government opted for a law that imposed an additional expenditure burden on industry. Equally surprising was the fact that the government itself willingly took on the awesome responsibility of providing water monitoring and treatment facilities, rather than providing social welfare services only a few years after raising the slogan of Garibi Hatao (Remove Poverty). In real terms, the commitment of the government at that time emphasized the removal of poverty, rather than the removal of water contamination.

The single most important factor that brought the environmental movement to the Indian door was Mrs. Gandhi's personal commitment toward environmental protection.[20] The three factors that shaped Mrs. Gandhi's perception of the environmental issue were her political strength at home, India's position in international politics, and Mrs. Gandhi's aspirations as a leader.

In terms of the political situation at home, the period from 1947 to 1974 was far from being favorable to the emergence of social issues. India was involved in three major wars—with China in 1962, with Pakistan in 1965 and again in 1971. Wars imposed a burden on the country's already limited social and economic resources, and they diverted the government's attention to defense and military issues. In addition to bearing the after-effects of the wars, India also became vulnerable to the changing economic tides. Droughts and floods were common occurrences making it impossible for the country to achieve self-sufficiency in food. By the late 1960s, the failure of the liberal economic policies adopted by the late Prime Minister Lal Bahadur Shastri led to a double crisis of economic stagnation and political instability.[21] Political violence instigated by Marxist and Naxalite revolutionary groups further threatened the stability of several states, especially of West Bengal and Kerala.

In addition, a challenge to Mrs. Gandhi's leadership came from the sharply fractionalized Congress Party. The 1967 election results, in which the Congress Party failed to secure majority in 40 percent of the states and got only 54 percent of the seats in the national parliament, revealed that voters disapproved of the in-fighting within the ruling party. Several prominent leaders, including the party president, lost to political newcomers.[22] The party grew even weaker after Mrs. Gandhi took over its leadership in 1967 following Shastri's sudden death. Mrs. Gandhi was favored to lead the party and, consequently, to head the nation, not because of her seniority or popularity, but because she was seen as a weak leader, who could provide some time for the major party fractions to strengthen their base. Once Mrs. Gandhi started to assert herself, the party experienced a sharp conflict between her progressive bloc and the conservative bloc of the senior party leaders, known as the "Syndicate." The conflict led to the first major split in the Congress Party in 1969. [23]

After the split of the Congress Party, Mrs. Gandhi's position was significantly weakened, and she searched for a new base among the electorate-- a base that would separate her from the "Syndicates," who also kept their party's name as Congress and claimed to be representing the real Congress interests. A surprise alliance with the Communist Party of India (CPI) provided Mrs. Gandhi with that political base.[24] Mrs. Gandhi's agenda tilted toward populist and socialist policies, which worked as a magnet to attract voters in the upcoming elections of 1971.[25] In addition, Mrs. Gandhi's claim of representing the real Congress was more convincing to the people because she was the daughter of Jawahar Lal Nehru, one of the founding fathers of the Congress.

Following a landslide victory by her party in the 1971 parliamentary elections and also India's decisive win in the 1971 war against Pakistan, Mrs. Gandhi emerged as a charismatic leader.[26] Her identification with the progressive ideology allowed her to expand her influence over political processes. "The message that Gandhi delivered during the 1971 election campaign strengthened the impression among the electorate that she personally, rather than the Congress Party, represented the renewed commitment to economic and social reform."[27] The policy context that prevailed after the elections was definitely favorable to progressive issues, such as environment. Mrs. Gandhi's charismatic power also gave her a "honeymoon" time in which to experiment with new and difficult policies. Mrs. Gandhi's stand on the environmental issue in the 1970s reflected her self-assured style of leadership, and also her willingness to confront challenges. Nevertheless, the worsening economic situation fuelled by the oil crisis, impaired any significant progress on the environmental issue.

International forces, undoubtedly, accelerated the process. On the international front, India had always considered itself as the leader of developing countries, especially of the non-aligned countries. The nation also received a large amount of economic aid from international sources during the 1960s and the 1970s. Thus, unlike many other developing countries, India could not remain isolated from international forces. Mrs. Gandhi did not ignore the international agenda on the environment. She not only took an active role in the United Nations Conference on Human Environment, but upon her return, she also displayed a renewed interest in environmental protection. According to Vohra, the ex-chairman of the National Committee on Environmental Planning and Coordination, Gandhi's personal commitment was the single most crucial element in the formation of India's environmental agenda.[28]

In addition to the political situation at home and the ambitious position in the international arena, Mrs. Gandhi's personality and the challenges that she faced as an individual also hold some explanatory power. What forced Gandhi to take an initiative role in the promotion of the environmental issue? She, like her father Jawahar Lal Nehru, was a strong believer in the idealistic and moral values of the society. In her speeches, she frequently referred to Mahatma Gandhi's ideology and Nehru's philosophy that emphasized harmony with nature. Even though Gandhi always remembered her childhood days as being lonely and fearful, she was by no means a weak personality. Despite the fact that she carried the Nehru name with her, she had to struggle hard to make the people accept her leadership. The extent of her struggle is apparent from the fact that "she did not succeed to her father's office because of her leadership qualities but because she was seen as lacking them. In 1966, she was chosen to lead the Congress by the party bosses because they wanted to exclude the ambitious Morarji Desai."[29]

Indira's biographers have noted that she developed a feeling of insecurity during her childhood, which she could never overcome. She never lost her sense of solitude in a hostile world. According to them, Mrs. Gandhi's problem was her "unending search for total security and total acceptance which made her intolerant of criticism and unwelcome advice."[30] Mrs. Gandhi's rule was marked by the concentration of power, the breaking of state party apparatus, the lack of competition and the prevalance of mistrust.

"Both within the party and the government, authority was centralized and personalized, with decision making concentrated in the hands of the Prime Minister. Cabinet members, party presidents, and chief ministers held tenure on the basis of personal loyalty to Mrs. Gandhi."[31] She, as a person and as a leader, also felt vulnerable to international opinions. During the 1970s, in the wake of the environmental movement in the West, she was very likely to have become sensitive to the environmental issue.

Another important aspect of Gandhi's personality which had significant impact on her political personality was her training as a child and adolescent that she must achieve, grow, and realize her potential.[32] This characteristic, along with her insecurity, made Gandhi an aggressive leader in her later years. She, in order to prove her merit, tried new approaches and took bold steps at both the national and international levels. Gandhi's personality was well reflected in her approach toward the environmental issue in the early 1970s. Portraying herself as a tough leader against Western influences, she denounced the issue of pollution at the United Nations Conference on Human Environment. Nevertheless, her feelings for the well-being of India (Gandhi always felt that India was her, and only her, responsibility.) forced her to accept the critical nature of the environmental problem as soon as she arrived home.

The law-making process, undoubtedly, was influenced by Mrs. Gandhi's personal commitment and international pressures which came in the form of conferences. The implementation of the law, however, required a totally different set of policy context—a clear cut law, a strong and willing bureaucracy, and a long-lasting commitment from the government to provide the needed political and financial support. Needless to say, the water pollution control law failed to get any of the three resources.

The Water Act of 1974

The Water (Prevention and Control of Pollution) Act passed in 1974 defined water pollution as:

> Such contamination of water or such alteration of the physical, chemical or biological properties of water or such discharge of any sewage or trade effluent or of any other liquid, gaseous or solid substance into water (whether directly or indirectly) as may, or is likely to, create a nuisance or render such water harmful or injurious to public health or safety, or to domestic, commercial, industrial,

agricultural, or other legitimate uses, or to the life and health of animals or plants or of aquatic organisms.[33]

The scope of the law, based on this definition of water pollution, was quite broad, for it covered all physical, chemical, and biological aspects of water pollution, and at the same time, it covered damage not only to human lives, but also to plants, animals, and aquatic organisms. To strengthen the enforcement of the law, the legislation mandated the creation of an extensive bureaucratic network—central board at federal level, state board at state level, and joint board at any level—to handle issues concerning central and state pollution. The central board at the federal level, was comprised of central and state officials: a chairman, five officials, three non-officials, two representatives of government-owned companies or corporations, and one official specializing in public health—all to be nominated and appointed by the central government.[34] Defining the primary objective of the board as "to promote cleanliness of streams and wells," the act specified certain functions of the board to meet this goal. The central board was asked to:

(1) advise the central government of any matter concerning the prevention and control of water pollution;

(2) plan a nationwide program for the prevention, control, or abatement of water pollution;

(3) coordinate the activities of the state boards;

(4) provide technical assistance and guidance to the state boards;

(5) plan and organize the training of persons engaged in programs for the prevention and control of pollution;

(6) organize, through mass media, a comprehensive program regarding the prevention, control and abatement of pollution;

(7) collect, compile, and publish technical and statistical data;

(8) disseminate the collected information;

(9) lay down, modify or annul in consultation with the central and state governments concerned, the standards for a stream or well.[35]

At the same time, a state board consisting of a chairman, five state government officials, five persons nominated by state government from among state authorities, three non-official members nominated by state government to represent interests of agriculture, fishery, or industry or any other interest, two persons representing companies or corporations managed by state government, and a full-time member-secretary from the public health engineering department was to be constituted in every state.[36] The power of state boards was not limited to advising and information collecting; instead, it also included the inspection of sewage plants for treatment effluent, and the setting up of effluent discharge standards.[37] The scope of the board's power was further broadened by Section 25, which clearly stated that without the consent of state boards, no new outlets could be operated or old ones altered for discharge of sewage or effluent into stream or well. State boards had the right to refuse the consent, if pollution control standards were not met.

The act specified penalties for various offenses. State boards played an important role in shaping the judicial process related to water pollution, since the law stated explicitly that "no court shall take cognizance of any offence under this Act except on a complaint made by, or with the previous sanction in writing of the state board."[38]

In addition to the central and state boards, the act also had a provision for a joint board by two or more states to ensure abatement of interstate water pollution.[39]

On its own merit, the Water Act was an excellent piece of legislation; however, when applied to the real policy world, the law failed miserably. Several factors, such as the center-state relations, intervention by feudalistic forces, control by the industry over local economy, level of corruption in the bureaucracy and lack of financial support, severely undermined the impact of the act. These factors will be discussed later in a more general context; however, the inherent pitfalls of the law itself are addressed here.

To begin with, the scope of the Act was restricted to streams and wells. The act did not cover ground water pollution caused by the leakage of toxic materials or accumulation of pesticide residues. In addition, the act did not necessarily apply to the whole state; instead, state government was authorized to restrict its application to specified areas. The act also failed to prescribe a uniform set of standards applicable to all states.

Problems related to the functioning of the boards were fairly serious. Boards were autonomous bodies; however, Section 18 of the act itself curtailed this autonomy by requiring the boards to follow such direction as their respective governments might give them. In addition, the government also reserved the right to review any order given by boards.[40] The act attempted to regulate pollution by insisting that a prior license be taken by industries before discharging any effluent into the water course. Boards had the right to refuse license to any new applicant; however, they did not have sufficient power to close the existing sources of water pollution. The boards lacked the authority to issue orders directly; instead, they were required to go through courts and judicial procedures which were very time-consuming, allowing the polluting industries to continue operation for a fairly long period of time.[41] Until March of 1983, out of 1,483 large- and medium-sized offending industries, only 16 were taken to courts by various boards.[42] The *Annual Report* of the central board read in defense:

> Cases against the industries have been filed for contravening the provisions of Section 25 of the Water Act of 1974. Since the accused have not appeared after the issuance of summons, the matter is being processed by the courts for serving warrants. The central board is actively pursuing but is being unable to achieve any progress due to the legal procedures involved.[43]

Other provisions in the act revealed a strong bureaucratic hold over political processes on one hand, and the symbolic nature of the policy itself on the other hand. Despite the fact that municipalities had been identified as the largest polluters because they were allowing the release of untreated sewage water into rivers, the act did not specifically make them liable for prosecution. They were not bound by law to provide water treatment facilities. The head of any governmental agency was not punishable for ignoring pollution control measures "if he proves that the offense was committed without his knowledge or that he exercised all due diligence to prevent it."[44]

Moreover, unlike similar legislation in the United States, Great Britain, West Germany, and Japan, the act included no provision for the affected public to litigate against polluters. The public was, instead, left to rely upon the boards, since the act stated that "no court shall take cognizance of any offense under this Act except on a complaint made by or with the previous sanction in writing of the state board."[45] Though this provision appeared appropriate in the light of the nation's predominantly illiterate, poor, and rural population, but the fact was that boards themselves were overburdened and were incapable of performing such a judicial function. According to a senior officer of the Gujarat Water Board, the boards were able to handle only 5 percent of such complaints.[46] The act also banned civil courts from entertaining any suit or proceeding in respect to any matter which an

appellate authority, as constituted under the act, was empowered to determine. The jurisdictional weaknesses of the act were obvious. The "third
party" rights, which make the backbone of the United States' policy, were
severely limited. Such an arrangement undermined the overall effectiveness
of the regulatory policy. Consider a hypothetical case in which the victim
was a third party, harmed by the effluent discharge of a polluting company.
As long as the polluting company had the consent order from the state board,
no one could be held responsible for compensating the victim party: the
polluting company was exempt because it acted with board consent, and the
board was free because it had the protection given to it by Section 50 of the
act. Ironically, the third party's right to prosecute is recognized under the
American and the British statutes from which the provisions of the Indian
act were taken.

The relationship between state boards and the Central Board was also
left unclear. The Central Board was only an advisory body: it lacked the
power of surveillance over the activities of state boards who were responsible
for local implementation. The Central Board was not granted any powers
to force the state governments to adopt uniform standards or to overtake
those cases where state governments were reluctant to enforce such standards.

The act was further weakened by its inability to provide for a definite
and independent source of financing for the boards. State boards suffered
from financial crunch as well as from political manipulation directed by state
governments and by the Central Board. In 1979, most state boards had fewer
than 50 staff personnel, and their total budget varied between Rs 20,000 and
Rs 350,000 (approximately between US $200 - $350 at that time's exchange
rate of 1:10). Their budgets increased significantly in later years; nevertheless, compared to their responsibilities, the budgets were always inadequate.
The *Annual Report* published by the Kerala State Pollution Control Board
summarized its dilemma in 1983 as follows.

> The board is still in its infancy and is working under severe handicaps
> of non-availability of funds to the extent required and consequent
> lack of manpower and infrastructure...The plan outlay under the
> prevention and control of water pollution is fixed at Rs. 50 lakhs
> [approximately US $500,000] in the Sixth Five-Year Plan against the
> proposed outlay of Rs. 3 crores [$3 million] spread over a period
> of five years...But, unfortunately, the government has very recently
> suggested that even this meager plan outlay of Rs. 50 lakhs should
> be reduced to Rs. 30 lakhs.[47]

Although the finances were limited, the responsibility of state boards continued to increase. According to the above report, the Kerala Water Board was expected to take the budget cuts and at the same time administer additional duties with regard to air pollution control.

In order to partially meet the requirement for funds, the central government passed the Water Cess Act in 1977, under which each industry and local body was to pay a nominal cess (tax) fee on water consumption.[48] This act, while augmenting the resources of state boards, provided incentives to waste-dischargers by allowing a 70 percent rebate on the cess if their wastes were treated according to the standards prescribed by boards. But because the cess fee was nominal, it did not provide enough funding to improve the financial situation of the state boards.[49] The Lok Sabha (Lower House) debate that followed the introduction of the Cess Act on the floor for discussion clearly indicated that despite an arrangement to collect nearly Rs 3.40 crores (or US $3.5 million) in revenue each year, the law was expected to be insufficient. "The expected revenue was too small to save human beings. We as Indians, unfortunately, are not alive to the problem," remarked one former Minister.[50] On the other hand, there were arguments against any tax at all: it was feared that small, as the cess might be, it could open the way for more cess in future.

Thus, from the very beginning, several loopholes existed in the Water Act, making it symbolic in nature and ineffective in practice. The impact of the law was further undermined by the existing political and social barriers, such as bureaucratic corruption, mass apathy, feudalistic economy, and the power of industry. Because of these conditions, water boards themselves turned into an instrument of bureaucratic exploitation and political bargining.

> ...in recent years these Boards have been 'politicalised' and appointments on these Boards are considered as berths for M.P.'s [Member of Parliament] or M.L.A.'s [Member of Legislative Assembly] who could not be accommodated as ministers. Often accusations are made against these Boards that they are soft to those industries who assist the political party either by donations or in other ways, while they prosecute those who do not find favour with the ruling party. The industry is also deprived of the right to approach a court against arbitrary exercise of power by regulatory agencies by provisions in the Law barring jurisdiction of civil courts against decisions of the Board.[51]

The Water Act was amended in 1988; however, the amended act did not deal with the fundamental problem of political malnutrition. The amendments made it mandatory for all "polluting" industries to obtain environmental clearance. This rule applied to all new and existing industries. Through amendements, the state boards were also vested with new powers to obtain information from industries and to stop water and electricity supply to offending industries. Penalties for non-compliance were also doubled. These amendments did not, however, touch the fundamental issue of power distribution between state boards and the Central Board and between industries and the boards. In fact, the basic weaknesses of the original Water Act, such as the third-party rights and an independence financial base, were never even considered. The effective implementation of the amended act remains as doubtful as of the original act in 1974.

The Air Act of 1981

Following the Water Act, the government passed yet another pollution control law in 1981--the Air (Prevention and Control of Pollution) Act. Once again, the international concern for the quality of air influenced the decision-making process. In addition, Mrs. Gandhi's return to power in 1980 also led to a renewed interest in environment-related issues. The Act defined air pollution as the presence of any "solid, liquid, or gaseous substance in such concentration as may be or tends to be injurious to human beings or other living creatures or plants or property or environment."[52]

Like the Water Act, the Air Act also attempted to institutionalize the commitment of the government to improve the nation's environment. However, once again, little, if any, attention was paid to the enforcement of the law at the time of its adoption. The law was given a step-motherly treatment and was meant to be toothless. There are provisions in the act for the creation of separate air pollution control boards to carry out enforcement responsibilities; nevertheless, this responsibility was assigned to the central and state water boards.[53] No time was specified in the law as to when separate air pollution control boards should be created. The responsibility of water boards with regard to improving air pollution was meant to be advisory and coordinative.[54] The enforcement and penal rights of water boards in this regard were identical to those specified in the Water Act: public participation was not specifically encouraged; citizens were not allowed to participate in the licensing procedures; and the third-party rights were non-existent.

The implementation of the act was limited, in part because the enforcement duties were vested with the already over-worked and under-funded water boards. Like the Water Act, the Air Act was also not a product of a participatory policy process; instead, it was a result of the bureaucratic policy process. However, the Air Act differed from the Water Act in one aspect: unlike its predecessor, the Air Act already had a solid support from environmentalists before it appeared on the policy agenda. The support was clearly identifiable by 1980 because of two major national controversies. One of the controversies, the Mathura Oil Refinery dealt with the visible damage caused by air pollution to the famous Taj Mahal. The other controversy, the construction of the Silent Valley Hydroelectric Plant, involved the issue of deforestation and conservation; nevertheless, it had aroused some serious reaction among the educated elite of the nation. Interestingly, a suggestion to include air quality control in the Water Act itself was rejected in 1974. Yet, just six years later, a new law was passed to deal with the so-called "unnecessary" issue.

The Air Act was another example of symbolism that existed in the environmental policy area throughout the 1970s and early 1980s. The law became ineffective due to political malnutrition. Without a proper power base and an adequate enforcement network, the act simply failed to withstand the pressure from adverse interests, particularly industry.

Several amendments to the Air Act were issued in 1987: noise pollution was included in the definition of "air pollution;" a mandatory air clearance was introduced for all industries; and finally, state boards were given wider powers to curb industrial pollution, which included the closure of electricity. However, the impact of these amendments is unlikely to be drastic.

Laws Against Deforestation

Unlike the pollution issue which was constitutionally under the domain of state governments until very recently, the deforestation issue has been on the central government's agenda since the days of the British. Before the British colonized the forests in the 18th century, social customs and religious traditions guided the relationship between the people and their forests. Since the lives of the people were not only closely linked to, but, were often totally dependent on the forests, a respectful relationship between the two necessarily evolved. The forests were often worshipped daily or periodically in elaborate social and family ceremonies. Superstitions played the role of laws and obtained compliance through inserting fear for the unknown. The belief was common that the forests were guarded by *Vandevi*, the goddess of forests, and any disrespect brought curse to individuals, and even to the entire village. Since the possibility existed that an entire village could be held responsible for individual acts, instituting the idea of respect for forests was accepted as an integral part of mass socialization.

The British intervention, however, broke this sacred and harmonious relationship between the people and their forests. It was the British who for the first time declared the forests as a value good—a good which needed protection and proper distribution. The conflict between the people and their forests was identified and later defined by several forest-related laws that were enacted. In 1865, a law decalred that the government was empowered (1) to declare any land covered with trees, brushwood, or jungles as government forest by notification, provided that such notification did not abridge or affect any existing rights of individuals or communalities; (2) to make rules relating to the preservation of trees; and (3) to prescribe punishment for the breach of the provisions of the act.[55]

Subsequently, a more comprehensive law, passed 13 years later in 1878, further institutionalized the governmental claim on forests by classifying the forests into three categories: (1) restricted forests, which were controlled by the government and, as the name implies, were restricted from the people; (2) protected forests, which were accessible to the people, but restrictions applied as to what could be taken away from them; and finally (3) village forests, which were declared as community forests and were to provide daily subsistence to the people.[56] For the first time, the act of 1878 also established a forest bureaucracy in the form of the Forest Settlement Officers (FSOs). FSOs were placed at the local level, and among other things were asked to protect forests from the nearby villagers.

The British policy of "commercialized forest-management" was further institutionalized in 1927 when the government passed the Indian Forest Act. The new law neither questioned, nor did it alter the old laws; it was only meant to bring all previous forest-related laws under one common umbrella. This unification gave the British more power on the use of forest resources. Surprisingly, the law passed by the colonial power in 1927 still provides the basis for forest management in the post-1980s.

The Indian Constituion, in 1950, placed "forests" under the state jurisdiction. The central government, therefore, became free from the responsibility of managing forests. Newly formed states accepted the responsibility for forest management, but were unwilling to make forest preservation one of their top priorities. Several concerns regarding the ability of state governments and the uniformity of the legal system were beginning to emerge. The result was the adoption of the 1952 Forest Policy Resolution by the central government. The resolution, ironically, accepted the need for economic growth more readily than it provided measures to protect the forests.

In actual practice the concept of national interest was interpreted in a very narrow sense. The destruction of forests for the construction of roads, building of irrigation and hydroelectricity projects, ammunition factories and other projects was justified in the name of national interest, whereas cultivation of lands shown as forest lands without any actual tree cover was treated as encroachment.[57]

Once again, the emphasis on rapid industrialization (which also resulted in fast urbanization) and the fast greening of the nation over-shadowed the environmental issue: the forests received a low priority. While the stress on the forests continued to grow, the pressure on the central government to make a policy change did not appear until the mid-1970s. At this time, "forests" that were kept under the state legislative list in the Constitution were declared to be under the concurrent list. Concurrent items in the Constitution refer to those items on which both state and central governments can legislate; however, in case of conflict, central laws prevail. This development spawned both positive and negative reactions: some argued that it was a step in the right direction, since the central government was now empowered to overrule the arbitrary decisions of state governments; but others feared that it was the beginning of the diminution of state powers.

The central government formalized its claim over forests in 1980, when it passed the Forest (Conservation) Act. The act prohibited state governments from allowing any forest land for any non-forest purpose without the prior approval of the central government. This act curbed the indiscriminate diversion of the forest land for non-forestry purpose. The success of the law was applauded by the Ministry of Environment and Forests in its Annual Report: "the average rate of deforestation, which was of the order of 1.5 lakhs [150,000] ha [hectares] per year prior to the promulgation of the Act, has come down to 5,500 ha. per annum after 25th October, 1980 when the Act came into force."[58] The Forest (Conservation) Act, a welcoming step from the central government, ran into troubled political waters when state governments themselves complained that the process of getting clearance from the central government was holding up their important developmental projects for months. Keeping this in mind, an amendment was proposed to the act--an amendment that was to make it mandatory for the central government to provide clearance within 15 days from the day of the application. The amendment was, nevertheless, repealed against severe opposition from environmentalists.[59]

The central government more recently attempted a proposal to prepare a new forest policy document. The prepared document, which was brought to the Prime Minister's cabinet for consideration in 1984, was, according to the critics, not much different from its predecessors. The government continued to deny the need to change the consumption-oriented lifestyle. The bureaucracy was still understood to be the only agent of forest management and forest protection.[60] In 1988-89, a revised National Forest Policy finally came in effect. This revised policy was much criticised for its resemblance to the old forest policy adopted in 1952. A newspaper analysis read, "...nothing has been proposed about the forest department, land laws, judiciary, panchayats and so on. If supplementary changes in socio-economic and administrative legal system are not required, why a new policy at all?"[61]

The history of the forest policy over the last one hundred years indicates that the policies are modified by "muddling through," rather than by any rational process. Also, the government tends to opt for incremental policies —policies where the feedback on existing policies works to strengthen the old approach. Needless to say, it means that once adopted, policies are difficult to change, regardless of their success or failure.

The implementation of the forest policy (as expressed in the Forest Act of 1927, and in subsequent policy efforts) was most dissatisfactory. Nearly 20 percent of the forest land was lost during the decade of 1975-85. In the states of Gujarat, Haryana, Punjab, and Rajasthan, half of the forests were lost during the time period of 1972-1982.[62] Despite the forest law, the destruction of the forest land was not stopped. Interestingly, the forest bureaucracy itself emerged as a villain in this game of forest management. The forest bureaucracy (forest department officers) was not only criticized for being ineffective, but in fact, studies indicated that it was also a contributing factor in the systematic destruction of the forests.[63] Among the reasons identified for this "villainous" profile of the forest bureaucracy was the indescretionary powers in the hands of the officials, and the alliance between the local industry and forest officials. There was also evidence of overwhelming corruption among forest officials. Moreover, the inherent principle of the policy that the forests need protection from the people, and not for the people, fostered a hostile relationship of mistrust and non-cooperation between the people and forest officials.

Laws Against Environmental Destruction

Although nearly 50 different pieces of legislation, 30 of these on the control of pollution alone, existed in India by the mid-1980s, the widespread destruction of environment still continued. The concern for environmental protection was fomented by the serious tragedy caused by the gas leak in the United Carbide Plant located in Bhopal in 1984. It was realized that several sources of environmental destruction, such as hazardous substances and acid rain, were not covered under existing laws; therefore, a comprehensive environmental law was needed. The Environment (Protection) Act, passed in May of 1986, reflected this major concern.[64]

The Environment (Protection) Act had three major objectives: (1) it was meant to be a supplementary rather than a new law; (2) it was to provide a clear focus of authority; and (3) it was to "plug loopholes" in existing laws.[65] The Act provided the first official definition of environment emphasizing the inter-relationship between the environment and the people:

> ..."environment" includes water, air and land and the inter-relationship which exists among and between water, air and land, and human beings, other living creatures, plants, micro-organism and property; "environmental pollutant" means any solid, liquid or gaseous substance present in such concentration as may be, or tends to be, injurious to environment.[66]

Surprisingly, the act did not ask for any new bureaucratic agencies to be established: the emphasis was to use the existing enforcing networks. Based on the provision of the Act, which allowed the central government to delegate its powers, at least 16 major agencies were used to enforce the law: Factories Inspectorate, Dock Safety Inspectorate, Indian Bureau of Mines, Port Authority, Inspectorate of Plantations, Marine Department, Central/State Pollution Control Boards, Transport Authorities of the States, Food Authorities of the States, Atomic Energy Regulatory Board, Drug Controllers and Inspectors, Chief Controller and other Controllers of Explosiveness, Insecticide Inspectors, Inspectorate of Boilers, and Directorate General of Shipping. In addition, Rajiv Gandhi made a personal appeal to state governments to form environmental councils consisting of representatives from all political parties, non-governmental groups, environmental experts, and the central government.[67] At the end of 1987, only three states—Jammu and Kashmir, Himachal Pradesh, and Orissa had agreed to set up such councils.

The Environment Act, a much-applauded legislation, offered no new solutions, neither did it indicate any significant policy shift. In fact, it was the same old wine being sold in the same old bottle but under a new lable. The similarity of tone, words and the emphasis between the Environment Act and the two previous acts, especially the Water Act, was amazing. The Environment Act, however, had certain added features. First, the amount of punishment put forth was significantly higher. Under the Environment Act, a failure to comply could result in imprisonment of up to five years or a fine of up to one lakh rupees or US $6,000 (compared to the imprisonment limit of three months and a fine limit of 5,000 rupees or US $3,000 set in the Water Act).[68] Second, the jurisdiction of the act applied to the whole of India (as opposed to the provision where state governments could restrict the Water Act's jurisdiction to certain declared areas). Third and last, the third-party right to prosecute was identified in the Environment Act, although to a very limited extent. The act stated that any person, after giving a notice of sixty days to the central government, may take an offensive party to the court[69] (no such right existed under the Water Act). Despite these improvements, the act barred civil courts from entertaining environmental complaints, freed company and departmental heads from taking full responsibility of an offense, and negated the right of the citizens to suit the government for ignoring its duties.

Interestingly, the Bhopal tragedy made the issue of environmental protection so politically volatile that the support for the act was unanimous. The bill, drafted by the Ministry of Environment and Forests, took only six months from the time of its conceptualization to the final signature by the President. It was not referred to any special parliamentary committees, and no significant opposition was formed to hamper its journey by the industrial or business community, the two most powerful organizations in the nation, and also the two most affected groups by the legislation.

Reconciliation Through Regulation

Thus, the policy approach favored by the government was, undoubtedly, regulatory, and it continues to remain so. The controlling legislation emphasizes the control of environmental deterioration through regulation rather than through cooperation. The role of the state, thus, is "policing," rather than "managing," and the policing act is to be performed by the bureaucracy. The regulatory aspect of the environmental policy is neither new, nor is it unique to India. In fact, most developed countries have relied on regulations to prevent the loss of this "common good." The assumption has been that since environment is a common good, it is irrationally used. Therefore, it is necessary that the government should step in to ensure the fair distribution of the good by avoiding the problem of "free riders." The history of regulatory environmental policies in the West, nevertheless, indicates that regulations are expensive, unreliable, and ineffective in the long run.[70] They require an extensive administrative network, a large revenue base, and a continuous support from the public to succeed. Needless to say, none of the prerequisites are met in India.

Three aspects of the Indian environmental policy are noteworthy. First, there is an emphasis on regulating the action rather than altering the behavior of individuals or groups. Unfortunately, in the environmental field, by the time the action appears, an irreparable damage is already done. Second, there is an acceptance of the tutelary role of the government, indicated by the willingness of the government to take enormous responsibilities that include not only regulating but also educating the people and collecting information. Third, there is a sense of leniency that permits enforcing agencies to maneuver. In fact, this leniency may often reflect the carelessness of the government toward the primary goal of environmental protection itself. The absence of set standards, the lack of time schedules, the laxity of punishments and the dearth of political power given to regulators are all excellent examples of policy leniency.

Ironically, these three aspects of the environmental policy—regulation, tutelage, and leniency—make the reconciliation between the goals of economic growth and environmental protection possible. The ineffectiveness of the policy makes the issue of environmental protection acceptable in a society that is economically deprived and politically vulnerable. The environmental policy, as it is designed, successfully embeds the sense of symbolism—a sense that provides superficial assurances to the masses, while keeping the basic structure of the society intact.

Action-oriented regulations, such as periodic inspections of sites and sampling of effluent, allow offenders to deal with local level officials who in India can easily be bribed and pressured. On the other hand, behavior-oriented regulations that aim at achieving a long-term solution, require a change in the basic values of the society and, therefore, are politically undesirable. Similarly, the idea of tutelage is mass-appealing, and provides credibility to the government. But at the same time, it is disruptive to the formation of a strong public lobby. Laws, such as the Water Act and the Environment Act, destroy the base on which environmentalists could appeal to the public. Consequently, the public fails to play its surveillant role--a role that is the backbone of a regulatory policy process. Elder and Cobb have noted this dilemma by saying that "it is the making of policy rather than its execution that the public is most sensitive to. In fact, satisfaction can accrue from the process even if the process fails for one reason or another to produce actual policy outputs."[71] The situation in India reflects this symbolism accurately. Now since a policy on environment already exists, the public must attack on the implementation inefficiencies, which are hard to prove and difficult to rally around.

In brief, the environmental policy with its characteristics of regulation, tutelage, and leniency provides an important political resource to the government. Without challenging the basic structure of the society and without altering the basic goal of the system, i.e., economic growth, the government is able to launch the environmental movement. It will be misleading to suggest that the government, especially Mrs. Gandhi, had no intention to protect the environment: the effect of the movement was expected to eventually trickle down to the bottom layer of the society. However, considering the international pressure that existed in the early 1970s and considering the ambitious, yet cautious, style of Mrs. Gandhi's leadership, it is safe to assume that the government was searching for a reconciliation, rather than a solution, to the environmental problem.

Notes

1. Anil Agarwal, Ravi Chopra and Kalpana Sharma, *The State of India's Environment, 1982: A Citizen's Report* (New Delhi: Centre for Science and Environment, 1982), 17.

2. In the first decade after the independence, mass education was considered to be a moral issue, while in the second decade, it was treated as an important part of the Green Revolution strategy. Today, it is felt that neither Indian industry, nor wealthy farmers feel the need for a larger literate labor force. J.P. Naik, *Equality, Quality and Quantity: The Elusive Triangle in Indian Education* (New Delhi: Allied, 1973); Krishna Kumar, "Education: Safer options," in *India Briefing: 1988*, ed. by Marshall M. Bouton and Philip Oldenburg (Boulder: Westview, 1988), 111-128.

3. India, National Committee on Environmental Planning and Coordination, Inaugural Function, April 12, 1972, 1.

4. India's response was one of many similar responses from the Third World. *Report of the Secretary-General on the United Nations Conference on the Human Environment, Stockholm, Sweden, 5-16 June 1972* (UN Doc. A/CONF.48) reports that the differences were resolved after several discussions. Conferences that provided the forum for discussion included "International Organization and the Human Environment" (cosponsored by the Institute on Man and Science and the Aspen Institute for Humanistic Studies, Rensselaerville, New York, May 21-23, 1971); "The Crisis of the Human Environment and International Action" (by International Studies Program, University of Toronto, Toronto, May 25-27, 1971); "Sixth Conference on the United Nations of the Next Decade" (Stanley Foundation, Sinaia, Romania, June 20-26, 1971); and "The UN System and the Human Enbvironment" (Institute for the Study of International Organization, Brighton, England, November 1-4, 1971).

5. Indira Gandhi, "Man and his Environment" (address at the plenary session of the United Nations Conference on Human Environment, Stockholm, Sweden, 14 June 1972).

6. *The Constitution of India* (New Delhi: Government of India, 1950), Article 252.

7. Ibid, Articles 249-252.

8. The Upper House in India is a permanent body, in which members are elected and sent by state legislatures to represent state interests. All states do not have equal representation: allocation of seats corresponds to state populations, although smaller states are given a proportionately larger share. Every alternate year, one-third of the members go back for re-election.

9. R.K. Bharadwaj, *Democracy in India* (New Delhi: Asia Books, 1980); M.M. Sankhdher, *Framework of Indian Politics* (New Delhi: Gitanjali, 1983).

10. Union Territories are those small regional units which, at the time of the state reorganization in the early 1950s, were left under the central administration. Union Territories have their own local governments for handling various day-to-day tasks. In fact, the system works like a unitary system in regard to Union Territories.

11. Cynthia Enloe in her book *The Politics of Pollution in a Comparative Perspective: Ecology and Power in Four Nations* (New York: David Mckay, 1975) cites this as an indicator of the emergence of the environmental issue in a society.

12. *Lok Sabha Debates* (New Delhi: Government of India Publications), 21 February 1974, 240.

13. Ibid, 241.

14. *Lok Sabha Debates* (New Delhi: Government of India, 16 April 1979), 7-10.

15. Thomas Mathew, "Governmental Response to Environmental Needs in India," *Indian International Centre Journal* (1982): 240-41.

16. I have discussed this point before in my earlier work "Environment as a Political Issue in Developing Countries: A Study of Environmental Pollution in India," *International Journal of Environmental Studies*, 23 (1984): 105-112.

17. Anthony Downs, "Up and Down with Ecology: The Issue Attention Cycle," *Public Interest*, 28 (1972): 28-50; Steven Reed, "Environmental Politics: Some Reflections based on the Japanese Case," *Comparative Politics*, 13 (1981): 253-70.

18. Mathew, *Governmental Response*, 240-41.

19. V.P. Arya, *A Guide to Industrial Licensing in India* (New Delhi: Iyengar Consultancy, 1981), 31-33.

20. This impression was given to me during all of my interviews with high level officials involved in the environmental decision-making process. Dr. R.S. Mehta (chairman, Gujarat Water Pollution Board, and one of the founding fathers of the National Environment Research Institute, Nagpur) and Mr. Brij Kishore (the then Director of Department of Environment) and Mr. B.B. Vohra all displayed their dissatisfaction with the current state of environment in the nation, but still pointed out that it was Mrs. Gandhi's personal commitment that is primarily responsible for making the environment a priority issue. These interviews were held on December 14, 22, and 28, 1983, respectively, in Ahmedabad and New Delhi.

21. F.R. Frankel, *India's Political Economy: 1947-1977* (Princeton: Princeton University Press, 1978), Ch.9.

22. Norman D. Palmer, "India's Fourth General Elections," *Asian Survey*, 7 (1967): 277.

23. For a detailed discussion on Mrs. Gandhi's challenge at that time, see A. Ghosh, *The Split in the Indian National Congress* (Calcutta: Vaibhav, 1970); Robert L. Hardgrave, Jr., "The Congress in India: Crisis and Split," *Asian Survey*, 10 (1970): 256-62; Mahendra Prasad Singh, *Split in a Predominant Party: The Indian National Congress in 1969* (New Delhi: Abhinav, 1981).

24. S. Ghose, *Indira Gandhi, The Resurgent Congress and Socialism* (New Delhi: Asia Books) 1975.

25. Myrone Weiner in "The 1971 Elections and the Indian Party System," *Asian Survey*, 11 (1971): pp. 1153-66 argues that Mrs. Gandhi also appealed directly to the people bypassing the "vote banks," which helped her relate better to the people in the 1971 elections.

26. Insights to Mrs. Gandhi's leadership are provided in M.C. Carras, *Indira Gandhi: In the Crucible of Leadership* (Boston, Beacon Press, 1979); N. Sahagal, *Indira Gandhi's Emergence and Style* (Durham: Carolina Academics, 1978).

27. Frankel, *India's Political Economy*, 454.

28. Based on my personal Interview with Mr. B.B. Vohra, Ex-chairman, National Committee on Environmental Planning and Coordination and the former Secretary to the Government of India in the Ministry of Petroleum and Chemicals (8 December 1983, New Delhi)

29. S. Mansingh, *India's Search for Power: Indira Gandhi's Foreign Policy 1966-82* (New Delhi: Sage, 1984), 8.

30. Ibid, 11.

31. Robert L. Hardgrave and Stanley A. Kochanek, *India: Government and Politics in a Developing Nation* (Harcourt Brace Jovanovich, 1986), 209.

32. Carras, *Indira Gandhi*, 36-40.

33. *The Water (Prevention and Control of Pollution) Act, 1974* (New Delhi: Government of India Publications, 1974), Section 2 [e].

34. Ibid, Section 3.2.

35. Ibid, Section 16.2.

36. Ibid, Section 4.2.

37. Ibid, Section 17.1.

38. Ibid, section 49.1.

39. Ibid, Sections 13-15.

40. Ibid, Section 29.

41. For a detailed discussion on the legal aspects of the law, refer to S. Bhatt, *Environmental Laws and Water Resources Management* (New Delhi: Radiant, 1986), especially Chapter 5.

42. *Annual Report* (New Delhi: Government of India, Central Board for Prevention and Control of Water Pollution, 1983).

43. *Annual Report* (New Delhi: Government of India, Central Board for Prevention and Control of Water, 1982), 36.

44. *The Water Act*, 1974, Section 48.

45. Ibid, Section 49.

46. Based on my personal interview with Dr. R.S. Mehta, Chairman, Gujarat Water Pollution Control Board, December 14, 1983.

47. *Annual Report* (Trivendram: Kerala State Government, Water Pollution Control Board, 1983) p.6.

48. *The Water (Prevention and Control of Pollution) Cess Act, 1977* (New Delhi: Government of India, 1977).

49. Based on my personal interview with Mr. Brij Kishore, the then Director of the Department of Environment (22 December, 1983, New Delhi).

50. "Comprehensive Bill to Check Pollution Soon," *The Hindustan Times*, 29 November 1977, 8.

51. G.H. Lalvani, "Law and pollution control," *India's Environment: Crises and Responses*, ed. by J. Bandopadhyay, et al., (Dehradun: Natraj, 1985), 288.

52. *The Air (Prevention and Control of Pollution) Act 1981* (New Delhi: Government of India, 1981), Section 2a.

53. Ibid, Section 3.

54. Ibid, Section 16.

55. *The Forest Act, 1865,"* passed by the British Government of India.

56. Sharad Kulkarni, "The Forest Policy and the Forest Bill: A Critique and Suggestions for Change," in Walter Fernandes and Sharad Kulkarni, *Towards a New Forest Policy: People's Rights and Environmental Needs* (New Delhi: Indian Social Institute, 1983), 87.

57. Ibid, 88.

58. *Annual Report: 1986-87* (New Delhi: Government of India, Ministry of Environment and Forests, 1987), 44.

59. The Ministry of Environment and Forestry has now set a new self-imposed deadline of three months for clearing projects. This action has come as a response to the sharp criticism that it is facing from state governments ("Developmental Dilemma," *India Today*, 30 November 1988, 61).

60. M. Gadgil, S. Narendra Prasad and Rauf Ali, *Forest Management in India: A Critical Review* (Bangalore: Indian Institute of Science, 1982).

61. Vikas Pandey, "Forest Policy: Cosmetic Changes," *The Hindu*, 3 June 1990.

62. Anil Agarwal and Sunita Narain, *The State of India's Environment, 1984-85* (New Delhi: Centre for Science and Environment, 1985), 80.

63. I have tested this hypothesis empirically in *Forest: The People and the Government: An Examination of the Indian Forest Policy* (New Delhi: National Book Organization, 1989) Chapters 3 and 4; Also see, Fernandes, *Towards a New Forest Policy*.

64. *Annual Report, 1986-87* (New Delhi: Government of India, Ministry of Environment and Forests, 1987), 10.

65. Ibid.

66. *The Environment (Protection) Act, 1986* (New Delhi: Government of India, 1986), Section 2.

67. Ibid, Section 13.

68. Ibid, Section 15.

69. Ibid, Section 19b.

70. See David Vogel, "Evaluating British and American Environmental Regulation: Effectiveness, Efficiency and the Politics of Compliance" (presented at the 1984 American Political Association's Meeting in Washington, DC). Vogel claims that the direct administrative cost of compliance, of course, is exorbitant, but there are several other costs which are equally threatening--loss of jobs, building of hostile relationship with the industry, cost of litigation, credibility of the government, closing of industries for not being able to meet the required cost, etc.

71. C.D. Elder and R.W. Cobb, *The Political Uses of Symbols* (New York: Longman, 1983) 21-22.

CHAPTER 4

Functioning of an Environmental Bureaucracy

T he bureaucracy is said to be one of the two major gifts given to the infant India by the British. It is also claimed to be one of the major hurdles in the nation's development today. The rigid nature of the Indian bureaucracy provides the political system its stability and continuity; but at the same time, it makes the system resistant to change. The bureaucracy in India is expected to perform multiple roles in an atmosphere of great expectations: it is supposed be a manager and distributor of society's resources, a designer of the nation's long-term strategies, and a regulator of society's behavior; and it is supposed to perform these functions while being responsive to the public and being rational to itself. Clearly, more is expected from the bureaucracy than it is capable of providing. In this chapter, the evolution of the environmental bureaucracy and its "regulatory" functions are analyzed.

Following with the central theme of the book, i.e., the "politicalness" of the environmental policy process, this chapter identifies various reasons for which the implementation of environment-related laws in India is either promoted or blocked. On one hand, the rights and duties of the environmental bureaucracy are analyzed in the light of the overall characteristics of the Indian bureaucracy. On the other hand, the implementation process is viewed from a participant's perspective (in this case from the perspective of regulators and regulatees).

Expansion and Consolidation

The creation of an environmental bureaucracy in the 1980s was not faddish, nor was it an experiment for India. A number of organizations, such as the Zoological Survey of India, the Botanical Survey of India, and the Man and the Biosphere, have long been a part of the Indian administration. The more formal response by the government in 1980 only reflected its willingness to bring these scattered organizations together under one umbrella.

The first attempt to institutionalize the environmental concern came in 1972, when a National Committee on Environmental Planning and Coordination (NCEPC) was created.[1] It is interesting to note that the Preparatory Committee for the United Nation's Conference on Human Environment was, in fact, the precursor of the NCEPC. The committee consisted of senior officers, chief engineers, professors and environmentalists representing various administrative ministries, research organizations, and public agencies whose work had a bearing on the environment. The NCEPC was an advisory body charged with the responsibility of suggesting and reviewing environmental policies and programs. The main task before the Committee was to "ensure that while the country pursues its legitimate desire to develop its economy as fast as technology and resources will allow, the environment and the quality of life that depends upon it is not unduly degraded."[2] Its prime success came in the form of the increased awareness for the environmental cause, both inside and outside of the government. The result was the creation of an extensive environmental bureaucratic network and the emergence of over 100 public interest groups within the next decade.

In the wake of the environmental movement, Mrs. Gandhi, after her return to power in January 1980, appointed a high-level committee consisting of 10 members from various government and research institutes to recommend legislative and administrative measures to enhance environmental protection.[3] Events leading to the formation of this committee were summarized by Digvijay Pratap Sinh as follows:

> I remember drafting, in consultation with my uncle Dr. Nagendra Singh, Judge of the International Court of Justice, a representation to the Prime Minister to set up a Ministry/Department of Environment and then taking the final draft for discussion with Dr. M.S. Swaminathan and Prof. M.G.K. Menon on the lawns of the latter's house on a cold winter morning, for giving the final shape to the recommendation.[4]

The committee, named after its chairman, N.D. Tiwari, submitted its report on November 15, 1980, and suggested two major solutions: one, tightening of the loopholes in existing policies; and two, the consolidation of the bureaucratic power into one agency.[5] Based on the recommendations of the Tiwari Committee, a full-fledged Department of Environment was created in 1980, under the chairmanship of the then Prime Minister Indira

Gandhi herself. The Department of Environment (DOE), like its counter-part of the same name in the United Kingdom, was formed by amalgamating components from different departments and independent agencies. Accord-ing to the Department's own report, the DOE was to play a "watchdog" role. While serving as a "nodal" agency,[6] the DOE was to carry out environmental appraisal of development projects (similar to the environmental impact assessment); to protect and conserve wildlife; to monitor and control air and water quality; to establish an environmental information system; to promote environmental research; and to sustain international cooperation. Another important task of the DOE was its role as the coordinator of activities between the federal, state, and local level agencies.[7]

However, the Department of Environment, despite its consolidated power base, failed to bring desired results. One may even argue that it was meant to be a failure due to the inherent conflict and vagueness that existed in the structure itself. The environmental policy (as reflected in laws adopted by the government) was regulatory in nature, but at the same time, the bureaucratic network that it created was non-regulatory. The Department of Environment was an advisory body with a small political base and even a smaller financial support. It was a "watchdog" who had no bark. The term "nodal agency," used by the government itself, indicated the frivolous nature of this important agency. Consequently, the criticism to the Department of Environment grew even before the Department could start its operation. Environmentalists claimed that once the pressure from the industrial and business sectors started to appear, the Department would loose its effective-ness. Considering the corrupt and rigid nature of the bureaucracy, it was not wise to leave the implementation solely in the hands of the local bureaucrats, who were vulnerable against various pressures. Moreover, the Department, which was to overlook other bureaucratic agencies, lacked the ability to withstand the pressure coming from within the government itself. Without an independent and competitive power base, the DOE was unable to oversee the activities of other development-oriented agencies, such as the ones dealing with forests, energy, transportation and industrialization.

The failure of the DOE did not force the government to re-evaluate its policy on environment; instead, it compelled decision-makers to tighten further the grip of the bureaucracy. The new attempt came in 1985, when the newly-elected Prime Minister Rajiv Gandhi elevated the status of the Department of Environment to an independent ministry. Thus, the Ministry of Environment and Forests was created, and several important organiza-tions, new and old, were brought under its jurisdiction. With the adoption of the Environment (Protection) Act and the creation of the Ministry of Environment and Forests (MEF), the environmental concern became fully institutionalized in 1986.

The organization of the MEF was comprehensive and elaborate. Comprising several agencies and divisions, the MEF offered one of the most impressive environmental law enforcing networks in the world. As Figure 4.1 indicates, in 1989, at the apex of the organization was the Minister of Environment and Forests, assisted by a Minister of State (both were political positions) and followed by a full-ranked secretary (a permanent civil service position). From the functional point of view, the MEF was divided into eighteen divisions (See Figure 4.1). In addition there were two separate and administratively independent units, Ganga Project Directorate and the National Mission on Wastelands Development, that reported directly to the Secretary. Divisions were further assisted by 11 autonomous agencies and 6 associated units. The autonomous agencies were only assisted by the Ministry, while the units were under the administrative control of the Ministry.

A notable feature of the MEF was its increasing diversification and specialization: Forest Conservation was added as a division in 1987; and in 1988, two additional divisions, Hazardous Substances Management and Forestry International Cooperation, joined the list. The Ministry also grew in its staff strength. The Department of Environment, Forests and Wildlife (housed in New Delhi) had the technical and clerical staff of 1,171.[8] A slow albeit steady growth marked the expansion of the department: 684 in 1986, 970 in 1987, 1,056 in 1988, and 1,171 in 1989. The figures indicate an increase of 41 percent from 1986 to 1987; 9 percent from 1987 to 1988; and 11 percent from 1988 to 1989.

Ministry of Environment and Forests

The functions of the MEF were divided into three major categories: custodial; regulatory; and finally, promotional. Custodial functions related to those functions where the MEF itself accepted the primary responsibility of controlling environmental deterioration. Functions, such as pollution monitoring and control, eco-regeneration, assessment of flora and fauna, forest resource development, wildlife conservation, and the development of wastelands fell under this category. In this context, the MEF worked more as a guardian and as a provider than as a regulator. It provided services, such as surveys and assessments, with no direct cost and benefit to anyone: neither the gainer nor the loser could be identified. The funds for these activities,

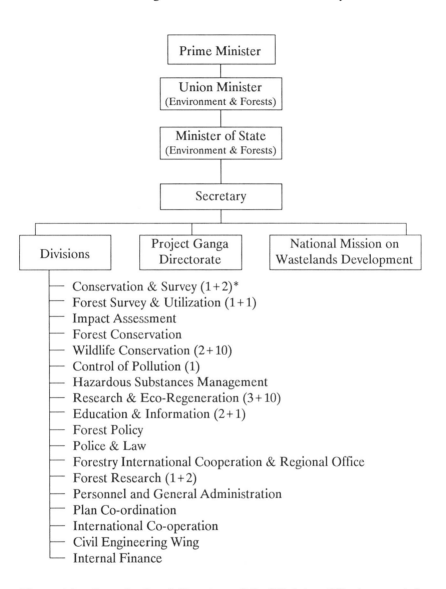

Figure 4.1. Organizational Structure of the Ministry of Environment & Forests

* The first number in parentheses indicates the number of autonomous agencies assisted by the division and the second number in parentheses indicates the number of units under the control of the division.

nevertheless, were identifiable--they came from the government's limited pot. Because of this characteristic, the MEF had a limited potential to build either the necessary political support or the desired mass appeal. In other words, the MEF had a small and a dispersed clientele; therefore, it had no choice but to depend on the ruling party's patronage for its basic survival.

The regulatory functions of the Ministry of Environment and Forests were the most visible and, thus, were under the heaviest scrutiny by the citizens and the media. Setting emission control standards for industries and conducting environment impact assessments for developmental projects formed the heart of the MEF's regulatory responsibilities. These functions are discussed in greater detail below.

Under the regulatory policy framework, extensive guidelines were set for emission discharges from industries, and minimal national standards (MINAS) were evolved for each specific industry, such as pesticide, caustic soda, synthetic, oil, sugar, thermal power, cotton textile, cement, electroplating and dyes.[9] Further, in order to assess the quality of air and water, the MEF also established an extensive network of local and regional monitoring stations and periodic surveys. In 1989, a two-tier water quality monitoring under the United Nations Global Environmental Monitoring Systems (GEMS)

Table 4.1
Water Quality Monitoring Stations Under GEMS Program

State	Stations	Rivers Covered
Andhra Pradesh	10	Godavari, Krishna, Pennar, Mahi
Bihar	4	Subarnarekha
Gujarat	9	Mahi, Marmada, Sabarmati, Tapti
Karnataka	5	Cauvery, Krishna
Kerala	9	Chaliyar, Kallada, Muvattupuzha Periyar
Madhya Pradesh	5	Tapti, Narmada
Maharashtra	5	Godavari, Krishna
Tamil Nadu	4	Cauvery
TOTAL	51	

Source: *Annual Report* (New Delhi: Government of India, Central Board for Prevention and Control of Water Pollution, 1986), 16.

Table 4.2
Water Quality Monitoring Stations Under MINARS Program

Name of State	Number of Stations (in 1986)	(in 1989)
Andhra Pradesh	-	21
Assam	3	8
Bihar	15	4
Delhi	3	3
Gujarat	-	20
Haryana	13	13
Himachal Pradesh	15	18
Karnataka	3	25
Kerala	-	5
Madhya Pradesh	3	30
Maharashtra	-	22
Orissa	14	29
Punjab	13	13
Rajasthan	-	1
Tamil Nadu	-	10
Uttar Pradesh	28	10
West Bengal	-	-
TOTAL	110	232

Source: *Annual Report* (New Delhi: Government of India, Central Board for Prevention and Control of Water Pollution, 1987), 16; Also *Annual Report* from the same source, 1989, 21.

and the Monitoring of Indian National Aquatic Resources (MINARS) consisting of 283 monitoring stations (51 under GEMS and 232 under MINARS) was in effect (see Tables 4.1 and 4.2).[10] In order to monitor the quality of air, a national network of ambient air quality monitoring stations was started in 1984. In 1989, the network consisted of 150 stations covering 41 cities and towns.[11]

The MEF's operations were often area-based, indicating the ability of the organization to direct resources in a "fire-brigade" fashion. The program that attracted the most attention was the Ganga Action Plan for the Prevention of Pollution of the Ganga. The plan was significant because it marked the beginning of a new era in the government's thinking toward environmental issues.

Ganga Action Plan: A Policy Shift:

The Ganga is not only a religious symbol for the millions of Hindus, it is also a basis for survival for the thousands of people in the states of Himachal Pradesh, Punjab, Haryana, Uttar Pradesh, Rajasthan, Madhya Pradesh, Bihar, West Bengal and the Union Territory of Delhi. Thirty-seven percent of the nation's population resides in the Ganga basin and 47 percent of the nation's total irrigated area is situated in this basin. In its 2,525 kilometer stretch from Gangotri in the Himalayas to its meeting point with the sea at Ganga Sagar in the Bay of Bengal, the Ganga passes along 29 major cities (with populations over 100,000), 23 small cities (with populations between 50,000 to 100,000) and about 48 towns (with populations of less than 50,000). It is estimated that 900 million liters of sewage is dumped into the Ganga every day.[12] In 1985, according to official sources[13], not a single small city

Table 4.3
Pollution of Ganga Through Residential Sources

	In Bihar	In Uttar Pradesh	In West Bengal
Number of major cities	4	6	27
Number having sewerage collection facility	1	4	6
Number having any treatment facility	1	0	5
Number of towns	4	4	15
Number having sewerage collection facility	0	0	0
Number having any treatment facility	0	0	0

Source: An Action Plan for Prevention of Pollution of the Ganga (New Delhi: Government of India, Department of Environment 1985), A1 and A2.

along the banks of the Ganga had any sewerage system. The effluent passed through open drains into the river. Other than Bhavnagar, Kalyani and Farakkatownship in West Bengal, and Uttarkashi and Rishikesh in Uttar Pradesh, no small town had either the sewerage system or the treatment facility. The situation was equally dismal in major urban areas, where more than half the cities had no sewerage system, and nearly ninety percent had no water treatment facility (Table 4.3).

Under the Ganga Action Plan, the government accepted a two-phase plan: the first was to build 262 different schemes in 27 major cities at a cost of Rs 283.68 crores (approximately US $180 million), and the second one was to construct sewerage facilities in small cities. As of July 1990, 148 schemes had been completed (62 percent in Uttar Pradesh, 69 percent in Bihar, and 46 percent of the target in West Bengal)[14]; however, no concrete estimates and schemes for the second phase were available. The strategies to reduce the pollution load as given in the Plan are listed below.

— renovation of existing trunk sewers and outfall to prevent the overflow of sewage into the Ganga;

— construction of interceptors to divert the flow of sewage;

— renovation of existing sewage pumping stations and sewage treatment plants and installation of new ones;

— arrangements for bringing human and animal wastes from locations proximate to the sewage/sullage digester for sanitary disposal, production of energy and manure;

— providing sullage or sewage pumping stations at the outfall points of open drains, to divert the discharge from the river into the nearest sewers and treatment plants;

— alternative arrangements to prevent discharge of animal and human wastes from cattle sheds located on the river banks;

— low cost sanitation schemes in areas adjoining the river;and

— pilot projects to establish the feasibility of technology applications in the treatment of wastes and resources/energy recovery.[15]

The Ganga Action Plan marked a dramatic policy shift in the environmental policy field: for the first time, the government recognized the "commonality" of the pollution source. The emphasis was placed on the domestic sources of pollution; consequently, the responsibility of the government shifted from setting of emission standards to actually being the provider itself. Since no single individual or group could be held responsible for domestic sewage, the government, under the banner of the welfare state, assumed the responsibility itself. Regulating and monitoring still remained important parts of the implementation process; however, the targets of regulation were not any outside organizations. They were the government agencies (municipalities) themselves. This new approach was bound to start a new rift between federal level bureaucrats and their local counterparts. In addition, the government was forced to generate additional avenues of resources to fund this new program. The cost of preventing the pollution of the Ganga was estimated to run into several hundred million dollars.

The Ganga Action Plan sought public support and covered even the minute details, such as the construction of cattlesheds and the prohibition of throwing of dead bodies into the river by building free or low-cost cremation centers. A series of exhibitions, *seva shivirs* (service clinics), and *padyatra* (public processions) were also planned at regular intervals and in various places to promote public awareness.

In order to carry out the Plan, another layer of bureaucracy, in the form of the Central Ganga Authority (CGA), was also established under the chairmanship of the Prime Minister.[16] The CGA consisted of the union finance minister, chief ministers of Uttar Pradesh, Bihar, and West Bengal, deputy chairman of Planning Commission, minister of state from Planning, minister of state from the MEF, minister of state from the Department of Science and Technology, and secretaries from various environment-related agencies. The CGA was assisted by a Steering Committee, consisting of 19 high-level (at the level of joint secretary, chief secretary, or director-general) bureaucrats representing 16 government agencies and three independent research centers. For functional purposes, the CGA granted the responsibility of regional administration to state level agencies. In Uttar Pradesh and Bihar, the Department of Urban Development and in West Bengal, the Department of Environment were made responsible for this task. Furthermore, state and city level task forces were also established by the state governments for the smooth functioning of the plan.

Needless to say, the Ganga Action Plan was one of the major commitments taken by the Indian government in the 1980s. The *Annual Report* of the MEF applauded the success achieved under the Plan, however, the follow-up reports by the media remained not only critical, but also skeptical of the program. Reporting on the progress of the scheme in July of 1987, *India Today* declared that:

> In fact there has been hardly any progress at all since the monumental project took off in June 1985. Out of the 66 projects in West Bengal, 47 have been delayed and in 33, no work had begun. In Calcutta, where the Ganga pollution is the highest, construction had not started on even a single project. And in Bihar and Varanasi, work is only crawling. The Ganga is still as filthy as it was two years ago... Scientists who were associated with the project are beginning to lose patience. More and more bureaucrats have moved in and taken over all the decision-making.[17]

Environmental Impact Assessments: A Bureaucratic Tool

The Environmental Impact Assessment (EIA), which was another regulatory responsibility given to the MEF under the Environment Protection Act, allowed the Ministry to play an important political role. Under the EIA, all projects were required to go through an environmental appraisal, conducted by the MEF technicians based on the information provided by the applicant. According to the government, "the objective of Environmental Impact Assessment is to achieve sustained development with minimal environmental degradation and prevention of long term adverse effects on environment by incorporating suitable preventive and control measures."[18] The environmental appraisal of projects was to be conducted by the Department of Environment within the MEF through various permanent and temporary committees. In 1988, four permanent committees existed to deal exclusively with projects related to river valley development, mining operations, industrial growth and thermal power projects.[19] Other than these, various special committees in Bombay, Delhi and in several coastal areas were also in operation.

The environmental appraisal provided the crux of the environmental policy in India, for it was this function that established the long-term policy priority. Unfortunately, the MEF was not appropriately guarded to perform this role. A large number of appraisals and the lack of information in many environment-related areas made it impossible for the appraisal committees to devote adequate time and energy for individual projects. It was reported that "as many as 115 big and small power, mining, chemical and steel projects have been held up by the ministry for nearly five years."[20] In fact, environmental appraisal itself turned into a political burden for the MEF and, consequently, for the government. To begin with, the MEF emerged as a target of criticism even within the federal government. Fingers were being pointed to the MEF for blocking major development schemes. The MEF, according to these complaints, was expected to play the role of a coordinator and planner, and not of a regulator.

Second, the appraisal process became a source of conflict between federal and state officials, simply because most of the projects for appraisal were brought by state level agencies. It was estimated by the department that it should take anywhere from eight months to two years to obtain the environmental clearance; however, in 1988, several projects were reported to be in the waiting line for more than five years. For example, the 200 MW Chalkudi Hydro Electric Project was proposed by the Kerala government in March of 1983; the 600 MW Sawalkot Hydro Electric Project and the 630 MW Bakreshwar Thermal Power Project were proposed by the state govern- ments of Jammu & Kashmir and West Bengal, respectively, in June of 1984; and the 2000 MW Bandhava Thermal Power Plant has been in line for the Madhya Pradesh government since August of 1984. While the state govern- ments pointed to the critical shortage of power supply in their states, the MEF claimed that it was unable to grant clearance for lack of data. Meanwhile, the political and financial burden continued to grow and the cost of construction doubled and, in some cases, even tripled.[21]

The conflict between the energy needs and the environmental needs has been growing. It is likely to intensify even more in the 1990s. It is interesting that while the MEF plans to implement its policy guidelines of environmental protection, the newly proposed Eighth Five-Year Plan proposes to add at least 38,000 MW of electricity through new hydro and thermal power plants.[22] Even after this investment, it is estimated that the nation will suffer a 20 percent power shortage during 1990-95 time period of the Eighth Five-Year Plan. It is difficult to see how the MEF will remain in the way of this mounting developmental pressure from the national and state governments.

Third, the impact of EIA on the bureaucratic behavior was also undesir- able. The appraisal process sharply divided the Ministry of Environment and Forests itself. More often than not, the conflict arose between technical experts, who focused their attention on the environmental impact of projects, and bureaucrats, who were pressured by politicians to favor a more balanced view on environment and development. Lastly, the environmental appraisal process, despite its good intentions, added another layer of bureaucratic maneuvering, often leading to corrupt practices. Since the criteria for appraisal, especially the quantifying of social costs, involved uncertainty and vagueness, the process was open to significant bureaucratic discretion.

The regulatory profile of the MEF was really a one-sided picture. In addition to the supervisory and regulatory duties, the MEF, under its promotional functions, also served as the major center for the collection and dissemination of environmental information and data. The Department of Environment, in 1980, established an Environmental Information System (ENVIS) network. In 1989, the network consisted of an ENVIS Focal Point located in the Ministry and ten other ENVIS centers throughout the nation and published several important documents including their annual report and Paryavaran Abstract, a quarterly journal reporting Indian research information on environment and related areas. The ENVIS also provided a link to the INFOTERRA (Global Information Network) and the United Nations Environment Program (UNEP).[23]

With its custodial, regulatory and promotional functions, the MEF was a textbook example of an environmental bureaucracy. Nevertheless, the effectiveness of the MEF was far from being exemplary. Several legal, political and social problems contributed to its inefficient performance. As discussed in the case of the Water Pollution Control Boards, the policy itself provided a weak foundation. The Department of Environment within the MEF, for example, was given a "watchdog" role: it was expected to protect the environment, punish polluters and challenge the industry; and ironically, it was expected to achieve these miracles with its coordinating and planning powers. Despite all the good intentions, the MEF failed to function with the same vigor and authority as the Environmental Protection Agency in the United States could. According to Mr. Vohra, the ex-chairman of the NCEPC, "...it [environmental bureaucracy] was never meant to have teeth...it will be long before we equip ourselves with any such sets of teeth."[24]

The thrust of the policy and, consequently, of the environmental bureaucracy was the idea of deterrence, which, needless to say, required a mental relationship between two competitive forces. In the case of environmental protection, the destructive force, whether visible or invisible, was clearly more powerful than the protective force. Political processes, ironically enough, only perpetuated this imbalance. The environmental policy, despite its comprehensiveness, and the environmental bureaucracy, despite its consolidated powers, remained inferior to the more powerful developmental bureaucracy.

The Enforcement Gap: An Analysis in Policy Effectiveness

Since the time of the creation of the environmental bureaucracy, the gap between expectations and performance has been widening. Causes and consequences of this gap directly relate to the future of environmental protection in the nation. It is indeed true that the environmental bureaucracy is still in its infancy, and is still being shaped and molded; nevertheless, it must be remembered that no time limits have been set for the bureaucracy to mature and show results. For example, the water boards have been in existence for 12 years--more time than was granted to the United States Environmental Protection Agency by the 1972 Amendments to the Clean Water Act which clearly demanded that all the nation's water was to become "fishable and swimmable" within 10 years.[25] The achievements of the environmental bureaucracy in India can be summed up in a few sentences: it has been successful in creating a new awareness for environmental protection, and it has also met its goal of establishing various monitoring and implementing networks. However, it has so far been unable to translate these achievements into direct policy outcomes. The rate of deforestation has not been reduced; the level of pollution in water has not been decreased; and the quality of air has not been improved in any significant way. So far, the government has made important environmental investments, which are expected to pay dividends in the future. But the questions to be answered remain: how much more investment is needed, and will there be any dividend return at all?

Faced by an strong developmental challenge, the government is forced to adopt a pretentious policy approach. Pretention is visible in governmental reports: even after ten years, the reports of the Central Water Pollution Control Board emphasize activities, rather than achievements. Policy outcomes are measured in terms of how many networks have been established, and how many emission standards have been set up, instead of whether the quality of water or air has been improved as a result of these networks and standards. The government is able to achieve a balance between its developmental goals and environmental goals by glorifying procedures, and as long as these procedures do not directly threaten the developmental goal, the government faces no political challenge by committing itself to environmental activities. Pretention, in fact, helps the government to reconcile the two seemingly conflicting goals.

The growth in the size of the environmental bureaucracy is particularly enticing, and it reflects the commitment on the part of the government to institutionalize the issue. Since its creation in 1981, the personnel strength of the Department of Environment has quadrupled and its budget has multiplied several times. As indicated in Table 4.4, the Seventh Five-Year Plan (1985-90) sanctioned Rs 427.91 crores (approximately US $357 million) for environmental protection activities by the central and state governments, as opposed to only Rs 40.05 crores (approximately US $40 million at that time's exchange rate) sanctioned under the Sixth Five-Year Plan (1980-85). These figures indicate one of the sharpest inclines in any federal agency's budget. The commitment displayed by the Planning Commission in its five-year plans had a trickle-down effect on the Department of Environment's budget, as the budget nearly doubled in 1985-86 (See Table 4.5). The increase came because of the Ganga Action Plan, for which the government committed Rs 240.00 crores (or US $167 million) over a five-year period (in 1985-86, the Ganga Action Plan was granted Rs 1,000 lakhs, or US $7 million). However, this sanction is likely to end or be curtailed under the Eighth Five-Year Plan beginning in 1990.

Despite budgetary increases, no major shift in the government's expenditure priorities is apparent. Table 4.6 indicates that the expenditure on pollution control has increased substantially, as nearly 70 percent of the DOE's budget in 1984-85 was allocated for this purpose, as opposed to only 13.4 percent in the previous year. The share of the pollution control programs dropped somewhat in the following year; nevertheless, it was still the most demanding category. It is important to note that the increase in this category

Table 4.4
Expenditure on Environmental Protection Efforts

Expenditures (in crore rupees)	6th Five-Year Plan	7th Five-Year Plan
Central Government	--	35.00*
State Governments	--	75.71
Joint	--	2.20
Total (from various sources)	40.05	427.91

* It includes Rs 240.00 crores sanctioned for the cleaning of Ganga

Source: *Seventh Five-Year Plan, 1985-90* (New Delhi: Government of India, The Planning Commmission, 1985), Part II, 339.

Table 4.5
Budget Increase for the Department of Environment

Year	Total Budget (in lakh Rs)	Percent of increase from previous year
1982-83	1,386.43	
1983-84	1,864.02	34.4
1984-85	2,093.91	12.3
1985-86	4,132.76*	97.4
1986-87	NA	
1987-88	18,040.00	
1988-89	18,200.00	(0.9)
1989-90	20,200.00**	11.0

* It does not include the budget sanctioned for the cleaning of Ganga.
** The figures are estimates.

came because of the Ganga Action Plan, which alone costed twice as much as the remaining pollution budget (Rs 1,000 lakhs out of a total pollution control budget of Rs 1,457 lakhs in 1984-85). The budget data indicates that the government spent between 20 to 25 percent on research and development, 10 to 15 percent on the Botanical and Zoological Surveys each, less than two percent on the collection of information through ENVIS, and less than one percent on the promotion of environmental awareness. This distribution did not change much over the years, and if one takes out the one-time expenditure on the cleaning of Ganga, then the pollution control figures remained around 15 to 20 percent of the total environment budget.

Even though environmental protection now commands a permanent place in the nation's long-term economic strategy and even though the allocation for environmental protection occupies an important position in the nation's planning strategy, it will be misleading to assume that the emphasis on environmental protection has in any way undermined the government's preference for fast economic growth. If the allocation of money indicates governmental priorities, then the figures in Table 4.7 reveal that environmental protection is still a secondary priority. The government is committed to improving the living standards of its population through industrialization and social welfare programs. Under the Seventh Five-Year Plan, only 0.2 percent of the total budget was committed for environmental protection: the

Table 4.6
Distribution of the Department of Environment's Budget
for Selected Categories

(in lakhs rupees)

Category	1982-83	1983-84	1984-85	1985-86
Pollution Control*	215.00	250.00	1,457.30	1,690.38
	(15.5)**	(13.4)	(69.6)	(40.9)
Research & Development	245.00	430.00	550.00	748.00
	(17.7)	(23.1)	(26.3)	(18.1)
Exhibition & Education	7.00	13.00	26.00	37.00
	(0.5)	(0.7)	(1.2)	(0.9)
ENVIS	10.00	45.00	40.00	75.00
	(0.7)	(2.4)	(1.9)	(1.8)
Botanical Survey	225.50	254.50	321.90	382.85
	(16.3)	(13.7)	(15.4)	(9.3)
Zoological Survey	191.60	240.50	297.87	345.95
	(13.8)	(12.9)	(14.2)	(8.4)

*   Include CBPCWP; Cess Reimbursement to State Boards; Laboratories; Environmental Pollution Cell; Waste Recycling and other pollution control schemes; and Clean Ganga Project.

**   Figures in parenthesis indicate percentage of total budget in that category.

***   Includes Centres of Excellence and Integrated Action Oriented Research.

amount was equal to or less than the government's budget for nuclear, space, or energy research programs. Irrigation, housing, urban development and water supply continue to take a major portion of the government's budget. Considering the government's strategy of playing the role of a provider, it is certain that the demand for additional expenditure on environmental protection efforts will rise in the future, making it more difficult for the government to maintain its reconciliatory approach.

Table 4.7
Allotment of Governmental Money to Selected Sectors Under
the Seventh Five-Year Plan

Sector Category	Rupees (crores)	Percent of Total Budget Outlay
National Rural Employment	3,473.99	1.9
Rural Co-operative Development	416.15	0.2
Irrigation Schemes	14,360.55	8.0
Development of New Energy Sources	519.55	
Rural and Small Sector Industrial Development	2,752.74	1.5
Nuclear Research	315.00	0.2
Space Program	700.00	0.4
Health & Medicine	3,392.89	1.9
Family Welfare	3,256.26	1.8
Housing & Urban Development	4,259.50	2.4
Water Supply	6,522.47	3.6
Environment Protection Including Ganga Action Plan	427.91	0.2

Source: *Seventh Five-Year Plan, 1985-90* (New Delhi: Government of India, The Planning Commission, 1985), Part I, 30-32.

The widening enforcement gap in the environmental policy is caused by the pretentious policy approach adopted by the government. In addition, several other contextual and behavioral factors also contribute to the failure of the policy. Five major factors are identified in the section below. These factors reveal the irrationality of assumptions and the futility of applying these assumptions to the real world. The factors include the high cost of regulation; high cost of compliance; complexity arising due to federal structure; bureaucratic rivalry; and finally, the highly political profile of the bureaucracy.

(I) Cost of Enforcement

The enforcement gap is directly related to the cost of enforcement on the part of those who are responsible for enforcement or, in this case, local bureaucrats. The enforcement of standards, for example, becomes difficult when local level officials, for one reason or the other, refuse to carry out the directions given to them by the central command. Since the setting of standards is very much a national issue, the participation of local officials in arriving at decisions is minimal. If local officials perceive the process to be an imposition, they may thwart the implementation, regardless of its merit. Conformation by local officials becomes more crucial when one considers the non-regulatory functions of the environmental policy, such as the establishment of monitoring networks, provision of treatment facilities, building of wildlife conservatories, etcetra. In all of these areas, decisions are made by central level officials, but are carried out by local level officials, who are not under any direct pressure from international agencies, nor are they accountable to the politicians who initiate the policy to begin with. In fact, local officials function in a context which is entirely different from the context faced by federal level officials: they are vulnerable to the pressures from the local elite. Consequently, while it is easy for federal level officials to provide symbolic support to the policy, for local officials, the policy is a real battlefield. They are pressured by their higher-up authorities to produce results, while at the same time they are challenged by the local industries or businesses to alter their implementation guidelines. The politics of implementation, in this case, remains basically local.

From an official's point of view, the cost of conforming with implementation guidelines depends on the willingness of the local elite to comply. The cost is reduced significantly if the elite are assured of the merits of complying (as in Great Britain[26]), or if they are made to believe that the cost of not complying is greater than the cost of complying (as in the United States[27]). While both methods have their pluses and minuses, it is recognized now that the long-term implications of voluntary compliance are far greater than the short-term effectiveness of forced compliance. Other than Great Britain, where local Alkali Inspectors are given enough authority to strike a deal with local industry, Japan also relies on the ability of local officials to bargain an optimum level of compliance from industry.[28] Both the nations assure this process by making flexible laws with little or no fixed standards and by not fixing any legally set time schedules. It is clear that the intent of the government in India is also similar, because Indian environmental laws are flexible, locally-oriented and do not impose time limits.

However, local bureaucrats in India face a significantly higher cost of compliance than their counterparts in Great Britain or Japan. The public's mistrust in local officials, who are known to be corrupt and anti-people, plays a major role in determining this cost. Faced by the lack of support from the public, officials find it difficult to establish an adverse relationship with the local elite.[29]

> There appears to be a complex attitudinal and perceptional set of expectations about the citizen's relationship with administration. The components of this syndrome are: lack of self-confidence on the part of the ordinary citizen in dealing directly with officials, a feeling that the best way to deal with administrators is by enlisting the support of others, particularly individuals with the right contacts and political pull, that administrators do not and will not treat all people equally and that their administrative actions are final, complaints availing very little or being difficult to process.[30]

Several studies have shown that bureaucrats in India are alienated from the people and suffer from an upper-class bias.[31] Most of the officials in the bureaucracy, especially in higher services, are drawn from the urban middle class, and there exists a gross under-representation of either the rural farmers and cultivators, or the urban workers and artisans. This limited class selection stems from the screening system for the civil services that has been in the existence since the British rule. Studies reveal that a high portion of the recruits attend expensive private schools and a few selected universities--both of which are unaccessible to the poor and uneducated. The domination of the urban professional class was expected to give the system a meritorious bureaucracy with a better understanding and vision; nevertheless, this domination has created severe paradoxes in the bureaucracy. On the outside and in their ideals, bureaucrats may believe in the moral values of the society; but in their behavior they often engage in practices which are impersonal, irrational and even immoral.

> Extreme impersonality combines with ready susceptibility to personal pressures and interventions. A bureaucrat may be theoretically preoccupied with correctness and propriety, but in practice he may go along with endless irregularities and improprieties. Similarly, his pursuit of absolute justice and uniformity in civil service rules, regulations and procedures often lead to glaring anomalies and injustices.[32]

In the environmental policy field, the public's image plays an important role. Local people, who are the direct victims of water pollution of rivers and streams, remain quiescent in the policy process because they lack the trust that officials will listen to them, and also because they are aware that the officials are in alliance with polluters. In other words, the environmental policy process in India does not suffer from the lack of awareness, but from the abundance of helplessness.

Another reason for the high cost of enforcement stems from the fact that local officials in India are not granted the same kind of freedom by the system as their counterparts are in Great Britain. While responsibility has been decentralized in the bureaucracy, the devolution of authority is yet to come. Local officials are simply not expected to localize the decision-making by striking deals with polluters. They are accountable for following the procedures given to them, and not for results. Consequently, they have little or no desire to implement a policy for its goals.

The Indian civil service suffers from excessive self-importance, indifference towards the feeling or the convenience of individuals and obsession with the binding and inflexible authority of departmental decisions, precedents, arrangements or forms, regardless of how badly or with what injustice they may work in individual cases. Additionally, the civil service suffers from a mania for regulations and formal procedures, a preoccupation with activities of particular units of administration and an inability to consider the government as a whole.[33]

Additionally, it is generally accepted that industries or forest contractors have "connections" with the next higher-up layer of officials. Local officials find their authority severely limited in forcing a polluting industry to comply by taking them to courts as in the United States or by striking deals with them as in the United Kingdom. Moreover, there is a general feeling among local officials that, if they ignore the power of the alliance between the industry and the higher-ups, then their career will suffer. Even though local officials are protected against losing their jobs due to the job security provided by the Indian Civil Services, the possibility of demotion or transfer to remote areas often works as an important tool to assure compliance by local officials. Thus, for officials, the cost of implementing tough standards far exceeds the cost of ignoring the standards, especially if the local industry is not willing to comply.

(II) The Cost of Compliance

The widening enforcement gap in the environment protection area is, to a great extent, due to the high cost of compliance for industry or for other destructive forces. The success of a regulatory policy depends on the ability of the regulator to seek compliance from the regulated, whether directly or indirectly, whether through coercion or through persuasion. The regulatory aspect of the environmental policy in India fails even before the implementation actually begins because of the previously mentioned inherent weaknesses of the regulators (local officials. What makes the situation even worse is the unwillingness of the industry or other sources to comply. Defiance, rather than compliance, has been the strategy of the mighty industry. Several reasons create this attitude. First is the mistrust of the industry for officials: the alliance between the industry and the bureaucracy depends on mutual suspicion, rather than on mutual interest. Bureaucratic procedures are viewed as unnecessary and in conflict with the interest of the industry. The following incident is just a reflection of this mistrust toward environment impact assessments.

> Plainly, companies believe that the official dawdling is uncalled for and that the Government indulges in nit-picking. The charge is not entirely unfounded. A transmission line in Maharashtra was delayed for 35 months just because it passed over 150 metres of notified forest land. In many places, the forest land may not have a single tree but only a few shrubs. Yet, because it is notified as forest land, we are refused permission to start project.[34]

Second, the image of officials as being susceptible and vulnerable allows the industry to ignore emission control guidelines. It is believed that officials can easily be "bought" and, therefore, it is cheaper to buy off a regulator than to comply with regulation. Moreover, the complexities of environmental laws and the impersonal behavior of bureaucrats further discourages industries to take the laws seriously. In general, industries can afford to display a sense of aloofness and casualness when it comes to the question of their compliance. The following case study[35] depicts this feeling.

Deenar Syntex Pvt. Ltd.,[36] a small scale textile firm with a capital investment of about US $3 million, was looking for a location in the state of Gujarat. Since this state hosts the largest number of textile industries in the country and most are located near Ahmedabad City, Kalol (in the district of Mahsana, 35 km. away from Ahmedabad) was selected as the preferred site by company experts. In compliance with Section 25 of the Water Act, the firm applied for a "No Objection Certificate" from the Gujarat State Water Board in January 1980. The application was promptly rejected by the board on the ground of "non-availability of satisfactory disposal site." A visit to the site indicated that there was no river or water source in the area. Waste was to be disposed via a storm drain. According to the board, the area was "land-locked," although four very large firms with substantial discharges and with questionable treatment facilities were already using it. In discussions between board officials and firm experts, a nearby site, Dholka, was suggested by the board as an alternative. Another application for a "No Objection Certificate" was forwarded by the firm in April 1980, and was approved by the board a year later in May 1981.

On July 1, 1981, the unit began construction. A water treatment facility advised by the company's own consultants and costing approximately US $17,000 was installed. The effluent from the unit was to be discharged in the Eastern Drain, a massive storm water drain which flows 14 km. to meet the Bhogara River. According to the board officials visiting the unit, the treated effluent was declared to be within the norms. As required by the Water Act, the next step for the firm was to seek the "Letter of Consent," which is granted by the board once it is satisfied with the quality of the treated discharge. According to the law, a unit must obtain this letter before starting production. Despite several visits by board officials and a satisfactory sample of the discharge, the firm did not have the letter of consent even in 1984. The firm, however, started production in 1982. A follow-up letter was received by the owner of the firm stating that, under the law, the firm could be prosecuted for beginning production without the proper consent. The owner, when asked about this case, replied to me that "the board can not do anything. The consent may not come for another ten years, and there are so many industries doing it without the letter." The chairman of the Gujarat Water Board until 1982, Dr. R.S. Mehta, also agreed that the delay as found in the case of Deenar Syntex was not uncommon.

This case study reflects the feeling of mutual mistrust, the burdensome nature of bureaucratic procedures, and the casualness of the industry.

The third reason for the increased cost of compliance on the part of the industry is the style of decision-making in India, which is predominantly exclusionary. Even though there exists a close alliance between the ruling Congress(I) Party and the industry/business class, the direct involvement of these sectors is not expected in the policy process. The influence by the industry/business is exerted through the back door, rather than through open discussions on the front porch.[37] While big industries are able to secure back door entries by directly keeping in touch with the prime minister and with other party bosses, medium and small scale businesses find themselves alienated from the decision-making process. Decisions, thus, are treated as impositions rather than as agreements reflecting mutual interest. The input of the industry is not built into the process of setting environmental goals and strategies. The history of the pollution policy in the United States reveals that this exclusion leads to an unnecessary and expensive strategy of defiance by the industry. The energy of industry is spent in proving the inadequacy of the law or the enforcing network, rather than in voluntary compliance. A regulatory law in this context becomes a challenge between the power of the environmental bureaucracy and the power of industry. In India, industry/ business has not shown much desire to participate in the decision-making process because, for them, the cost of lobbying for favorable results at the time of policy formulation is far higher than the cost of non-compliance at the time of policy implementation. In other words, industry plays a passive role in the process of policy formulation, but it assumes an active role in the process of implementation. The cost of non-compliance is minimized due to the prevailing corruption, where "buying off" of regulators can be easily achieved. Additionally, the payment of fines (which is not drastic) or going through litigation (which process may drag for several years while the company continues its operation) is viewed as cheaper than installing a treatment facility. Also, the highly competitive nature of the industrial market makes the cost of compliance beyond the reach of most industries. They are unlikely to invest in pollution control devices, if their competitors can afford to continue being "free-riders."

The compliance by industry is also adversely affected by the impersonal nature of the bureaucracy. It is believed that bureaucrats merely follow procedures and are unwilling to take a case on its merit. This lack of individual consideration translates into confusion regarding the law itself. The control of pollution is not sought through optimum and feasible means, but through universal means which make solutions seem unnecessary and often even irrelevant. In case of India where the level of information is not adequate, the localized decision-making may prove to be cheaper, more relevant and more convincing. Another advantage of the localized decision-making process is that it can utilize the research and information capabilities of the industry, thus, putting less burden on governmental resources.

The last, but certainly not the least important, reason for industry's non-compliance is the complex and lengthy process that an industry has to go through in order to obtain environmental clearance. As in the case of Deenar Syntex, the process results in a feeling of frustration. Even in those cases where the compliance is finally secured, a feeling of hostility, rather than real compliance, remains. The regulated industry feels that the compliance is nothing more than a nuisance, and because of this attitude, it looks for any possible way of getting out of the compliance or at least ignoring it. The Ministry of Environment and Forestry admits that, for most major ventures, a triple clearance may be required: forest clearance, pollution measure clearance, and finally the social clearance involving the rehabilitation of people being displaced. For each of these clearances, one may have to go through a seven-layered process. It is ironic that despite this lengthy and supposedly strict procedure, many ventures in the past have faced trouble after acquiring the clearance and even in the middle of the construction stage. The Mathura Oil Refinery and Tehri Dam in Uttar Pradesh and the Sardar Sarover Project in Gujarat are good examples of this obstacle, where environmentalists claimed that the clearance was not granted on adequate grounds. The Tehri Dam, under construction at a cost of US \$2.1 billion, is expected to be the world's fifth-highest dam with extraordinary developmental benefits in the form of 2,000 megawatts of energy, irrigation for 270,000 hectares of land, and 12,000 jobs.[38] However, the dam faces severe criticism from environmentalists, and media reports indicate that under the pressure, the Soviets, who are providing the collaboration, may withdraw their support. The reason given by Soviet scientists are the same as given by environmentalists, that among other things, the dam will bring the level of seismicity in the area to a 9 point on the Richter scale. While the government still plans to finish the Dam, such actions are making the credibility of the MEF and the government questionable.

(III) Implementation within Federal Boundaries

The implementation of the environmental policy must take place within the federal structure prescribed by the constitution. The enforcement gap in this context emerges from the unique "centralized federalism" that exists in the nation. To begin with, unlike the American federalism, the Indian federalism did not emerge as a result of the union of various independent units. Instead, federalism emerged in India as more a matter of administrative convenience than of political reality. Powers were granted to states by the center and not vice versa. This structure led to a dominant-center-weak-states federalism in India. In addition, various economic and foreign crises that the nation faced in its infancy further necessitated the concentration of power in the center. The drive toward centralization, which reached its peak during Mrs. Gandhi's rule[39], did not lead to a unitary system; instead, it led to an imbalanced growth of federalism--federalism where state responsibilities gradually increased, while at the same time state abilities decreased. The pattern led to enforcement gaps in virtually every policy area. Faced with increasing responsibilities and decreasing resources, state bureaucracies are now more inclined to support their performance through an emphasis on statistics rather than on real impact on society. Moreover, the manipulation of achievement-related statistics and the emphasis on actions, rather than on results, has also become a common behavioral trait of the bureaucracy.

It is interesting that both water and forests were originally considered as local or state responsibilities; therefore, they were kept under the state list in the Constitution. Nevertheless, since the central government's interference in these areas, there has been a devolution of state resources, but there has

Table 4.8
Distribution of Budget Between the Center and States for
Selected Sectors Under the Seventh Five-Year Plan

Category	Central Government (percentage)*	State Government (percentage)
Agriculture	38.4	59.0
Rural Development	54.0	45.7
Irrigation and Flood Control	4.9	93.9
Energy	57.3	41.6
Industry	82.6	16.9
Transportation	71.7	25.1
Information and Broadcasting	98.4	1.5
Social Welfare	35.3	58.5
Environment Protection	81.8	17.7

* Percentages of the center and states will not add up to 100 because a small percentage of the budget is allocated for Union Territories, and is administered by the central government.

Source: Compiled from *The Seventh Five-Year Plan, 1985-90* (New Delhi: Government of India, The Planning Commission, 1985), Part I, 30-32.

not been any devolution of their responsibility. The formulation of policy now falls under the control of the central government, but its implementation is still under the jurisdiction of state governments. State governments, nevertheless, are expected to conform to national policies and are supposed to generate their own funds to carry out these new responsibilities.

Table 4.8 reveals the direction set forth by the Planning Commission for the environmental policy. The ratio of responsibility, according to the expected expenditures under the Seventh Five-Year Plan, is 7:1 (81 to 18 percent) in favor of the central government. Regardless of the provisions made in various environmental laws, the Planning Commission's view in 1985 was that the central government will be bearing the major cost of environmental protection. The ratio of expenditure in social policy areas, such as rural development and social welfare, was nearly equal. The central government, however, took a major responsibility in infrastructural or growth-related activities, such as transportation, communication and industry. The expenditure ratio reveals only an indirect measure of responsibility distribution; and while it gives some important information, its reliance should not be over-stated.

The funding support of state level environmental protection agencies has been a major source of discontent. The Tiwari Committee, appointed in 1980 by then-Prime Minister Indira Gandhi to suggest measures to strengthen the environmental enforcement network, displayed its disappointment over existing arrangements and showed little faith in either the ability or the willingness of state governments to fund their environmental agencies. Citing their shortcomings, the report read:

> Most of the members attending the above meeting [a meeting of the Member Secretaries of State Environment Committees] expressed difficulty in carrying out the useful programmes effectively mainly owing to utter paucity of staff. There was mostly no technical personnel for secretariat work for environmental appraisal of projects. Paucity of funds was a serious handicap so much so that some SECs [State Environment Committees] did not even have financial support for setting up of expert committees and for meeting expenses on their deputation while visiting project sites.

> There are two alternative schemes for providing financial assistance to the SECs, viz: (1) a Centrally-sponsored scheme with 50 percent of the expenditure met by the Centre and the remaining 50 percent borne by the state; (2) a fully Central scheme, i.e. the entire

expenditure would be borne by the Centre. Owing to the financial stringency in the states, the first alternative does not look feasible. The states may be reluctant to meet the remaining 50 percent of the budget expenditure. It, therefore, appears that only a fully Central scheme at this stage can bring about the desired activation in the SECs.[40]

The centralization of the environmental decision-making process was considered to be necessary to avoid the overlapping of jurisdictions and to assure the uniformity of environmental standards. Also, it was expected that the centralized decision-making process would be able to provide the maximum utilization of information and research in an area where both had a premium price. Nevertheless, under the existing federal structure, the expectations failed to turn into reality. State governments failed to generate resources because of their limited extractive ability; and at the same time, they also failed to enforce national standards because of their minimal coercive ability. In fact, the arrangements under the environmental policy created a double protection shield for governments--state governments could protect themselves by accusing the central government for failing to provide adequate funding, while the central government could pass the blame on to state governments for failing to implement laws.

Surprisingly, there is a lot of animosity between the central and state governments. The representation and input of state governments is assured in the decision-making process: every committee assigned to design the environmental policy has representatives from state governments. However, beyond a formal recognition, there is little consideration for the individual needs of state governments. Now as the environmental impact assessment becomes an integral part of the licensing process, the resentment on the part of state governments is likely to grow even more. The evidence indicates that the environmental assessment process is being viewed as a delaying tool and as a weapon in the hands of the central government to interfere in the autonomy of state governments. This perception has developed because of the lack of individual attention paid to states' needs and because of the absence of any participation by state level developmental agencies. The dilemma of the Maharashtra government is expressed well in the quote below.

The State governments, anxious as they are to attract projects to their states, are generally unwilling to raise any awkward questions, least of all about the environmental impact of these projects. Occasionally, however, various agencies of the State Governments do take a hand and when necessary, sometimes refuse to give clearance to these projects. In such cases the concerned department in the Central Government then generally takes up the matter with the State Government [of Maharashtra] at a political level with the always implicit threat that they would relocate their projects outside Maharashtra unless given what amounts to a virtual blank cheque. Faced with this threat, the State Government capitulates overruling its own expert bodies.[41]

The location of West Coast Fertilizer plant is a good case in point. The plant was first proposed to be established inside the Bombay city limits, which according to reports was an environmentally unwise decision. The chief minister of Maharashtra, Sharad Pawar, himself proposed an alternative site, but later on under the pressure from the central government supported the original disastrous site. His decision resulted in considerable delay in the construction of the plant due to litigations and petitions, which continued for years and went up to the World Bank.[42] One of the organizers of the campaign against the location of the plant within the city limits of Bombay notes, "The reason given by the Chief Minister to us and to other was that the State Government were [sic] under extreme pressure from the Ministry of Chemicals & Fertilizers to adhere to the original decision with the threat that otherwise the project would be located in Gujarat or at Tarapur close to the Gujarat border."[43]

The center-state relationship, thus, works in a similar context at the national level as the agency-industry relationship at the local level. Mutual understanding is lacking in both relationships.

(IV) Bureaucratic Power and Rivalry

Politics within the bureaucratic network creates another source of enforcement difficulties. The environmental bureaucracy suffers from the lack of essential resources that determine an agency's place in the bureaucratic network: information, clientele and legal support. Consequently, it fails to compete with other bureaucratic agencies. Since the field of environmental protection as a science is relatively new, there is a dearth of information and reliable data on various aspects of environmental deterioration. The awareness and research in the West has certainly provided a lead; nevertheless, scholars agree by now that environmental problems and their solutions in the Third World differ from the problems and solutions identified in the industrialized world of Europe and North America. This realization leaves developing countries with an enormous responsibility of conducting their independent research while using the lead given to them by developed countries. Indian scientists are aware of the situation and have initiated several efforts to increase their level of information; however, much remains to be explored at this point. While the physical cost of environmental deterioration may be easily obtained, the identification of the social cost of this deterioration may still be a challenge. In many areas, enough information may exist to indicate a general adverse impact of environmental deterioration, but more information is needed to pinpoint the nature and scope of this adverse impact.

In a policy process, information is power. But the environmental bureaucracy fails to compete with other agencies because it lacks this power base. If the cost of "no-action" for a problem is not known, but the cost of "action" is easily identified, then it is unlikely that the "action" will be supported. Similarly, if it is easier to identify the cost than to pinpoint the benefit of a given action, then the support for action becomes an unwise decision. Often, the cost of environmental protection, such as the construction of a dam or the installment of a treatment facility, is quantifiable, while the benefit is long-ranged and hidden, such as avoiding earthquakes and stopping siltation. For the environmental bureaucracy, the lack of information becomes a policy barrier. Faced with these limitations, the environmental bureaucracy finds it difficult to present its case more forcefully and also to defend itself for its "economically tough" decisions. The case of the Sardar Sarover Project, which received governmental clearance only in 1988, and which is to foster the development of the State of Gujarat is an excellent example of this dilemma.

> Gujarat has backed its argument by jugglery on the most important criterion: the cost-benefit ratio. The Planning Commission laid down that the benefit of a dam project should be at least one and a half times that of its cost. For the Sardar Sarover, the Tata Economic Consultancy Services (TECS) commissioned by the state, worked out that the cost-benefit ratio was a healthy 1:1.84. But that analysis is warped. The cost estimates are based on 1981-82 figures; since then, project costs have doubled. TECS relied mainly on the state's projected potential of irrigation--hardly a credible source. Also, the costs don't cover environmental loss, only loss of revenue from forest

produce. To justify the magical 1:1.84 ratio--now raised to 1:2--the project's planners have discovered new benefits. These include: savings in various costs because of use of hydel instead of thermal power: Rs 13,000 crore, and an addition of Rs. 14,441 crore for "increased industrial production."[44]

In addition to the lack of information, the absence of a visible and reliable clientele has also undermined the competitiveness of the environmental bureaucracy. A project's clientele is of great significance, since it provides the basic support to an agency at the time of its creation, and then the political nourishment throughout its life. There are two types of clienteles: the public and the organized interest groups. While analyzing the determining factors for an agency's power, Rourke admits that "the size and dispersion of an agency's clientele have a very significant bearing upon the scope of its influence .... [however] a small clientele that is highly self-conscious and dedicated to the pursuit of certain tangible objectives that it shares with the agency can in the last analysis be much more helpful than a large clientele that has neither of these characteristics."[45] The environmental bureaucracy loses on both counts. Unfortunately, the nature of environmental protection is such that it serves a constituency that may not even be aware of its services. It attempts at improving the air quality of a metropolitan city; however, the people in that city may not even be aware of the effects of air pollution. Unless the immediate health or welfare of the people is threatened by environmental destruction, they fail to provide an active clientele to the environmental agency.

Catastrophes, such as the Bhopal Tragedy, often help the development of a clientele. Within a year of the tragedy, nearly two dozen environmental groups emerged in the city of Bhopal alone. Mass protests were staged, and continue to be staged, in various cities that host similar industries as Union Carbide. However, a fast growth of clientele is not necessarily healthy, as is clear from Charles Jones' study of air pollution in the United States, where the people started to expect more from their agency than it could possibly provide. The result was an ambitious environmental policy which was impractical to implement. In the case of Bhopal also, the rapidly-growing clientele forced the government to restructure the issue as an issue of the control of multinational corporations, rather than as the issue of environmental safety and protection. Similarly, the sudden growth in the size of the environmentally oriented elite in the 1970s also led to symbolism in the general environmental policy area.

In addition to not having an aware clientele, the environmental bureaucracy also suffers from an abundance of attackers. Environmental bureaucracy is primarily a regulatory agency; therefore, it makes identifiable enemies more easily than it does identifiable supporters. According to some scholars, it is equally important for an agency to avoid enemies as it is to make friends.[46] Unfortunately, because of the kind of service the environmental bureaucracy provides, it tends to make more enemies than friends.

The dependency of an agency on its clientele is far more critical in a presidential system than it is in a parliamentary system because parliamentary systems lack any separation of power between the executive and legislative branches of government. In a presidential system, an agency must constantly maintain a support in the executive (which is responsible for direction) and in the legislature (which is responsible for appropriations). On the contrary, in a parliamentary system, an agency requires support primarily from the ruling party bosses, who control both--the direction and the appropriations for a policy. Mrs. Gandhi's support, for example, was sufficient for the creation of the environmental bureaucracy in India. It is not to suggest here that agencies are merely puppets in the hands of the ruling party. In fact, in India and in Great Britain, the bureaucracy has shown a remarkable commitment to neutrality. Moreover, the Indian bureaucracy was established with the ideas of rationality and merit. Agencies in India typically have resisted any serious attempt to appeal directly to the public to counterbalance the power of the ruling party. Nevertheless, their responsibility to serve to the public is well engraved in the political culture. Agencies are supposed to be rational and are expected to remain over and above politics.

The third and critical source of an agency's power is the legal support that it gets through laws and statutes. According to the environmental policy, the Department of Environment provides "the administrative structure for planning, promotion and coordination of environmental programmes." The environmental bureaucracy is a coordinative agency: it is supposed to supervise the process of decision-making by ensuring that environmental considerations are taken into account. Coordination, however, requires a hierarchical arrangement, without which the process becomes meaningless, especially when other agencies are not willing to cooperate. In other words, the efficiency of the environmental agency as a coordinator is not an independent factor; it is dependent on the mercy of other presumably cooperative agencies. The assumption behind this arrangement is that agencies are basically rational actors; theoretically, once the costs of environmental deterioration are known to them, they will automatically incorporate environmental concerns in their decision-making process. So far, other agencies, especially the ones related with development-related work, have resisted any attempt to make the environmental aspect an integral part of the policy process.

The scarcity of the three resources--information, clientele and legal support--hampers the growth of the power of the environmental bureaucracy. Even though there has been an increase in the size of the agency's budget (which Fenno[47] has used to measure the strength of an agency), the power of the environmental agency in India is severely limited.

(V) The Politicization of Bureaucracy

The politicization of the Indian bureaucracy in general, and the environmental bureaucracy in particular, leads to a situation in which bureaucratic authority can be used to reward political loyalties. Appointments and appropriations in this context become the instruments of securing political support. Among the consequences of the politicization of the bureaucracy are the erosion of the bureaucratic neutrality and the increasing gap between policy expectations and policy performance.

The politicized bureaucracy of today emerged in direct response to the concept of "development bureaucracy,"[48] which became a popular phenomenon in the 1960s and early 1970s. Unlike the Weberian bureaucracy, the idea of the development bureaucracy rested on three basic assumptions: (1) that centralized long-term planning was essential for the steady development of the newly emerging nations; (2) that political institutions in developing countries were undeveloped and unreliable and, therefore, the long-term planning should be carried out by an institution which was presumably free from political pressures; and (3) that the bureaucracy, created on the basis of merit, designed to be disciplined and trained to be rational, was the only viable institution. The development bureaucracy received its major support from international agencies, from donor nations and from other lending institutions, who felt more comfortable in dealing with a permanent institution, such as the bureaucracy, rather than with ever-changing and unpredictable political institutions. The bureaucracy in the Third World was viewed by national and international planners as a necessary tool in promoting the mobilization of the society.

Nevertheless, it became clear by the 1970s that the development bureaucracy not only failed to bring the expected development but, with the newly acquired powers, it also transformed itself into a leviathan. Since the thrust of the development bureaucracy was its rationality and superiority, it allowed bureaucrats to free themselves from any type of public or political accountability. Moreover, in order to insure rationality, the emphasis was put on procedures and rules, which according to some scholars, worked as impediments to the development itself.[49]

The Indian bureaucracy, being shaped by the idea of the development bureaucracy, suffers from a "great hiatus between its emotional awareness of the desirability of change and the willingness to accept it in practice."[50] This hiatus result is a peculiar kind of bureaucratic behavior--behavior that is characterized by personality and performance gaps. Bureaucrats may talk about change, such as the change pertaining to environmental protection, but when it comes to practice, they are resistant to the very basic idea of change that they so openly support.[51] This inherent gap in the bureaucratic behavior is widely accepted in the society, and it makes bureaucrats vulnerable to political pressures. While continuing to uphold their rational ideals in general, bureaucrats easily succumb to political pressures in their daily actions.

> In a major breakthrough, politicians are moved by a determination not to allow officials to stand between them and the exploitation of even the details of administration for political-cum-personal ends. In the war of benefits and concessions for clients, the dividing line between the policymaking and field administration has been eroded. The bureaucratic fort has given way and officials are adjusting themselves to new ways even to the extent of doing and saying what might please the political masters.[52]

The environmental bureaucracy, which to begin with has few resources, is particularly hurt by political interference. Its power as the coordinator of various governmental agencies and as the regulator of industry are both curtailed because of its close association with politicians. Since the appointments to the agency positions, especially to high positions, are viewed as political patronage, appointees (who are also coordinators of various agencies) are unable to take a stand independent of their patron's wishes. According to Lalvani, "Earlier, the chairman and members of these Boards [state water boards] were appointed on the basis of their professional skills and experience, in recent years these Boards have been 'politicised' and appointments on these Boards are considered as berths for M.P.'s [Member of Parliament] or M.L.A.'s [Member of Legislative Assembly] who could not be accommodated as ministers."[53] It must be remembered that appointees continue to keep their position as long as they remain loyal to the ones who appoint them.

Similarly, the existence of political patronage also undermines the authority of officials to regulate industry, because industry is closely aligned with the ruling party as well. In other words, the environmental bureaucracy, because of its politicization, has become a "captive agency."[54] It is allowed to survive, but not permitted to regulate. It is not to suggest here that other agencies are not politicized in India, or that agencies do not try to hold politicians on ransom through their leviathanian powers. The point is that the environmental bureaucracy, because of its age and its small resource base, is at a greater disadvantage. So far, it has been unable to develop the political clout to exercise its influence either on politicians or on other agencies. The following example illustrates the political maneuvering involved in granting of licensing.

> Technical advice of governmental departments or expert agencies are often over-ruled at a political level for political motives. The BMRDA [Bombay Metropolitan Region Development Authority] and relevant State Government agencies had recommended that the township be located further away from Bombay. The Rashtriya Chemicals & Fertilizers (RCF) authorities, however, established a portion of their housing colony inside the Green Belt. The BMRDA protested to the Maharashtra Government in the Department of Revenue which instructed the Collector of Alibag District to take necessary penal action against RCF--which penal action was started. Some of these events took place during President's rule in Maharashtra in 1980. Having cut no ice with the officials, right up to the Chief Secretary level, as soon as the elected Government came into power in mid 1980, the RCF authorities approached the then Chief Minister Shri Antulay, who summarily over-ruled his own officers and in fact had the Collector immediately transferred.[55]

The tragedy of Bhopal is also a reflection of the politicization of bureaucracy. The operation of Union Carbide "was welcomed by all, because it meant jobs and money for Bhopal, and saving in foreign exchange for the country, with the rising demand for pesticides after the Green Revolution."[56] The plant was established in 1979, and it began pesticide manufacturing in 1983. In 1982, three experts from Union Carbide Corporation, USA, pointed out safety lapses in their investigations. Their reports were also published in the local newspaper Rapat. It is coincidental that only a few weeks before the gas leak, the factory had been granted the environmental clearance by the Madhya Pradesh Water Pollution Board. The Department of Environment in New Delhi granted the license permit in 1983 without following the prescribed procedures for granting license for a hazardous substance company. While explaining the reason for this implementation loophole, a media report exposed the nature of alliance: "The company employs the relatives of powerful politicians and bureaucrats. Its legal adviser is an important leader of the Congress(I) and the public relations officer is the nephew of a former education minister of the state. The company's well-furnished guest house at Shyamala Hills was reported always at the disposal of the chief minister, and many union ministers stayed there during a Congress convention in 1983. Arjun Singh [chief minister of Madhya Pradesh] himself is facing a court case alleging that he had personally received favors from Union Carbide: his wife received favors from the company during visits to the US."[57] In brief, the case illustrates the highly political profile of the environmental bureaucracy and the close relationship between regulators, industry and politicians in general.

Politics Behind Reconciliatory Enforcement

The implementation process in the environmental field depends, to a great extent, on the political profitability of the issue. Since implementation is a local issue, political calculations based on local conditions become the most important elements. The policy variables that we identified in Chapter Three are no longer the influencing variables. It was argued that Mrs. Gandhi's personal commitment and international forces together gave the necessary impetus to the environmental movement and sparked the legislative support for the environmental issue. The analysis suggested that personalities and international pressures are significant inputs to the process of issue-creation and policy formulation. Nevertheless, the implementation history of the environmental policy process indicates that the influence of these factors declined considerably as the policy was put into practice. The single most important variable that determined the tone of the implementation process was the local policy culture--a term that I will define and discuss more fully in Chapter Five. It is sufficient to say here that the local policy culture results from the intermingling of the interests of regulators, regulatees, and other policy actors. The local policy culture did not favor the implementation of the environmental policy. All the involved actors--regulators, regulatees and politicians--benefitted with the symbolic implementation of the policy.

The bureaucratic network, like the legal network, fostered the process of reconciliation between the goals of environmental protection and economic growth. The bureaucratic behavior--its neutrality, rationality, self-centeredness, non-accountability and political dependency--all tended to create a policy context, where it was safe to enforce environmental laws without challenging the overall goal of fast economic growth. In order to achieve this reconciliation, however, certain paradoxes were accepted in the environmental policy area. The environmental bureaucracy was given the role of a coordinator without any hierarchical authority, and was given the role of a regulator without any independent power base. In brief, the environmental bureaucracy was expected to bite without any teeth.

While in general, the performance of the environmental bureaucracy in curbing the destruction has been disappointing, in certain areas it has made a dent. The most important contribution of the environmental bureaucracy has been the spread of environmental awareness at all levels of society. Even though environmental assessments by the Department of Environment have not been as forceful as one might have thought, they have helped to integrate the need for assessment in the general project evaluation process. Similarly, even though the public may criticize the inefficiencies of the bureaucracy, it is clear that the process of criticism also reflects awareness. The environmental movement has reached to the grassroots, and it is partly due to the increased level of awareness in the government itself. The problem is not that officials are not aware of the environmental destruction (even the media accepts that they are); the problem is that they are able to separate the two: the morality of the environmental issue which they accept and the practicality of the issue which they continue to ignore.

In brief, the failure of the environmental bureaucracy was due less to the weakness of the bureaucracy itself, than it was due to the general policy context that exists in India: lack of rationality and neutrality in officials; absence of the public trust in the bureaucracy; presence of corruption and the acceptance of this corruption by the society; existence of the alliance between the elite and the ruling party; non-accountability of technicians; and finally, the domination of political patronage in policy process. The same factors, however, contributed to the process of reconciliation. What has hurt the environmental bureaucracy most is its lack of credibility. Even now the reports by the Ministry of Environment and Forestry sharply differ from the similar reports from independent agencies. While the government continues to claim that the performance of the agency is satisfactory and that the environment is being improved, independent sources, such as the media, reveal that the process of environmental destruction is not reversed. The presumptuous attitude of the government is evident. This attitude, however, is likely to come under greater attack in the future as the environment of the nation deteriorates further and as the frustration of the public towards the government continues to build.

Notes

1. *National Committee on Environmental Planning and Coordination Terms of Reference* (New Delhi: Government of India, Department of Science and Technology, 1972, Resolution No. H.11013/2/72-Admn.I).

2. O.P. Dwivedi, "India: Pollution Control Policy and Programmes," *International Review of Administrative Science* (Brussels), 43 (1977): 128.

3. The Committee was created by Resolution No. 1/4/80 (February 29, 1980). Several other events were going on at that time that provided moral support to this committee. The President of India, in his Joint Session of the Seventh Parliament on 23 January, referred to the need for setting up a specialized machinery; while launching the World Conservation Strategy on March 6, Mrs Gandhi emphasized the connection between the Indian heritage and environmental protection; a major debate was initiated in the Lok Sabha on the subject of "Rape of the Earth" on August 11; and finally, the Planning Commission agreed to include a specific mention to environmental protection in the forthcoming Sixth Five-Year Plan on August 30 and 31.

4. Digvijay Pratap Sinh, *The Eco-vote: People's Representatives and Global Environment* (New Delhi: Prentice-Hall, 1985), 70-71.

5. *Report of the Committee for Recommending Legislative Measures and Administrative Machinery for Ensuring Environmental Protection* (New Delhi: Government of India, Department of Science and Technology, 15 September 1980). It is subsequently referred to as the Tiwari Committee.

6. Both the terms "watchdog role" and "nodal agency" were used by the Tiwari Committee to describe the nature and scope of the proposed Department of Environment.

7. *A Profile*, (New Delhi: Government of India, Department of Science and Technology, 1981), 2.

8. *Annual Report* (New Delhi: Government of India, Ministry of Environment and Forests, 1990), 80.

9. *Annual Report: 1986-87*, (New Delhi: Government of India, Central Board for Prevention and Control of Water Pollution, 1987), 14.

10. *Annual Report, 1988-89* (New Delhi: Government of India, Central Pollution Control Board, 1990), 20-21.

11. Ibid, 36.

12. *Ganga Action Plan* (New Delhi: Government of India, Ministry of Environment and Forests, no date given).

13. *An Action Plan for Prevention of Pollution of the Ganga* (New Delhi: Government of India, Department of Environment, July, 1985), A/1.

14. Information provided by the Office of Ganga Project Directorate, August 1990.

15. *An Action Plan*, 4-5.

16. Ibid, 11.

17. "An Unholy Mess," *India Today*, 31 July 1987, 84.

18. *Annual Report 1986-87*, 28.

19. Ibid, 21.

20. S.D. Gupta, "Development Dilemma," *India Today*, 30 November 1988, 60.

21. Ibid, 60-61.

22. Raj Chengappa, "Seeking Radical Solutions," *India Today*, 31 January 1989, 62-64.

23. *Annual Report, 1984-85* (New Delhi: Government of India, Ministry of Environment and Forests, 1985), 95-99.

24. Thomas Mathew, "Interview: Environment for Survival", *Indian International Centre Journal*, December 1982, 358.

25. Morris A. Ward, *The Clean Water Act: The Second Decade* (Washington, DC: E. Bruce Harrison, 1982), 3.

26. David Vogel, *National Styles of Regulations: Environmental Policy in Great Britain and the United States* (Ithaca: Cornell University Press, 1986).

27. Charles O. Jones, *Clean Air: The Policies and Politics of Pollution Control* (Pittsburgh: United Pittsburgh Press, 1975).

28. Steven R. Reed, *Japanese Prefectures and Policy Making* (Pittsburgh: University of Pittsburgh Press, 1986), Ch. 4.

29. Samuel J. Eldersveld and B. Ahmed, *Citizen and Politics: Mass Political Behavior in India* (Chicago: University of Chicago Press, 1978).

30. Samuel J. Eldersveld, et al., *The Citizen and the Administrator in a Developing Democracy: An Empirical Study in Delhi State* (Chicago: Scott, Foresman, 1968), 27.

31. D.N. Rao, "Disparities of Representation Among the Direct Recruits to the IAS," *The Indian Journal of Public Administration*, 11 (1963): 88-89; Hardwar Rai and S.P. Singh, "Indian Bureaucracy: A Case for Representativeness," *Indian Journal of Public Administration*, 19 (1973): 73-77.

32. O.P. Dwivedi and R.B. Jain, *India's Administrative State* (New Delhi: Gitanjali, 1985), 43.

33. *Ibid*, 44.

34. Gupta, "Development Dilemma," 60.

35. The case study is based on my personal conversations with various people involved.

36. The name has been changed to respect annonymity.

37. Stanley A. Kochanek, *Business and Politics in India* (Berkeley: University of California Press, 1974).

38. Shantanu Ray, "Soviets Losing Interest in Tehri Dam," *India Abroad*, 17 February 1989, 19.

39. Stanley Kochanek, " Mrs. Gandhi's Pyramid: The New Congress," in *Indira Gandhi's India: A Political System Reappraised*, ed. by Henry C. Hart (Boulder: Westview Press, 1976), 93-124; W.H. Morris-Jones, "India--More Questions than Answers," *Asian Survey*, 14 (1984): 811.

40. The Tiwari Committee (see note #5).

41. S. Chainani, "Bombay Environmental Action Group," in *India's Environment: Crises and Responses* ed. by J. Bandopadhyay, et. al., (Dehradun: Natraj, 1985), 239.

42. Ibid, 39-40.

43. Ibid, 240.

44. "A Flood of Controversies," *India Today*, 31 October 1988, 76.

45. Francis E. Rourke, *Bureaucracy, Politics, and Public Policy* (Boston: Little Brown, 1976), 86.

46. Murray Edelman, "Governmental Organization and Public Policy," *Public Administration Review*, 12 (1952). Edelman says that there always exists a group of people who hold the power to kill an agency if it does not pursue their wishes. Having a strong group of killers may create problems for an agency's survival, for the agency may not be able to satisfy their undue demands.

47. Richard F. Fenno, *The Power of the Purse* (Boston: Little, Brown and Co., 1966).

48. Dwivedi and Jain define development bureaucracy "as that aspect of public administration that focuses on government-influenced change towards progressive, political, economic and social objectives." (*The Administrative State*, 214). For a detailed discussion of development bureaucracy, refer to Edward W. Weidner, *Technical Assistance in Public Administration: The Case for Development* (Chicago, 1964); F.W. Riggs, *The Ecology of Development* (Bloomington: Indiana University, 1964); G.F. Gant, "A Notion Application of Development Administration," *Public Policy*, 15 (1966); United Nations, *Development Administration: Current Approaches and Trends in Public Administration for National Development* (New York, 1975).

49. R.S. Milne, "Bureaucracy and Development Administration," *Public Administration*, 51 (1973): 712; Richard P. Taub, *Bureaucrats Under Stress* (Berkeley: University of California Press, 1969).

50. Dwivedi, *The Administrative State*, 225.

51. For individual case studies, see R. Roy, *Bureaucracy and Development: The Case Study of Indian Agriculture* (New Delhi: Abhinav, 1975); H.R.Chaturvedi, *Bureaucracy and Local Community: Dynamics of Rural Development* (Delhi: Allied, 1977); N.K. Singhi, *Bureaucracy: Positions and Persons: Role Structures, Interactions and Value Orientations of Bureaucracy in Rajasthan* (New Delhi: Abhinav, 1974); P.L. Bansal, *Administrative Development in India* (New Delhi, 1974).

52. Quoted in Dwivedi and Jain, *The Administrative State*, 84-85.

53. G.H. Lalvani, "Law and Pollution Control," in Bandopadhyay,

India's Environment, 288.

54. The term "captive agency" was used by Rourke *(Bureaucracy, Politics and Public Policy)* to describe the agency that was unreasonably dependent on organizations to whom it provides tangible benefits. The environmental agency in India is equally captive in the sense that it is dependent for its survival on some outside force, although its dependence is not on social organizations, but is on politicians.

55. Chainani, *Bombay Environmental Action Group*, 235.

56. Anil Agarwal, "Who is to blame?," in *The State of India's Environment, 1984-85*, ed. by Anil Agarwal and Sunita Narain, (New Delhi: Centre for Science and Environment, 1985), 216.

57. Ibid.

CHAPTER 5

Environmental Bureaucracy and Its Non-regulatory Functions

E nvironmental bureaucracy in the Third World is expected to perform several non-regulatory functions. These functions include the spread of environmental literacy, collection and dissemination of information, construction of treatment facilities and distribution of natural resources. In fact, this distributive and redistributive role is often the major role of the environmental bureaucracy. In contrast to the role played by environmental bureaucracy in developed countries, the environmental bureaucracy in developing countries must adopt a tutelary role. More often than not, environmental bureaucracy in developed countries is the result of public awareness. It is created in direct response to the public outcry for governmental action. However, environmental bureaucracy in developing countries, as is revealed in the case of India, is the product of leadership initiative and international pressure. Public, in this context, is quiescent. Information is also unavailable. Environmental bureaucracy, thus, is forced to be initiative and innovative. It is expected to lead the public opinion, rather than follow it. It is also expected to make the public responsive to governmental actions, rather than making governmental actions responsive to the needs of the public. In brief, the scope of its power and responsibility in developing countries is much greater than is commonly realized.

In addition, the thinking behind environmental policy in developing countries also makes it inevitable for the environmental bureaucracy to engage in non-regulatory functions. More often than not, Western countries' concern for the environment is the result of their excessive use of natural resources. In contrast, developing countries are faced with the problem of imprudent use of natural resources. Consequently, they can not afford to ban the use of natural resources. Instead, their strategy is to use natural resources in an ecologically sound albeit development-oriented way. Environmental policy in developing countries, therefore, is often closely linked with developmental policy and environmental programs are closely associated with developmental programs. Or else, environmental programs have an explicit developmental objective. The thinking behind environmental policy is, thus, eco-development, which puts an extra burden on environmental bureaucracy. In sum, even when regulation is the nexus of environmental policy, in reality, environmental bureaucracy finds that it is forced to perform a large number of non-regulatory functions. In this chapter, we evaluate the performance of the Indian environment bureaucracy in its non-regulatory role.

Under its policy thinking of eco-development, the government of India initiated several programs, most notably the social forestry program. Social forestry was adopted in direct response to the problem of serious deforestation in the nation. It was launched with a dual purpose: environmental (to protect natural forests from reckless destruction) and developmental (to satisfy the basic forest-related needs of the people). Launched in 1980, social forestry as a policy program now has the implementation history of nearly a decade. This enables us to take a micro-look at the implementation process and to examine the government's priorities and abilities through its specific policy programs. However, before embarking on the evaluative analysis, it is essential that we establish the context of social forestry by assessing the form and nature of the society's dependence on forests.

Forests: The Triangle of Dependence

India's 57 million hectares of forests present a critical political dilemma for policy makers because the society's dependence on forests is multifaceted: people are dependent on forests for different, and often even conflicting, reasons. At least three major forms of forest dependency can be readily identified: (1) ecological preservation, (2) industrial production, and (3) direct consumption. The significance of forests for ecological preservation is hardly an issue for debate. It has been long realized that forests are essential for the sustenance of the physical environment and, therefore, they must be preserved. The ecological role of the forests is not limited to providing forest resources, but it extends to several other critical tasks, such as the prevention of soil erosion, floods, and siltation.

The second form of forest dependency is economic. Other than being essential for the protection of Mother Earth, forests also fulfill an important economic obligation by providing basic raw materials, such as timber, paper and bamboo. Several of India's top industries, such as paper, packaging, tobacco, timber, furniture, and housing rely on the availability of forest ma-

terials. Paper and timber industries have the greatest reliance on forests.
At present, India has over 175 paper mills with an annual production
capability of 1.91 million tons. According to sources, only 59 percent of this
capability is currently being utilized. The Development Council for Paper,
Pulp and Allied Industries estimates that by the year 2000, the production
of paper in the nation will double, escalating the demand for forest raw
materials from 3.09 million tons to over 6.70 million tons. The estimates
are reasonable, as the present consumption rate of paper in India is less than
2 kilograms per person, very modest indeed when compared with the per
capita consumption figure of 272 kilograms in the United States, 124
kilograms in the United Kingdom, 115 kilograms in France, 11 kilograms
in Thailand and 10 kilograms in Egypt.[1] Even with this low consumption
figure, paper mills in India have already destroyed a large number of natural
bamboo forests, and have created a serious bamboo famine.

The packaging industry is also a heavy user of forest materials,
especially wood. Their demand for wood is also growing at an alarming rate:
it is expected to rise from the current level of 0.5 million cubic meters to
1.2 million cubic meters within the next 15 years.[2] Thus, the stress on forests
is likely to rise, and not recede, in the future. Yet another important
consumer of forest material is the tobacco industry, which uses the flue-
curing process—a unique process involving the slow drying of green leaves
in wood-burning furnaces. India, according to some estimates, is the third
largest producer of flue-cured tobacco after the United States and China,
and earns over Rs 700 crores (approximately US $467 million) in excise
earnings and nearly Rs 120 crores in export earnings every year.[3] Needless
to say, the tobacco industry is essential for export-import planning. This
creates a serious paradox for policy planners. In order to keep the tobacco
industry competitive in the international market as well as to keep it afloat
in the domestic sphere, the government is forced to view forests as a
significant source of raw material. Considering the current unfavorable
foreign trade balance sheet, the government of India cannot afford to enforce
those environmental regulations that are potentially harmful for the production capacity of its forest-dependent industries.

The third and most critical dependence on forests comes from the people
themselves who require forest material for their daily survival. It is this aspect
of forest dependency that affects the lives of the people most directly. For
the rural poor, forests are an important source of food, fuel, fodder and cash-
earning opportunities: wood collected from nearby forests is used for
cooking and heating fuel; leaves are shaped into brooms, plates, bowls,

roofing material and mattresses; fodder is fed to animals; and sticks and stems are utilized to produce a variety of marketable items, such as baskets, hand-held fans and ropes. It is estimated that over 40 million people in the nation rely on minor forest produce (MFP) for up to 90 percent of their daily needs.[4]   Historically, the MFP has existed in abundance and has been available to the people at no cost. The lifestyle of these people, therefore, is primitive, yet simple and non-demanding. Moreover, forests also fulfill a crucial social need of the forest-dwelling populace by providing them with a permanent source of identity and belonging. Anthropologists and social activists in India point out that the life style of the forest-dwelling population is entirely dependent on forests: their songs are written about forests; their dances reflect various moods of forests; their festivals are associated with the seasonal changes of forests; and even their celebrations are directed toward various gods protecting the forests.

Other than the consumption-oriented lifestyle of the forest-dwelling people, the growing population in general also creates stress on forests. Wood is essential for the construction of new houses and bullock carts, as well as for providing fuel needs for the 75 percent of the nation's population living in the countryside, whether near forests or not. In addition, the growing population also increases the demand for land for residential purposes.

The multiple form of forest dependency creates a policy dilemma for forest planners. How should the issue of forests be defined? Should forests be preserved for their ecological necessity? Or should they be produced for industrial use? Or should they be protected for the direct consumption of the masses? The Indian forestry policy, as reflected through various forest-related laws, is sensitive to all the three needs and is based on the assumption that a balanced fulfillment of all needs is essential for the efficient management of forests. Despite this balanced policy goal, scholars concede that the enforcement of the policy favors one side over the other two. The industrial production aspect, according to them, gets preference over the ecological and consumption aspects. The evolution of the forestry policy also indicates that it was economic exploitation that formed the basis for policy initiation under the British. Since then, the direction of policy has changed; however, the commercial use of the forests still forms an important policy objective. In the following section, a brief history of the forestry policy is undertaken.

Forest Management and Policy Priorities

The history of forest management in India is more than a century old. During the British rule, forests were clearly seen as the nucleus of economic activity and growth. As discussed earlier, the British government with its inherent policy of economic exploitation transformed forests from a "free common good" to a "priced market commodity." Consequently, the industrial and commercial use of forests emerged as an over-emphasized policy goal. The role of the government, as shaped by the 1927 Forest Act, related to the management of forests with one specific goal--governmental control over the distribution of forest resources. The forest policy, thus, emerged as a regulatory policy albeit with an explicit commercial objective.

After the nation's independence in 1947, the perception of the government regarding forest management remained basically unchanged, although a greater lip service to forest preservation was provided under the new leadership of Jawahar Lal Nehru. The government retained the 1927 Forest Act and passed another legislation, the Forest Policy Act, in 1952. The 1952 Act did not alter the direction in any way; instead it further formalized the government's control over forest resources. Under the new act, the government granted itself the explicit right of identifying and classifying forest area. Despite its basic similarity with the 1927 Forest Act, the 1952 Forest Policy Act differed in one aspect. Its focus was broader than its predecessors's: it formally recognized the people's dependency on forests. The act clearly defined six major goals for forest management: (1) to evolve a system of balanced land use; (2) to check environmental destruction, such as siltation and soil erosion; (3) to keep an adequate tree cover; (4) to ensure the supply of pasture and small woods; (5) to provide the supply of raw material for industry; and finally (6) to obtain enough revenue to fulfill the above objectives.[5] The 1952 Forest Policy Act, however, proved to be ineffectual in fulfilling any of its policy goals. Other than providing symbolic assurances to the people, the act did not meet with any policy objectives. Its real impact on forests was not only negligible, it was even negative. The nation's tree cover which was reported to be 20 percent in 1952, was reduced to 14 percent by 1988. The government simply lacked the political commitment and the financial base needed to implement the Forestry Act.

It was only during the 1970s that the government's attention turned toward making more serious efforts to protect and preserve the eroding forests. This shift came partly as a result of the emergence of the worldwide environmental movement and partly as a result of the publication of several scientific reports exposing heavy losses in the forest cover, even when the cover was under the direct control of the government. The discovery of the rapid rate of deforestation across the nation led to a never-ending debate between social activists and governmental officials. Social activists accused the government for indiscriminately destroying the forests, while government officials blamed the people for recklessly using the forests for their daily needs. Furthermore, environmentalists added to the debate by arguing that the government had become the captive of those interests to whom it was supposed to regulate. Therefore, the governmental intervention in the

Table 5.1
Forest Revenue of State Governments (1978-79)

Name of State	Net Profit in rupees (000)	Total Outlay from forest Produce (000)
Andhra Pradesh	67,625	1,40,021
Assam	24,679	47,337
Bihar	53,080	1,12,934
Gujarat	4,322	85,954
Haryana	3,840	9,427
Himachal Pradesh	10,182	1,42,852
Jammu & Kashmir	33,423	2,74,868
Karnataka	1,69,614	3,34,131
Kerala	1,26,977	1,66,805
Madhya Pradesh	3,16,491	5,06,640
Maharashtra	55,539	1,92,510
Manipur	—	2,319
Meghalaya	—	2,939
Nagaland	—	890
Orissa	—	79,755
Punjab	(-)6,612	12,267
Rajasthan	(-)13,859	63,426
Tamilnadu	31,589	90,392
Tripura	(-)6,699	4,267
Uttar Pradesh	2,81,782	3,23,405
West Bengal	—	43,805

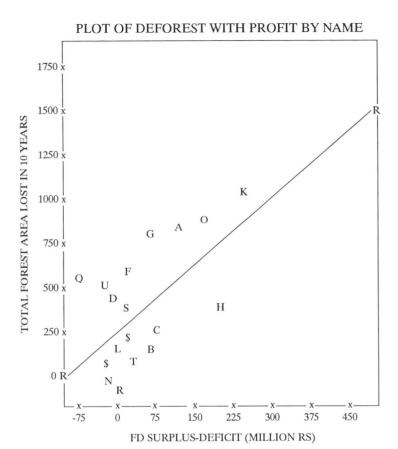

Figure 5.1. Scatterplot of State Profits and Forest Losses

| Correlation | .50342 | R-Squared | .25343 | S.E. of Est | 396.5 |
| 2-tail SIG. | .0169 | Intercept | 216.89 | Slope | 58.74 |

The following letter key is used for the plot.

A = Andhra Pradesh	H = Kerala	Q = Rajasthan
B = Assam	I = Madhya Pradesh	R = Sikkim
C = Birah	J = Maharashtra	S = Tamil Nadu
D = Gujarat	L = Manipur	T = Tripura
D = Haryana	M = Meghalaya	U = Uttar Pradesh
E = Himachal Pradesh	N = Nagaland	V = West Bengal
F = Jammu & Kashmir	O = Orissa	$ = Multiple Occurance
G = Karnataka	P = Punjab	

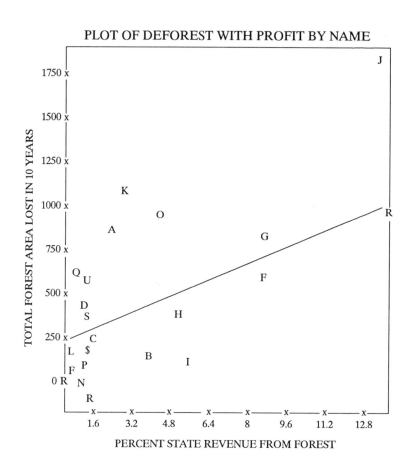

Figure 5.2. Scatterplot of State Revenue and Forest Losses

Correlation	.50342	R-Squared	.25343	S.E. of Est	396.5
2-tail SIG.	.0169	Intercept	216.89	Slope	58.74

The following letter key is used for the plot.

A	= Andhra Pradesh	H	= Kerala	Q	= Rajasthan
B	= Assam	I	= Madhya Pradesh	R	= Sikkim
C	= Birah	J	= Maharashtra	S	= Tamil Nadu
D	= Gujarat	L	= Manipur	T	= Tripura
D	= Haryana	M	= Meghalaya	U	= Uttar Pradesh
E	= Himachal Pradesh	N	= Nagaland	V	= West Bengal
F	= Jammu & Kashmir	O	= Orissa	$	= Multiple Occurance
G	= Karnataka	P	= Punjab		

management of forests had become a liability. They claimed that forest resources were being used for political purposes, particularly to buy patronage from the economic elite.

In addition, the government was also criticized for exploiting forests for financial gains. The criticism was well founded, as forests provided a significant source of revenue for financially starved state governments.[6] The data in Table 5.1 reveals the share of the forest-generated revenue for state governments during 1972-82. The information is significant because state governments in India enjoy considerable discretion and autonomy in the management of their forests. Even though broad policy guidelines are set at the national level, it is ultimately the state governments who design operational strategies based on their own emphasis. Revenue-related dependency on forest resources is unlikely to motivate a state government to protect its forests from destruction. Table 5.1 also presents data on the amount of profit (gross revenue from forests minus the cost of maintaining and regenerating them) made by state governments. A comparison of these figures with the figures for the amount of forest loss in the ten-year period between 1972 and 1982 indicates that forests have been a lucrative business for state governments. A scatterplot of the two variables, namely the amount of profit earned by state governments and the amount of forest area lost by them, is given in Figure 5.1. A Pearson's correlation coefficient of 0.73 and an R-squared value of 0.53 suggests that over 50 percent of the variance in the loss of forests can be accounted for by the amount of profit made by state governments. The relationship between state profits and the amount of forest loss is positive and is statistically significant. The results, thus, indicate that state governments, in the 1970s, used forest resources as a source of revenue earning. Figure 5.2, which produces a scatterplot for the share of forest revenue and forest losses, is also supportive of the argument.

Contrary to these figures, the government claimed that forests were basically a losing venture for them. They denied extracting any political and financial benefits from them. Reports from the Forest Department claimed that the stress on forests was caused by the people who were illegally entering the protected forest areas and were collecting forest produce for their daily consumption. The National Commission on Agriculture, while giving its report in 1976 on the loss of forests stated that:

Free supply of forest produce to the rural population and their rights and privileges have brought destruction to the forests and so it is necessary to reverse the process. The rural people have not contributed much toward the maintenance or regeneration of the forests. Having over-exploited the reserves they cannot in all fairness expect that somebody else will take the trouble of providing them with forest produce free of charge.[7]

Needless to say, this policy perception led to the policy strategy of "protecting forests from the people" throughout the 1970s. It was claimed by the government that a huge loss, amounting to several millions dollars a year, was caused by the reckless and illegal felling of trees by the forest-dwelling population. Not only were the forests being destroyed in this manner, but at the same time, the government was losing the revenue which it could otherwise use for the maintenance and regeneration of forests. This bold assertion by the government aroused much public discontent. Even though the report offered some significant positive solutions to the problem, it was still denounced by the press, environmentalists and social workers alike. Under public pressure, the government recognized the problem as being more complicated than envisioned in the National Commission's Report. Consequently, it designed a two-sided reform strategy in the late 1970s. On one side, the government applied restrictions on its own discretionary powers by introducing new checks on its licensing abilities. Since it was obvious that the large areas of forests were being destroyed by insensitive governmental decisions to build development-related projects, the legislature passed the Forest (Conservation) Act in 1980 to "check indiscriminate deforestation/diversion of forest lands for non-forestry purposes."[8] This step was necessary to satisfy the demand of environmental groups.

On the other side of the reform strategy, the government launched an innovative program of social forestry, which involved forest-cropping on public or private lands to provide for the fuel and fodder needs of the people. This step won the approval of the social activists who were opposing any environmental check by the government that denied the survival needs of the people.

It was with the social forestry program that, for the first time, the people's dependency on forests became an issue for policy makers. It was finally realized that this dependency was real and that it had an important implication for forest management. This realization introduced a significant shift in the forestry policy. The role of the government in forest management turned from being a regulator (as was established under the 1927 Forest Act) to being a "provider" of fuel and fodder.

Social Forestry

Social forestry as a policy program was launched in 1980. Its explicit objective was to reduce the direct dependency of the local people on forests. The strategy was not to change the lifestyle of the people, which has traditionally been dependent on forest materials; instead, it was to provide the same materials to them from sources other than natural forests. Social forestry, thus, involved the plantation of "forest crops" for the consumption of the society. Two major components of social forestry were identified by the government:

(1) Farm forestry, which involved the planting of trees on farm lands. The government, in this case, was to distribute free or subsidized seedlings of fuel and fodder-generating plants as incentives to farmers. The care, maintenance, and sale of "forest crops" was assumed to be the responsibility of private farm owners.

(2) Community forestry, which involved the planting of "forest crops" by forest departments or local cooperatives on public property, such as river banks, canal sides and along rail road tracks. In this case, the care, maintenance and distribution of crops was the responsibility of the nearby communities, although governmental supervision, if needed, was guaranteed. "Forest crops" were expected to fill the fuel and fodder needs of the rural people.

The social forestry program had a specific pro-people orientation; therefore, it became a political blessing for policy makers. The program was clearly designed to (1) fulfill the fuel- and fodder-related needs of the rural poor, and (2) to benefit local economies by creating self-sufficiency and employment opportunities. An important component of the program was the direct involvement of the people in the process of producing "common goods." The community approach was perceived to be of particular significance in minimizing the extra cost usually generated by "free riders." In other words, it was assumed that if people were involved in producing forest resources, they would also be cautious in their use.

However, the social forestry program, after an enthusiastic start, ran into serious difficulties when it was realized that the system of identifying "usable" lands and distributing program benefits was producing unintended, and even adverse, effects. Consequently, a new layer of bureaucratic authority in the form of the National Wasteland Development Board (NWDP) was introduced within the Ministry of Environment and Forests. The NWDP was set up in May of 1985 (1) to achieve a quantum leap in afforestation activities; (2) to take the program of afforestation to the people, especially to farmers and the landless; (3) to secure widespread involvement of other governmental and non-governmental agencies; (4) to place greater emphasis on the development of fuelwood and fodder; and finally (5) to evolve ways and means of securing institutional support.[9] The NWDP was responsible for identifying wastelands, establishing decentralized nurseries in villages and increasing cooperation from the people. It is too early to specifically evaluate the performance of the board; nevertheless, it is evident that other than institutionalizing the social forestry program, the board did not affect the implementation of social forestry in any significant way.

Social forestry as a policy program was accepted because of the political benefits that it provided to the government. The ready acceptance of social forestry was enticing, especially if one considers the enormous cost of the program. The government, under social forestry, assumed the responsibility of generating resources to provide: (1) free seeds and saplings to farmers, (2) field expertise through its forest departments, (3) a commitment of supervision, and (4) the willingness to tolerate encroachment on public property. In addition, the government was committed to generate resources to operationalize the program.

What are the factors, then, that prompted the government to champion the program? From the political perspective, at least four contributing factors can be identified. First, social forestry corresponded well with the government's general policy on rural development: it coincided with other social programs aimed at land distribution and social welfare, such as rural employment, property ownership, small-scale industries, household production, and agricultural subsidies. Social problems are easy to identify; however, social program are difficult to put into practice. When compared to the cost of tangible solutions needed to solve the problems of land distribution and rural welfare, the social forestry solution was very cost-effective. It required no change in the existing structure and was expected to generate little, if any, controversy. Contrary to the government's efforts to control water pollution where industries viewed themselves as potential losers, social forestry identified everyone to be a potential benefactor. Additionally, political benefits from the program were also invaluable: social forestry promoted government's credibility with the people by giving them the feeling of governmental presence in their constituencies. At the same time, the program also attracted the local elite by offering them new opportunities to expand their powers. Under farm forestry, rich farmers saw the possibility of switching to cash-cropping. The symbolic appeal of the program was immense, even if the program eventually failed to meet the broad objective of the forestry policy.

Second, the style of social forestry agreed with the general style of administration in India. The Indian administration, over the years, has assumed a paternalistic role in the management of social affairs. The role has been further strengthened due to the idea of development administration. Social forestry, with its "care-taking" tone fitted well in this mold of paternalistic ruling.

Third, the funding for social forestry was easily obtainable from outside sources. Unlike other developmental programs where the burden to finance programs fell on the government's shoulders, social forestry was financed with international money. Major programs under social forestry were funded by prominent international donor agencies, such as the World Bank, the Swedish International Development Authority, the United States Agency for International Development, the Overseas Development Administration (of

Table 5.2
Social Forestry Projects with Foreign Assistance

State	Total Cost	Estimated Foreign Assistance	Period	Donor Agency	Area Covered
Uttar Pradesh	40.0	23.0	1979-84	World Bank	52,680
Gujarat	67.0	37.0	1980-85	World Bank	1,05,440
Tamilnadu	47.0	33.0	1981-86	SIDA	
Madhya Pradesh	40.0	25.0	1981-86	USAID	1,00,000
West Bengal	34.0	29.0	1981-87	World Bank	93,000
Maharashtra	56.0	30.0	1982-87	USAID	N/A
Jammu/Kashmir	28.0	13.0	1982-87	World Bank	44,000
Haryana	33.0	20.0	1982-87	World Bank	67,000
Karnataka	55.0	27.0	1983-88	World Bank/ODA	1,49,000
Andhra Pradesh	40.0	40.0	1983-88	CIDA	1,38,000

* Abbreviations refer to the following:
    SIDA = Swedish International Development Authority
    USAID = United States Agency for International Development
    ODA = Overseas Development Administration
    CIDA = Canadian International Development Agency

the United Kingdom), and the Canadian International Development Agency. As Table 5.2 indicates, more than 50 percent of the cost of social forestry came from these donor agencies. In addition, technical expertise and planning assistance was also made available by the World Bank at no cost.

Last, other than the political and economic support, social forestry also had an unfailing moral and ideological appeal. The program received a zealous support from the Gandhian philosophy, which was, and still is, the inherent political ideology of the nation. Under the Gandhian philosophy, rural development is encouraged through several small steps taken by the people themselves, rather than through a single giant step taken by the state. Such a strategy, it is claimed, feeds self-sufficiency by creating an independent base for future economic growth. Social forestry with its emphasis on rural welfare, self-sufficiency, nature-preservation and community focus, readily agreed with the Gandhian vision of a decentralized economic and political system.

Social Forestry in Practice

Social forestry received an unprecedented support from the government.[10]   According to estimates, apart from the money given by international agencies, the government itself invested nearly Rs 600 crores (approximately US $400 million) in various social forestry schemes. About 1.93 million hectares of previously unused land was brought under social forestry plantation. Nearly 4,000 million seedlings were distributed to farmers under the farm forestry program alone. So far, over 3 million hectares of area has been planted and approximately 740 million seeds have been distributed under the community forestry program in 157 villages with severe fuel and fodder shortage.[11]   Moreover, the Seventh Five-Year Plan envisioned another 1.8 million hectares of land under social forestry and made provisions to distribute 40 billion seeds by the year 1990.[12]

Nevertheless, the performance of social forestry is ambivalent. Different perspectives make different assumptions; therefore, they arrive at disparate conclusions. On one hand, the government, through its numerous reports, claims the program to be a success. Its claim is backed by the impressive figures on the amount of area brought under "forest cropping" and on the number of seedlings distributed to the people for various social forestry purposes. Contrary to the governmental perspective, independent sources offer a negative report on the performance of social forestry. Viewed from their perspective, social forestry is a disaster because it failed to reduce the fuel and fodder dependency of the people. On the contrary, it created fuel and fodder shortage in practically every state.

The discrepancy between the governmental perspective and the independent perspective emerges because, although both measure performance, the former uses policy output while the latter uses policy impact to be the criterion for performance. Ironically, while the outcome of social forestry (measured by physical indicators, such as the area covered by the program or the seedlings distributed under the program) appears to be positive, its final impact is neutral, if not negative. This gap emerges from the local policy culture that allows the separation of policy outcomes from policy impact, and makes the government liable for the previous rather than the latter. Reasons for the failure of social forestry, therefore, are to be found not in the forestry policy itself, but in the social, economic and political context in which the program is implemented. The identification of this context is necessary to evaluate the performance of social forestry.

Social Forestry and the Local Policy Culture

Policies are almost always implemented locally. The local context of policy implementation, therefore, is an important controlling variable. Even though different policies are designed with different specific objectives in mind, they always share a certain degree of commonality. This commonality usually comes in the form of policy environment, or the general context of policy making and implementing. The context defines the boundaries within which policies are designed and enforced. During the policy-making stage, for example, policies are required to reflect society's broad values, such as democracy, capitalism or socialism. Policies are also made adaptable to basic political structures, such as federalism, parliamentarism, and political party structures.

Similarly, a general policy context for implementation is provided at the local level. This context, where the interests of policy participants intermingle, can be called local policy culture (LPC). The LPC, thus, is the reflection of attitudes, beliefs and orientations of policy participants toward public policies. The LPC is generic in the sense that all policies are implemented within the same broad context. It is not to suggest here that policies do not have their own implementation guidelines or that they are identical in their strategies. Instead, the idea is to contend that beyond individual priorities and guidelines, policies are often bound by the boundaries defined by a society's local policy culture. The LPC in India is predominantly shaped by the perceptions of governmental officials (who implement policies), the economic elite (who control the local environment) and the general public (who is the target of policies).

Among other things, the LPC in India rests on several general perceptions: (1) that governmental officials are corrupt, incompetent and vulnerable; (2) that governmental policies are insensitive to the needs of the general public; (3) that political institutions are designed to benefit the elite; (4) that the power of the elite is overwhelming; (5) that the public does not trust the government; and finally (6) that policies do not change anything. The implementation history of pollution control laws undertaken in the previous chapter has already indicated the inherent incompatibility of the laws with the LPC. It was found there that the LPC created a situation where non-implementation rather than implementation became the most cost-effective strategy for implementors. In the section below, I evaluate the program of social forestry: first, by revealing its irrational assumptions; and then, by highlighting its incompatibility with the LPC.

Social forestry, as mentioned above, comprised various sub-programs, most notably farm forestry and community forestry. A quick look at the implementation history of social forestry reveals that three vital problems gradually emerged: (1) performance variation, which resulted from the overwhelming success of some schemes and the total failure of others; (2) uneven distribution of governmental resources, which resulted in an even greater discrepancy in the distribution of benefits; and (3) adverse effect on the nation's physical environment. Performance variation is apparent: while farm forestry programs exceeded their goals in most states, community forestry programs failed to even take off. The reason for this performance gap is easy to detect: while farm forestry was an individual effort, community forestry was a "common" effort. Individual farmers, under farm forestry, had control over the plantation and distribution of their forest crops, while communities under community forestry had no control over individual incentives; therefore, they were unable to avoid the "tragedy of commons."

The basic assumption behind community forestry was also faulty. To begin with, it was assumed that human behavior was rational in an irrational system. Community forestry assumed that the "commonness" of individual interests could be easily agreed upon; that the fairness of labor in production could be readily established; and finally, that the fruits of "common" crops could be equally distributed. Nevertheless, it was overlooked that the same people who were to take this monumental task lived in a system that favored few while exploiting others. The context provided by the LPC, in other words, was quite different from the context envisioned by social forestry.

In general, the social fabric of the countryside in India is colored with the colors of several ethnic identities and kinship ties. Consequently, local community decisions are influenced by casteism, nepotism, religious beliefs and language preferences. In every village, one or more communities with their traditional hold over wealth, status and political power can be identified. For our purpose in this study, these communities are referred as the local elite. The local elite of today are semi-feudal: unlike their predecessors, the new elite are more educated and are better exposed to the market-oriented economy; nevertheless, they also rely on ethnic identities, such as caste, religion and language, to gather support from the masses. As a result, resources and benefits generated from national programs are disseminated by the local elite for the purpose of strengthening ethnic identities of the masses.

The "expansive" elite, as Rosenthal labelled them, are a product of democratic forces, yet they are also the biggest barriers in the implementation of policies based on the principles of democratic freedom and social equality. Their personal benefit, thus, works as an impediment to national development.

> Rural elite have proven themselves highly insensitive to the long-range consequences of their behavior. Increasingly, they have become a source of institutional restraint, standing in the way of more participatory and more redistributive patterns of political development. State and national political leadership has sometimes found itself fighting to keep open channels of opportunity that influential local leaders have attempted to consolidate into larger spheres of personal influence.[13]

Several case studies have already highlighted the incongruity between the interests of the local elite and that of the society. The studies have repeatedly shown that the power of the elite is not only overwhelming, but it is also counterproductive to the successful performance of social policies.[14] Like other rural development programs such as IRDP (Integrated Rural Development Program), NREP (National Rural Employment Program) and TRYSEM (Training of Rural Youth for Self-employment), social forestry programs were also shaped by the interests and strengths of the local elite. The elite, for example, selected and preferred those components within social forestry that agreed with their interests, and either discarded or modified the remaining to correspond to their interests.

An excellent example of program modification is the selection of seeds/ saplings for farm forestry. Several media reports indicated that eucalyptus was favored over other more suitable plants for forest-cropping. Eucalyptus offered a return of three to four times higher than other cash crops and required only a minimal maintenance. As a result, there was a great demand for eucalyptus. Nearly 80 percent of the seedlings distributed by the government were of eucalyptus. More and more farms were planted with eucalyptus: By the end of 1987, over 40,000 hectares in Haryana, 150,000 hectares in Maharashtra, 82,000 hectares in Uttar Pradesh, and 1,033,000 hectares in Karnataka were under eucalyptus farming. The preference for eucalyptus was so strong that saplings of plants other than eucalyptus were being wasted in government nurseries because of the lack of demand from the people.

The choice of eucalyptus reflected a rational behavior on the part of the people. Nevertheless, from the policy standpoint, eucalyptus farming was a disaster. Despite its good returns and low maintenance, eucalyptus failed to satisfy the major goals of the social forestry program. Because of its nature, eucalyptus was unable to meet the fuel and fodder needs of the local people: its leaves were not palatable to animals and its sticks were too few to provide a substantial fuel base. Since the plant required minimal maintenance, its farming did not offer employment opportunities to the landless poor. According to one study, "for each hectare of land shifted from field crops to eucalyptus, there is a loss of about 250 person days of employment per year."[15] In addition, eucalyptus had an adverse effect on the quality of the physical environment. The plant weakened, rather than strengthened, the long-term productive capacity of the soil. Partly due to the heavy planting and partly due to its root structure, eucalyptus damaged the soil permanently by extracting nutrients from it over a relatively short period of time. This also resulted in the draining of the water table in nearby areas. In addition, eucalyptus planting on private farms had an adverse impact on other related policies. It altered the pattern of farming; consequently, it changed the supply of essential commodities. Contrary to the intent of the policy, which specifically asked for forest cropping on non-agricultural lands, eucalyptus was farmed on good fertile land. Table 5.3 reveals that only 27 percent of the farmers who opted for eucalyptus farming used fallow land. More than half of the trees, according to the estimates in Gujarat, were planted on farms, and not on farm boundaries and along

Table 5.3
Patterns of Farm Forestry in Gujarat (by 1982-83)

Type of Land	Percentage of Farmers
Fallow Land	27
Land earlier under cash crop	37
Land earlier under food crop	27
Land earlier under mixed crop	9

Source: Anil Agarwal & Sunita Narain, *The State of India's Environment, 1984-85* (New Delhi:Centre for Science and Environment, 1985), 54.

irrigated channels. The lure of quick profit attracted many people to eucalyptus farming on the farms that were previously used either for agricultural farming or for other cash crops. The shifting created the shortage of basic survival commodities, particularly cotton. In addition, it also left the soil unfit for any other type of plantation.

It is evident that the benefits of farm forestry flew in the direction of the rich, who used governmental resources to earn individual profits. Social forestry was used by the local elite to solidify their interests. Small and marginal farmers were weary of the arrangements and were skeptical of getting any benefits from it. A study conducted in 1981 in the Chengalpattu district in Tamilnadu found that 61 percent of the villagers had no land to consider for farm forestry, 24 percent were unwilling to take up any farming that could not give them immediate returns, and only 15 percent were in favor of the program.[16]

Like farm forestry, community forestry also failed to reduce the people's dependence on forests. To begin with, the mortality rate of the plants under community forestry was very high. Moreover, the people themselves displayed resistance from participating in the program for fear of not getting a fair share of benefits. In addition, serious structural flaws also limited the scope of the program. Under community forestry, the responsibility of distribution rested with village-level units, such as co-operatives and *panchayats*. However, the power base of these village units was limited. Co-operatives were handicapped because they did not have any legal base; and *panchayats*, despite having legal jurisdiction, were crippled because they lacked the social commitment. Ironically, *panchayats*, the basic units of democracy, were themselves the victims of democratic developments.

The *panchayat raj* with a three-tier system was initially promoted during the Nehru administration as a model of decentralized democracy.[17] As introduced formally in 1959, it was to have a *gram panchayat* (village level) elected through popular vote, a *panchayat samiti* (intermediate level) consisting of the chairpersons of *gram panchayats* in a designated block area and a *zila parishad* (district level) comprising the chairpersons of *panchayat samitis* in a given district and under the district magistrate. Under this decentralized form of democracy, it was hoped that *panchayats* would provide a forum for negotiation and bargaining in a society as diverse as India. Nevertheless, several factors contributed to the diminution of *the panchayats'* powers. In most states, *panchayats* proved to be ineffectual. As early as the late 1960s, *panchayats* were reported "to be torn by factional rivalries, aggravated by elections based on separatism arising out of caste distinctions."[18] Even though *panchayats* existed, they were unable to exercise any power in favor of the masses.[19] This weakness was also pointed out boldly by several governmental committees analyzing the status of the *panchayati raj* system.

> Our second reservation about the role of the panchayati raj institutions in the formulation of micro-level plans arises from a widely shared view that the weaker sections of the rural community do not feel that their interests will be protected under the panchayat raj institutions. A strong version of this feeling is that the leadership of the panchayat raj institutions acts as a gate-keeper and prevents the flow of benefits to the weaker sections of the rural community.[20]

The operational failure of *panchayats*, however, did not leave any administrative vacuum. The vacuum, if any, was filled by other local bureaucratic agencies under the banner of "development administration." Development-oriented bureaucracies were expected to fulfill the political as well as administrative needs of the system. Nevertheless, their performance was as destitute as that of their predecessor, the *panchayati raj*.[21] Developmental agencies were limited by their own structural weaknesses. Local bureaucratic units lacked a clearly specified jurisdiction. Furthermore, they were overburdened with administrative and political responsibilities.

Historically, the emergence of development agencies in India was more for the purpose of filling the gap left by the popularly elected units of *panchayats*, than for the actual policy implementation. According to the careful study of B.B. Misra, "the extent of expansion that took place in the name of local development administration was more a function of patronage than administrative necessity."[22]   Consequently, local bureaucratic units emerged as political units. They facilitated interaction between the newly emerging and fast politicizing elite classes. They also provided strength and stability to political institutions by allowing various groups to counterbalance each others' powers. Thus, local bureaucrats were neither equipped nor were they willing to challenge the power of the local elite. Few, if any, incentives were offered to them to challenge their power. As discussed earlier, local bureaucrats found it in their best interest to implement a policy for its procedural obligations rather than for its policy intent. They achieved this by adhering to strict rules and ignoring their responsibility for policy performance.   The following case illustrates the frustration created by the procedure-oriented bureaucracy.

> An allottee [of land] states, 'the government has allotted land to me. At first the landlord who was its previous owner did not resist. I sowed and raised the crop. At the time of harvest the previous landlord wanted me not to cut the crop. I approached the Revenue Inspector in this connection, but did not receive any favorable response, rather he co-operated with the land owner. The land owner even threatened to kill me when I went to harvest the crop. I registered a case at the police station. The police seized the crop and gave charge of it to the ward member. In this struggle the crop got damaged. It was harvested and shared by the police and ward member. I approached the Tehsildar. He said, 'Government has given you land. Now it is your responsibility to take possession of that land. Why should we take such unnecessary burden over our head?'[23]

Considering the limitations of the policy environment, one may infer that the social forestry program failed because it was implemented in a system that offered no incentives for effectual implementation. The implementation network provided by the program guidelines was easily alterable so as to benefit the local elite and not the masses. The masses, to whom the program was meant to benefit, were also unresponsive to it. Thus, the elite's control over the implementation process and the public's low trust in the program produced unintended results.

After launching the program so enthusiastically in 1980, the government also became doubtful of its success by 1985. Among other problems, the unfair distribution of benefits was considered to be the most glaring problem. The government itself offered several solutions to make the program more effective.[24] The Seventh Five-Year Plan, for instance, suggested that in order to deal with the problem of unfair distribution of benefits from community forestry, more direct consultative contacts with *panchayats* must be established by the government. The government was also inclined to offer long-term loans to small and marginal farmers to facilitate the process. Some institutional arrangements to legally grant the right of benefits to those who planted the trees were also in the list of suggestions. Nevertheless, none of the solutions offered any concrete strategy for changing the adverse local policy culture.

Implications of Social Forestry

Social forestry is a program that provides reconciliation between the goals of economic development and environmental protection. It is based on the strategy of eco-development, i.e., ecologically sound development. The success of social forestry is vital for rural development and for forest conservation. Nevertheless, the performance record of social forestry indicates that eco-development policies, despite their emphasis on the improvement of the overall social environment, face stiff resistance during the implementation stage. The shameful greed for reckless development may not be entirely responsible for ecological destruction; instead, the social and political system that impedes the ecologically sound development of the society also shares the blame for deterioration. What makes the situation worse in developing societies, such as India, is the existence of the feudal economy which relies on personal loyalties to the extent that the forces of capitalism fail to penetrate the system. Therefore, market-oriented solutions, which, to an extent, are successful in developed countries, fail to work in the "limited capitalist" economies of developing countries. The tight control of the local elite over the economic and political system renders any reform--whether economic or political--ineffectual.

Notes

1. Anil Agarwal & Sunita Narain, *The State of India's Environment: 1984-85* (New Delhi: Centre for Science and Environment, 1985), 72.

2. Sunita Narain, "The Commercial Connection," in *State of India's Environment*, by Agarwal and Narain, 92.

3. Ibid.

4. Based on the *Census of India, 1981* and *The Report of the Study Team on Tribal Development Programmes*, (New Delhi: Government of India Publications, n.d.).

5. Walter Fernandes and Sharad Kulkarni, *Towards A New Forest Policy: People's Rights and Environmental Needs* (New Delhi: Indian Social Institute, 1983); Renu Khator, *Forests: The People and the Government* (New Delhi: National Book Organization, 1989).

6. Fernandes, *New Forest Policy*, 16.

7. Taken from the *Report of the National Commission on Agriculture, Part IX: Forestry* (New Delhi: Government of India, Ministry of Agriculture and Irrigation, 1976), 25.

8. *Annual Report, 1986-87* (New Delhi: Government of India, Ministry of Environment and Forests, 1987), 6.

9. Ibid, 45.

10. The workshop on a New Forest Policy, held at the Indian Social Institute in New Delhi (April 12-14, 1982) concluded with the note that the social forestry had failed. For other studies, refer to Marcus Moench and J. Bandyopadhyay, "Local Needs and Forest Resource Management in the Himalaya," in J. Bandyopadhyay, N.D. Jayal, U. Schoettli & Chhatrapati Singh, *India's Environment: Crises and Responses* (Dehradun: Natraj, 1985), 52-72; Deepak Bhattachrya, *Fuel, Food or Forest?* (Honolulu: Resource Systems Institute, working paper WP-83-1); Vandana Shiva, H.C. Sharatchandra and J. Bandyopadhyay, "The Challenge of Social Forestry," in Fernandes, *New Forest Policy*, 48-72.

11. *The Seventh Five-Year Plan, 1985-90* (New Delhi: Government of India, Planning Commission, 1985), Part B, 30-31.

12. Ibid, 33.

13. Donald B. Rosenthal, *The Expansive Elite: District Politics and State Policy-making in India* (Berkeley: University of California Press, 1977), 323.

14. L.C. Jain, *Grass Without Roots: Rural Development under Government Auspices* (New Delhi: Sage, 1985).

15. Agarawal, *State of India's Environment*, 57.

16. Sevanti Ninan, "Tamil Nadu: Credibility Gap," in *State of India's Environment*, by Agarwal, 56.

17. S.R. Maheshwari, *Rural Development in India* (New Delhi: Sage, 1985), 52-53.

18. B.B. Misra, *Government and Bureaucracy in India: 1947-1976* (New Delhi: Oxford University Press, 1986), 347.

19. For evaluation of the "panchayati raj," refer to Ashok Mehta, *Report of the Committee on Panchayati Raj Institutions* (New Delhi: Government of India, Ministry of Agriculture and Irrigation, 1978).

20. *Report of the Working Group on Block Level Planning* (New Delhi: Government of India, Planning Commission, 1978), 8.

21. Jain, *Grass Without Roots*, 196-220.

22. Misra, *Government and Bureaucracy*, 375.

23. Jain, *Grass Without Roots*, 211.

24. *The Seventh Five-Year Plan*, 33-34.

CHAPTER 6

Response from the People

P ublic participation is considered to be one of the decisive factors in the ultimate success of environmental policies in any country. In fact, it is often claimed to be the factor that separates the environmental policy process of industrialized economies from the similar process in developing economies.[1] According to several studies in Japan, the United States, the United Kingdom, Canada and Sweden, the public plays a crucial role, first, in bringing the issue of environmental protection to policy agenda and, then, in ensuring the implementation of policy choices.[2] For Anthony Downs, the process of issue creation starts with the public's realization of the consequences of environmental deterioration. The public outcry, then, pushes the issue of environmental protection to the government's agenda in a stage that Downs refers to as the "up" stage of the issue-creation cycle. The response from the people, however, is short-lived, for as the cost of achieving environmental protection becomes clear, the enthusiasm starts to fade away. Downs labels this stage as the "down" stage of the issue-attention cycle.

Similarly, Cynthia Enloe, while providing an insightful analysis of the emergence of the environmental issue in a cross-cultural context, also stresses the importance of public participation in the environmental policy cycle.[3] She lists several indicators of "issueness"; and surprisingly, more than half of them refer to the public's response, whether direct or indirect. The response, according to her, is manifested through non-governmental organizations, political parties, election campaigns, media coverage and mass protests.

When it comes to public participation, it is difficult to classify India either as a "politically developed country" where demands from the masses are supposed to be clearly expressed, or as a "politically undeveloped country," where the public remains basically apathetic toward political processes. The development of the Indian democracy has defied the predictions made by developmentalists in the 1960s. Contrary to their thesis,[4] the development of democracy in India did not depend on the development of social and economic forces. The nation did not keep a balance between modernization and democratization. Yet, the imbalance did not result in political decay or instability—the theme so strongly supported by Samuel Huntington in his analysis of developing societies.[5] In fact, the imbalance made India a unique system, where a surprisingly high level of political awareness could exist amidst an atmosphere of social inequality and mass poverty.

The level of mass political awareness in India is considerably higher than the levels found in most developing countries and even in some developed countries. For instance, the voter turnout in the 1984 parliamentary elections was an impressive 63.4 percent, compared to the 53.9 percent turnout in the United States' presidential elections of the same year. Even beyond voter turnout, the level of active participation in India compares favorably with the similar levels in the developed polities of the West. Eldersveld and Ahmed's comparative study provides some interesting insights to voter activities in India. For instance, the study reveals that during the 1967 and 1971 elections, 6 to 25 percent of the Indian electorates engaged themselves in activities other than voting: 6-10 percent in canvassing, 5 percent in demonstrations and processions, and 20-25 percent in political rallies.[6] In addition, in 1971, over 70 percent of the electorate "identified" themselves with one or the other political party, while 50 percent classified themselves as "strong" partisans.

Several studies focusing on the characteristics of mass political awareness in India point out another interesting characteristic of the Indian voting behavior. According to them, the difference between the political orientations of the privileged (urban, rich or educated) and the underprivileged (rural, poor or uneducated) populations is not significant. It appears that the rural poor are as much aware of their political surroundings as are the urban rich. The gap which existed 40 years ago has been largely bridged due to the high speed of rural politicization.[7] Eldersveld and Ahmed also point out that there is a remarkable similarity between the rural and urban areas in terms of their level of political participation. Their study concludes that "India's urban constituencies tend to resemble—both in voter turnout and in party preferences—the rural areas in which they are located more closely than they resemble each other."[8]

While the statistical figures on mass participation are impressive, the figures on the sense of "political efficacy," which are more relevant to policy process, are discouraging. Despite their high involvement, people in the nation have very little faith in the government, and almost a negligible trust in the abilities of their bureaucrats to work for their cause. However, it is intriguing that the people still make an attempt to influence the decision-making process even when they already know that the influence may be negligible. Research studies reveal that the complex nature of mass participation in India is a result of the local power struggle between various factions. Village-level factions based on race, caste, language and religion are exploited, and often even encouraged, for political purposes. Ironically, the competitive nature of elections makes factional in-fighting the most reliable strategy for acquiring electoral support and allegiance.

> Expansion of participation in rural areas is closely related to the impact of competitive elections. A critical determinant of the rural turnout is the degree to which local conflicts are identified with struggles at the constituency level. Factions become the vehicle of political mobilization and voting turnout. Almost every village is torn by factionalism, and almost inevitably village conflicts are drawn into the wider political arena. Party struggles thus become an opportunity for each village faction to further its interests and solidify its positions within the village.[9]

In fact, the extent of localization is so great that voting, more often than not, reflects issues and conflicts that are specifically related to a local area alone and virtually unrelated to the issues of the larger constituency. Voters, despite their strong partisanship feelings, often fail to pinpoint basic policy priorities of that party. However, regardless of the general pessimism, scholars agree that the Indian electorate of today is more sophisticated and more aware of the strength of its vote than it has ever been in the nation's history.[10]

In the environmental policy area, implications of this high public awareness, along with the limited sense of political efficacy, are worth analyzing. When it comes to the issue of environmental protection, the Indian public is not a silent spectator, yet it does not display any desire to assume the lead either. The level of public awareness and interest in the environmental issue is not stagnant; it has been growing consistently since the 1970s. In fact, several case studies below indicate that the role of the public in the environmental policy field is changing from being passive to being semi-active.

In the following section, I analyze the Indian public's response to the environmental crisis: first, in the direct form through mass protests and demonstrations; and second, in the semi-direct form as mediated through group and party activity.

Public Protests and Demonstrations: Some Examples

The public participates directly in policy process through protests and demonstrations. Protests and demonstrations are not rare events in India: as a matter of fact, the nation ranks among the top ten countries in the reported number of political strikes and anti-regime demonstrations in the world, according to the *World Handbook of Political and Economic Indicators*.[11] In the environmental area, there have been several cases of protests by the Indians. However, considering the intensity of the problem, the number of these protests pales significantly.

Most reported public protests in the past have focused on two basic environmental issues—pollution from a nearby industry, or tree-felling by contractors. The majority of the protests, surprisingly, originated in rural areas and involved those people that were directly affected by pollution or deforestation. Dead fish and cattle, unknown diseases, and floods all entered the consciousness of the people and ignited the flare of frustration. Local industries were easily identifiable; therefore, they were the first targets of public protests. Attacks were also directed at local governments and forest contractors. Now, however, the recent target is the central government itself. A few case studies[12] are undertaken below to reveal the form and nature of environmentally oriented public protests. The case studies form a sample of protests that emerged during the period of 1960 through 1988.

The Orient Paper Mills, at Amlai in Madhya Pradesh, was among the first serious targets of mass protest against water pollution. The mill was owned by the Birlas, one of the three industrial giants in the nation. The mill started its operation in 1965, after it assured the state government agency granting industrial licenses that all necessary steps would be taken to treat its effluent before discharging it into the nearby Sone River. However, fish and cattle started to die within two years. According to reports, villagers from more than 25 nearby villages became actively involved in organizing protests and in sending complaints to government authorities. The government did not respond to the problem; but, as a result of the public outcry, the mill agreed to install a water treatment plant. Despite the fact that the mill's officials claimed that the installed treatment plant was adequate, frequent fish and cattle deaths were still reported throughout the area. By 1980, despite the nation's general emphasis on environmental protection, the intensity of the protests had declined considerably. In the absence of any political support from political parties and from environmental groups, the protest could not challenge the strength of the rival industrial power. The people were appeased through religious and community presentation: "They [the mill owners] pre-empted all the efforts to mobilize opinion. A temple was built and Hanuman mandals [prayer sessions for Lord Hanuman] were organized to sing bhajans [religious songs]; booklets of bhajans, musical instruments, clothes for children, exercise books, and blankets were distributed free," according to a villager.[13]

A similar protest story originated in Mavoor, Kerala, where Gwalior Rayon Unit (another Birla enterprise) faced strong public opposition ever since its opening in 1958. The local people, mainly farmers, organized various protests throughout the 1960s when cattle losses and skin diseases started to increase rapidly because of the pollution in the nearby Chaliyar River. The protests ceased once the industry promised to install facilities to treat the effluent. However, since the situation continued to deteriorate, in 1974 the Kerala Water Board (established in the same year) took an interest in the case, and an agreement was reached between the mill and the board. The mill officials agreed to build another pipeline to discharge the effluent in another nearby water stream. When the firm ignored the agreement for five years, the protests became violent in 1979. Under public pressure, the mill installed the proposed pipeline in 1979. But, "it was a poor job, leaking effluent throughout its length, and the effluent was more toxic now because waste water treatment had been virtually stopped."[14]

In 1979, the government studies confirmed the existence of mercury in the water of Chaliyar River. Even though the Kerala Water Board had been involved in this case since 1974, it took seven years—until 1981—before the board succeeded in taking legal action against the industry. The failure of the board was partially explained in its report, which read that "...all the functions contemplated under the Water Act have not been carried out to the fullest extent. The Board is in its infancy and is working under severe handicap of non-availability of funds to the extent required and consequent lack of manpower and infrastructure."[15]

Yet another case of public protest involved the Zuari Agro Chemicals of Goa, during the 1970s. The company is owned by the Birlas, but is supported by United States Steel. This case is significant because it displays an active role played by political parties and interest groups. Despite the fact that company officials claimed to have provided all the necessary safeguards against pollution, when the company began its operation in 1973, "within a year cattle were also dying; and in another year, coconut trees began to wither away."[16] The affected villagers formed a citizen's Anti-pollution Committee, and organized a massive rally in March 1975. A number of political parties—the United Goans (local level), the Goa Pradesh Congress (state level), and the Communist Party of India (national level)—offered their support to the protesters. The All India Port and Dock Worker's Federation, a powerful union, also supported the protest. Political support in this case was possible since the target was a foreign subsidiary. The company was forced to provide compensation to villagers, and to install an additional waste treatment plant in 1977.

In general, support from political brokers, such as political parties and politicians, is hard to obtain; and, even after obtaining it, there is no guarantee that the public can compete with local industries. The case of ARC Cement Factory, which operates near Rajpur in the Doon Valley, exposes the nature of the local power struggle. Operating since 1981, the plant has become one of the most controversial cases of environmental destruction. The public and the local party support forced Rajiv Gandhi in April 1986 to write a letter to the Chief Minister of Uttar Pradesh to apply appropriate measures, including the enclosure of the plant, if necessary.[17] Despite the intensity of the public protest and the support from the leadership, the plant continued, and still continues, its operation because of the legal loopholes in environmental laws.

> Citizens groups are unable to file direct complaints in the courts since the Air Pollution Act does not give them the right to file third party judicial complaints....Undeterred, environmentalists then complained to the Uttar Pradesh State Pollution Control Board which had issued ARC a "no objection certificate" (NOC) in 1981 with certain conditions for setting up the factory. When the board discovered that ARC had not followed several pollution control standards, it withdrew the NOC... The district administration, despite acknowledging the withdrawal of the NOC, insisted they were helpless in closing down the plant since the licence to operate it was given by the Government [Central Government]. The Government responded that the Air Pollution Act does not give it the power to close down a plant even after a NOC has been withdrawn.
>
> The pollution board was left with only one remedy—to file a complaint with the chief judicial magistrate (CJM). But under the law,

the CJM is only empowered to impose a maximum fine of Rs 10,000 [US $667] and jail the equipment operator—not the owner or the management—for three months. Finally, the valley's Rural Litigation Centre filed a writ petition in the Supreme Court.[18]

In the Bhopal Tragedy, in which 2,500 people died and another 100,000 suffered irreparable physical damage from a gas leak at the Union Carbide Plant in 1984, the protests by the angry public were turned into a ritual. Nearly a month after the tragedy, public protests against the government began. First, there was *Chakkajam* (Stop the Wheels) organized by the Nagrik Rahat aur Punarwas Committee. Then, there was *Dhikkar Divas* (Day of Condemnation) initiated by the Zahareeli Gas Kand Sangharsha Committee. The *Rail Roko* (Stop the Trains) followed other protesting events, and lasted for nearly ten days. In this case, the protests were not staged by the affected people, but by the public at large. Even though these demonstrations were different from the ones discussed earlier in the sense that they were organized by one or the other group, one has to remember that the group activity was also a form of protest because the groups sprang immediately after the tragedy. Every year, several protests were organized on the day of the Bhopal tragedy; however, the focus of the protests changed significantly over the years. While in 1985 the government was blamed for collaborating with foreign companies and for not fulfilling its responsibility of inspecting the site, in 1988 the attack focused on the government itself for not taking care of the victims and for not stopping the exploitation of the victims by the local elite (such as doctors, lawyers and local officials who have been accused of making a fortune as a result of the tragedy).[19]

Street protests, such as discussed above, are only one dimension of public protests. The other dimension involves the protesting activities by the environmentally literate populations, such as social activists, environmentalists, researchers and scientists. Their activities may or may not correspond with mass activities. Moreover, these activists may or may not be members of environmental groups. Nevertheless, they try to influence the decision-making process by writing to legislators, signing petitions, and publishing in newspapers. Contrary to the scope and nature of public protests in the case studies above, the scope of the activists' protests for the same time period was broad. Their role was more focused and, therefore, was more influential. Protests from this environmentally literate sector attracted the media attention throughout the 1970s. For instance, the protests against the construction of the hydro-electric power plant in the nation's only remaining evergreen forest, the Silent Valley, filled most English newpapers for several months. The project was finally stopped in 1980. Another series of protests came in 1988-89 focusing on the Narmada Valley Project Scheme. Over one hundred prominent scientists, social workers and environmentalists, including Baba Amte, M.S. Swaminathan, Satish Dhawan and Anil Agarwal, applied pressure on Prime Minister Rajiv Gandhi. The scheme withstood a forty-year long debate but was finally approved by the central government in October of 1988. These two cases of environmental controversy indicate that the government is neither immune to environmental pressures, nor is it bound by them. While protests from environmentalists brought positive results and stopped the construction of the Silent Valley Project, similar protests could not prevent the approval of the Narmada Valley Scheme.

People in Action: A Case Study of Chipko Aandolan[20]

While the level of environmental literacy of the people is low and while the impact of environmental organizations on the society is minimal, it would be misleading to infer that the people of India are quiescent about environmental issues. In fact, the expression of demands and mobilization of interests is achieved through cultural means, indicating an intertwined relationship between social culture and politics. An example is the Chipko Aandolan, which is one of the most popular and result-oriented environmental organizations in the nation. The group received international recognition and acclaim in the late 1970s. Despite its success, the group is not even a "group" in political terminology. It has no identifiable goal, no planned strategy, and no formal membership.

Chipko Aandolan (literally translated as the "hugging" movement) emerged in the remote Himalayan hill town of Gopeshwar in the Chamoli District in March of 1973. It is reported that:

> On that fateful day, representatives from a sports goods factory situated in Allahabad reached Gopeshwar to cut 10 ash trees near village Mandal. The villagers courteously told them not to do so but when the contractors persisted, they hit upon the idea of hugging the earmarked trees. Sports goods manufacturers had to return empty-handed.[21]

Chipko has since then become a symbol of affection for trees. In 1974, Chipko Aandolan received national recognition when women of the nearby village Reni, led by 50 year-old illiterate Gaura Devi, made hugging of trees their daily routine. Their strategy was to lie down on streets and to hug trees so as to make it impossible for anyone to harm them. The scope of their activity slowly increased to cover all the surrounding villages. A typical demonstration involved planning, strategy and coordination. It also involved several stages of activities. First, the information regarding the schedule of contractors would be delivered to Gaura Devi, or someone in a similar position. Second, Gaura Devi would send this message along with the time and place of the meeting to other women through village children. Third, women would march to the designated area with drums and songs, thus attracting other people on their way. Fourth, they would request contractors to leave the property. And last, the women would either lie down on streets to prevent equipment from going to the forest or would form a human ring around the earmarked trees to stop the operation of the equipment.

Several confrontations between the women of Chamoli and various contractors occurred during the late 1970s. Some of the important confrontations were in Rampur Phata in 1973, in Byundar Valley in 1978, and in Dungari-Paitoli in 1979. Each time, contractors were forced to leave the forest area. Because of the primitive, but successful style of operation, the Chipko Aandolan became widespread in the nation. Consequently, several organizations with similar names emerged in other states. One example is the Appiko (which also means "to hug" in the Kannada language) in the state of Karnataka. Appiko's influence went even farther than Chipko's. It attracted the young population and received the support and leadership of village youth.

The emergence of Chipko Aandolan was not sudden, although it appeared to be spontaneous. What motivated the women to take a stand? According to some observers, Chipko was not an environmental movement, rather it was a voice against economic exploitation of village people. However, others argue that the genesis of the Chipko Aandolan had both an ecological and an economic reason. From an economic perspective, Chipko Aandolan simply reflected the growing dissatisfaction among village people about uneven and unjust distribution of profits from forest resources. During the 1960s, the targets of this movement were the state governments, local bureaucrats and forest contractors. Villagers basically resented the government's policy of a "contract system," which allowed the extraction of resources from the nearby forests. Forests resources were sold in urban markets benefitting only a few people. The contract system was a part of the government's policy which was shaped by the patterns established under the British government. The British government, during colonization, made policies which were aimed at exploiting natural resources for commercial gains. The Forest Act of 1927, which was aimed at protecting forests from the people, rather than for the people, was just a reflection of this policy thinking.

Under the traditional contract system, the local people did not receive any share of the profit. They were benefitted only in the sense that they could sell their labor and earn a living. Moreover, despite the governmental policy of declaring forests as national property, villagers perceived forests as "common goods" given by the god. Therefore, they claimed that they deserved a bigger and better share of forest resources. As early as in the 1970s, the village people expressed their voices collectively. The organizational support came from the two already existing village-level welfare societies: Gangotri Gram Swarajya Sangh (GGSS) in Uttarkashi and Dasholi Gram Swarajya Sangh (DGSS) in Gopeshwar. The strategy of action for the local people was to stop physically the government or contractors from harming the trees.

The Chipko Aandolan was definitely influenced by the Gandhian philosophy of non-violence and non-cooperation. The strategy used by the villagers brought considerable sympathy and curiosity to the movement from all over the nation. The villagers claimed their first official victory in the early 1970s when the "contract system" was abolished by the government and was replaced by the Uttar Pradesh Forest Development Corporation (UPFDC). Under this new system, the extraction of resources was encouraged through local cooperative societies. While the agents of extraction changed, no change was made in the basic policy thinking. Extraction and exploitation still remained the primary goals of forest management. The over-exploitation and reckless felling of trees still could not be avoided. Consequently, during the late 1970s, the Chipko Aandolan became an ecological movement whose prime responsibility was to question the government for its forest policy.

From an ecological perspective, the Chipko Aandolan really emerged around 1976. Once villagers achieved their goal of fair share, their attention shifted to other ecological issues. At this time, the movement was led by village women who fought against their own male family members for accepting jobs that destroyed the forests. The women promoted the Chipko slogan:

What do the forests bear?
Soil, Water, and Pure Air.
Soil, Water, and Pure Air
Are the Basis of life.

The Chipko Aandolan transformed itself into a vocal ecological movement for various reasons. The Alkananda Valley, where the movement
began, experienced an unprecedented chain of floods in the 1970s. Although
the area was declared as ecologically fragile in 1974, tree-felling continued,
resulting in more floods throughout the decade. Moreover, there were
several big landslides in 1977 and 1978 in Tawaghat and Kanodiagad,
respectively, which blocked the Bhagirathi river and caused serious flooding.
These landslides convinced the local people of the importance of trees in
hill areas.

The Chipko Aandolan, during the 1980s, was dominated by two distinct
schools of thought. The first was directed by Chandi Prasad Bhatt, who was
the pioneer of the movement and was the chairman of the DGSS. Bhatt,
based on my personal correspondence with him, is an eco-developmentalist,
who believes in conserving and developing natural resources in a way that
benefits the local economy while preserving the ecological balance. The main
objectives and activities of the Chipko Aandolan and the DGSS, according
to Bhatt, were[22]:

- to conduct and convene eco-development camps for afforestation;

- to educate the masses regarding their surroundings and environment, use of fuel and energy;

- to construct and build natural walls around the farms, forests, river
  catchments and to plant trees in these areas which ultimately hold
  the soil together and in due course of time, provide fodder and
  grass for domestic cattle;

- to put a complete ban on tree-felling in sensitive areas for commercial and other purposes;

- to establish a co-operative for forest management and use;

- to encourage agro-forestry;

- to press for environmental impact studies of landslides, floods, and
  soil erosion.

The second school of thought was led by Sunderlal Bahuguna, who is a politician and a journalist. Bahuguna is an ecologist and believes in promoting the Chipko message outside the region. He does not support agroforestry or the establishment of local industries which use forest resources in any way.[23] Although Bahuguna expresses his concern about meeting the needs of the local people through social forestry, the local economy per se is of secondary importance to him. Bahuguna has organized several activities in the region, which have received wide media coverage.

The Chipko Aandolan undoubtedly stirred interest and awareness for ecology among Indians. However, the Aandolan remained a local and spontaneous movement. Bahuguna's efforts to make it an organized, formal group did not have much success. Even in 1987, there was no office space for the Chipko's so-called officers. The only official linkage that the Aandolan had was through the DGSM. It is interesting to note that the DGSM itself had only ten formal members.[24] Nevertheless, the DGSM was a good training ground, as many women of the nearby villages, including those who were active in Chipko, worked in enterprises managed by the DGSS. While the Chipko Aandolan had a definite influence on governmental decisions at the state level, it had no political base either at the local or at the national level.

The Chipko Aandolan—its composition, strategy, and success—has some interesting implications for political scientists. To begin with, it is obvious, that despite a general feeling of apathy and disillusionment, people do participate in political processes. However, this form of participation is difficult to tap through macro-level analyses of political participation. The participation exists at the very grass-roots level for very basic issues. People's interests may not be mobilized in a formal way; however, they adopt informal means to express their demands. Often, their demands have a clear-cut, objective which is to influence not only the decision making process but also the very basic structural arrangement in the society. Like the Chipko Aandolan, the Ganga Mukti Aandolan's methods of protest are also unique and predominantly cultural. In early 1983, it organized a boat procession in which 80 small and big boats decorated with banners participated. Singing songs and gathering crowds along the river bank, they sailed from Kahalgaon to a public meeting in a nearby village almost 40 kilometers away.[25] Similarly, in the North Arcot District of Tamilnadu, on June 5, 1984, groups of men, women and children, carrying pitchers of water went in a procession through the main streets of the district and broke the pitchers in front of the municipal office. They played drums, which are usually associated with funeral processions, and burnt an "effluent monster."[26] Actions such as these are never pre-planned and are rarely taken seriously by the government; however, they leave a lasting impact on the perceptions of the local people.

The second implication refers to the unstructured and unintentional nature of public participation. The women of Chamoli did not seek to alter the overall governmental policy; in fact, their knowledge about the specifics of the policy were questionable. Nevertheless, they wanted an immediate and a visible result. Their strategy was not well-thought out and well-planned, but it was successful in mobilizing the people by displaying immediate results. The women of Chamoli, thus, challenged the conventional wisdom that public opinion is influential only when it is structured. Chipko's case study reveals that it is the persistence, and not necessarily the organization, that brings results.

The third implication refers directly to the group culture in India. Group activity in India clearly has a necessary cultural dimension: people are likely to accept those goals and strategies which are culturally suited to them. Showing respect for Mother Nature is a well-accepted aspect of the Indian philosophy. What is surprising is the aggressive role played by the illiterate women. Women, under the social philosophy and according to the Indian Constitution, have an equal status with men. Nevertheless, the society is protective of its women. Women are supposed to play an "indoor" role in the society and are supposed to follow their father/husband/son's wishes. However, in this case, the women of Chamoli took a leading role which, in the beginning, went against the wishes of their menfolk. The women of Chamoli represented a silent constituency (being women, illiterate, rural, and agricultural laborers); however, as the case reveals, this silent constituency had a potential to transform itself into political constituency when its basic interests were threatened.

The Chipko Aandolan's case study also highlights the relationship between the people and the government in India. More often than not, the targets of the movement were the officials themselves, who were understood to be in alliance with contractors. The people did not perceive the government as a protector; instead, for them, the government was a culprit which had to be stopped. Unlike Western countries, where the role of the public is to draw their government's attention to environmental problems, in India public protests tend to be against the government, indicating a low level of political efficacy. As Bhatt, who has been the spokesperson for the Aandolan, said, "All during the 1960s we would run from the hills to the state capital Lucknow to plead our case before government officials there. But finally, we saw the futility of this exercise. It would take years to convince an official and then he would get transferred. We would begin afresh with the new one."[27] In brief, the spirit of the Chipko Aandolan was to become "actors" rather than "promoters" of the environmental cause; and, thus, it was to undermine the state authority itself.

Politics Behind Public Protests

The selected cases of public protests reveal that the focus of public protest against environmental degradation was predominantly local. The target was often one local industry or one particular pollution source. The goal, more often than not, was to achieve an optimum solution to any one existing problem. The protests, nevertheless, were likely to be the reflection of a deeper, yet still local, power struggle, such as the struggle between two castes, or two communities, or between workers and managers etc. The process of resolution, as in the case of the Orient Paper Mill in Amlai, included the giving away of individual and community benefits to sidetrack the main issue.

The nature of the public protest was spontaneous, albeit not short-lived. As in the case of Gwalior Rayons in Mavoor, and of Orient Paper Mills in Amlai, the protests lasted for several years, indicating the endurance of the protesters, who were often poor and illiterate. Since the power of the local elite far exceeded the power of the masses, the protests could not make a dent unless they continued for a long time or they got diffused to other areas. On the other side, offenders found it cost effective to build temples and to give other community benefits, such as building community halls, providing new facilities (drinking water taps, for instance), or distributing blankets, rather than installing new water and air treatment plants. As a result of these symbolic gestures, protests often got stifled, at least until a new pollution problem could spark the protesters again.

In most cases, the power of the bureaucrats also worked against the public, for the alliance between the local officials and the industrialists prohibited any official inquiry into the matters. The bribing of the officials was a common occurrence, and villagers were usually aware of it. Consequently, villagers found it difficult to trust the government. The feeling of helplessness was prevalent: villagers could not boycott industries, for industries were the primary employers in the area. I was told during my interviews that, at the time of the annual inspection, government inspectors were often brought in luxurious company cars, were given the finest hotels to stay in and were honored in elaborate receptions. In addition, direct or indirect cash bribes were also offered. Inspectors, earning less than the socially acceptable wages, found the temptation hard to resist.

Another significant aspect of the public protests was that they were oriented more toward health problems than toward ecological issues per se. The death of cattle and fish, people's contraction of rashes and breathing problems, and the loss of human lives formed the major complaints against polluters. Not surprisingly, then, the protests were lodged primarily by the affected public. Given the social and economic attributes of the involved public, the "up-down" nature of the protests was understandable. The people who were directly affected by the pollution of rivers or by the felling of trees were living in rural areas, were poor and were illiterate. When they became aware of the environmental problem, their first reaction was to adjust to the situation. The involved industry or the contract business was important for village; for not only did it provide employment, but it also contributed to the overall local economy and, thus, increased the spending power of the rural people. More often than not, village economies were fully dependent on the local industry. In one family (India has the concept of extended family), as many as four or five members were employed by the local industry. This complete reliance on the local industry forced the people not to engage themselves in protest activities, for such activities could also mean the loss of jobs, something which is avoided in a country where finding a job, to begin with, is a major achievement.

In addition, the cases also indicate that the people had to be threatened by the degradation of the environment to an extent where their immediate survival was in danger before they would protest against the local elite. In most of the examples above, the people perceived their lives in danger. However, the power and tactics of the local elite were also evident. The elite tried to manipulate public opinion by distributing free commodities. They utilized the religious and cultural orientation of the people by organizing various activities. These commodities and activities did not cost much; nevertheless, they helped build the industry's rapport with the people.

In general, the case studies display a significant level of rural activism in the environmental policy area. However, any inference to the level of rural environmental awareness will be misleading. In fact, a high rate of general environmental illiteracy still existed. In several interviews[28] with the villagers in the state of Haryana, respondents identified the problem of pollution, but failed to pinpoint the source of pollution (no nearby industry existed in the area, but water ponds were polluted from the heavy use of pesticide and the effluent being discharged from small sugar mills). Several villagers blamed the deterioration of the water quality on super natural powers, while few thought that it was the government's responsibility to investigate, and not theirs. When asked how the government should spend the money allotted for the area, everyone, without exception, mentioned economic issues, such as transportation, housing, cattle and seeds, rather than any of the ecological issues. The high level of mass environmental illiteracy was also questioned by Vohra, the ex-chairman of the National Committee on Environmental Planning and Coordination in one of his printed interviews.

> We must not, however, forget that the typical Indian, and this includes the poor Indian, suffers from a spirit of apathy, fatalism and resignation to whatever comes to him. I think there is no other way to explain some of the things that we as a nation have been putting up with. For instance, take this business of water-logging and salinisation of land. The area which has been already lost is at least seven million hectares, and these were all once good lands, with access to canal irrigation. If we assume the price of such land on a conservative basis to be around Rs 30,000 [US $2,000] a hectare, then the loss suffered by the peasantry of India on this account alone is of the order of Rs 21,000 crores. Now whatever way you may look at it, this is a very big figure. But our people have accepted this loss without a murmur, they have accepted it as an act of God, more or less. We also accept the actual losses of Rs 1,000 crores or so caused by floods in a similar spirit. So there is this strain in our character of viewing even man-made disasters as part of a preordained fate.[29]

Contrary to rural areas, the level of environmental awareness in urban areas was relatively high. Even then, the involvement of the people in environment-related activities, such as protests, was surprisingly low. A public opinion poll survey in Jaipur city in the state of Rajasthan revealed that 42 percent of the students surveyed were aware of the air pollution in the city and perceived it as a health hazard.[30] Three-quarters of them identified the source of the pollution as industrial. However, few had directly participated in any environmental activity. Conceivably, the press played a significant role in raising the environmental awareness among the urban educated people. However, since the realization of the problem for these people was through a secondary source, rather than through their own experience (as it was for the rural people), the urban people were less inclined to engage themselves in environment-oriented activities. The following section analyzes the ability of the media to influence the environmental policy process.

The Role of the Media: A Content Analysis

The independent, mature and experienced image of the press in India is both a cause and a result of the democratic experience. Its near autonomous and powerful position makes the press an active participant in the nation's political game. In order to assess the role of the media in the environmental policy area, I undertook a content analysis of a national newspaper—*The Hindustan Times*—from 1976 to 1981. This time period was selected because the visibility of the environmental issue was the highest during this time: new laws were passed, new agencies were created and new organizations were established during this short period of five years. *The Hindustan Times* is one of the most reputed national newspapers; but since its printing is in English, its readership is limited to only the selected few. However, a preliminary investigation of several regional and local language newspapers revealed that the environmental coverage during the period was too limited to be taken for statistical analysis. In addition, the study by Sekar also indicated that the local press was, in general, silent over the environmental issue.[31]

For the analysis, the contents of all the environment-related articles were coded in terms of the size, placement, type (reportorial versus analytical), and level (national, state, or local) of the coverage. The contents were also categorized for the kind of environmental issues that they dealt with, and for their focus of attention (problem aspect versus solution aspect). The results of this analysis are presented in Figures 6.1 and 6.2, and in Tables 6.1 and 6.2.

According to the results, the coverage of the environmental news in *The Hindustan Times* doubled between 1976 and 1981. The debates over the two major controversies—the Silent Valley Hydroelectric Project and the Mathura Oil Refinery—were primarily responsible for the increase, totalling 37 percent of the total environmental news coverage during the years 1979 and 1980. Following the government's actions to resolve the controversies, the media interest declined, as clearly shown in Figure 6.1. However, the total environmental coverage did not drop proportionately. In 1981, fifty-

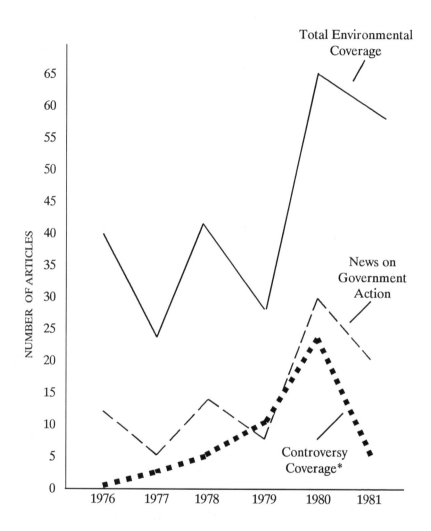

Figure 6.1. Environemntal News Coverage of Specific Controversies

* *Controversy coverage includes coverage on Silent Valley Hydroelectric Project and Mathura Refinery.*

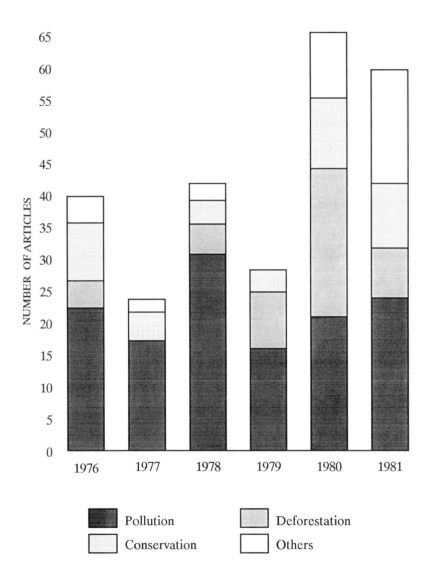

Figure 6.2. Distribution of News Coverage by Type of Environmental Problem

eight news articles appeared, suggesting the frequency of the coverage being more than once a week. As shown in Figure 6.2, of all the environment-related issues, pollution received the most coverage. In 1978, as much as 71 percent of the total environmental news items were about water, air, and land pollution. Since the paper caters to mostly urban readers, it is likely that the urban environmental problems, such as pollution, are of greater interest to it. The coverage on deforestation was highest during 1980, suggesting that it was triggered by the Silent Valley controversy.

Several other interesting patterns were also revealed by the analysis. First, nearly one-third of the news items in these years were nothing more than the simple reporting of governmental activities (Table 6.1), suggesting that the media interest was stimulated by the policy process, and not vice versa. The interest shown by the media was due to the initiative taken by the government in the environmental policy area. In this case, the process in India differs from the similar processes in other countries. In the United States, for example, the media played a role of an "exposer" of governmental apathy and neglect. In India, however, the media became a mouthpiece of the government, and played a role of a "messenger." It is noteworthy that this passive role of the media existed only in the initial stages of policy for-mulation. The media coverage of the 1980s, which is not covered in this content analysis, is quite different in its nature and scope from the coverage in the 1970s. Once the policy was in place, the media started to play a more active and aggressive role. Today, environmental news is covered substan-tially in non-English as well as in local newspapers. The tone of the coverage is also anti-government and increasingly critical of the interference by the government.

Second, nearly 40 percent of the environmental news items were edi-torials, or special assignments, indicating an effort on the part of the media to shape the public opinion. Third, only 9 percent of the news items appeared on the first page, while 19 percent were placed on the pages devoted to editorials. A significant portion of the coverage appeared in the magazine section, suggesting a low-priority, low-key and low-attention position of the environmental issue. Last, although the amount of the coverage doubled over the years, there was no change in the pattern of the coverage.

The content analysis examines the time period up to 1981. It is also limited in its scope and application. Therefore, it is essential to draw some inferences on the overall role of the media based on non-empirical obser-vations, especially after the post-1981 years. The coverage of environmental issues increased tremendously during the 1980s, and continues to grow in

Table 6.1
Distribution of News Coverage by Type of Coverage

	Type of Coverage		
Year	Reportive	Analytical/Informative	Total
1976	22	16	38
	(57.9%)	(42.1%)	(100.0%)
1977	13	10	23
	(56.5%)	(43.5%)	(100.0%)
1978	23	19	42
	(54.8%)	(45.2%)	(100.0%)
1979	21	6	27
	(77.8%)	(22.2%)	(100.0%)
1980	42	23	65
	(64.6%)	(35.4%)	(100.0%)
1981	34	26	60
	(56.7%)	(43.3%)	(100.0%)

the 90s. The Centre for Science and Environment[32] now brings out a publication, *Green File*, based solely on the reproduction of news articles from 30 major newspapers and 15 major news magazines. The *Green File* is printed every month and, despite its frequency, its editors claim that every month, the Centre collects about 2,500 to 3,500 news clippings, out of which only 300 to 400 are printed in the *Green Files*.

Several indicators suggest that the role of the media also changed significantly in the 1980s. Two changes were particularly noticeable. First, the media coverage was localized and regionalized. Most local and regional language newspapers started to cover environmental issues. The Bhopal Tragedy, for instance, was covered by local, regional and national newspapers alike. The catastrophic nature of the tragedy generated an atmosphere of fear toward local industries. Consequently, the media accepted the surveillant role and questioned the implementation of environmental laws. Similarly, the construction of Tehri Dam, despite its localized implications, was covered by all newspapers. Throughout the 1980s, the media continued to provide a forum to environmentalists.

The second change came in the style and tone of the media coverage. Compared to the 1970s, the tone of the coverage became more anti-government in the post 1980 years. The radicalization of the media began with the coverage of the Silent Valley Project and it continued throughout the decade. At present, the media plays a two-fold role: the watchdog role where a critical look is kept over governmental activities; and the instrumental role where the media is used by the government to promote its policies. Even though, the media, in general, is anti-government (for instance, it even accused several ministers including the prime minister Rajiv Gandhi himself for being involved in political scandals), the government still views it as a ready channel to reach to the people. The All-India radio reaches 90 percent of the population; newspapers are read by 10 percent; and the television is accessible to 14 percent of the people.

The government is successfully using the media to communicate to the people on environmental issues. For example, the government's newest plan to clean the Ganga river uses the media as an important tool to arouse the public's interest. The Ministry of Environment and Forests also emphasizes the use of media as the corner stone of its strategy to protect the environment. Although media is an important channel of communication, it is certainly not the only one. In rural areas, environmentalists and government campaign agencies also use folk songs, open-air theatres, festivals, and puppet shows. Compared to the rhetoric of the media, these traditional methods are more agreeable to the rural lifestyle.

Interest Groups and the Environmental Issue

Interest groups and political parties have been linked with the emergence of environmental movement in developed countries. Sandbach noted a sharp increase in the number of environmental organizations in Britain and in the United States during the peak of the environmental movement of the early 1970s.[33] Cynthia Enloe also noted the emergence of environmental organizations as an important, if not determining, factor in establishing the viability of the environment as a political issue.[34]

It is generally believed that interest groups and political parties perform an important infrastructural function in a democratic nation by articulating the needs of the people. While groups provide "commonness" to society's needs, political parties incorporate these needs into political agenda. In brief, these political brokers often shape and mobilize public opinion.

Despite low levels of political efficacy, group activity in India is significant. Over 25,000 public groups fulfilling a variety of purposes exist in the nation today. The pro-group culture is visible in the environmental policy area as well. By 1983, as many as 250 registered groups (also referred to as non-governmental groups or NGOs) were registered in the nation. The number is likely to be twice as many if the groups not formally registered were also counted. Figure 6.3 depicts a 600 percent increase in the number of environmental interest groups during a period of 20 years, from 1963 to 1983. Until 1970, only a handful of groups existed and even these groups were not exclusively organized for the environmental cause. The start of the accelerated growth came in 1972, when the United Nation's Conference on Human Environment convened in Stockholm, and also when the government established its first national level governmental agency charged exclusively for the cause of environmental protection.

The year 1980 marked the second point of sharp growth in the number of environmental interest groups. Three possible explanations can be offered for this sudden increase. First, the nation faced two major national level controversies in the late 1970s that drew the public's attention toward environmental protection--the Silent Valley Hydro-electric Plant and the Mathura Oil Refinery. Second, the government established a full-fledged organization, the Department of Environment, in 1980. Such an act was likely to have stirred some public interest. Third and last, the media coverage of the issue (which was aimed at stimulating the public interest) was also at an unprecedented level in 1980. Other than the outside variables, disasters and tragedies also force people to organize. It is not the pollution, but the realization of the effects of pollution that stimulates the organizational response. The obvious example is the incidence of gas leak from the Union Carbide Plant in Bhopal.. In response to the crisis, 13 new groups surfaced within two months of the tragedy for this cause alone.

Figure 6.3 also depicts the geographical distribution and growth of environmental groups in the northern (comprising Uttar Pradesh, Madhya Pradesh, Rajasthan, Punjab, Himachal Pradesh, Haryana, Jammu & Kashmir, and the Union Territories of New Delhi and Chandigarh), the southern (with Kerala, Andhra Pradesh, Tamil Nadu, and Karnataka), the eastern (with Assam, Bihar, Orissa and West Bengal) and the western (with Maharashtra, Gujarat and Goa) regions. Since the population distribution in the four regions is not equal, any comparison based on the absolute number of groups should not be made. However, a comparison based on the pattern of growth is valid and reveals that with the exception of the northern region (where group activity increased sharply toward the early 1980s), the pattern

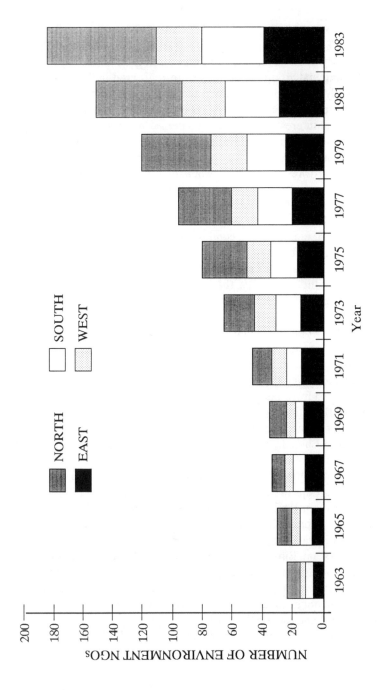

Figure 6.3. Growth of Environmental NGOs

of growth in the regions was identical regardless of any economic and political differences among them. In addition, after New Delhi (whose cosmopolitan culture naturally allowed the highest number of environmental groups to emerge), the states of Uttar Pradesh, West Bengal, Maharashtra and Kerala displayed the sharpest increase in the number of environmental groups.

Despite their large number, environmental groups had only a limited influence on the society or even on the policy-making process. The groups were not politicized; therefore, they remained outside of the political arena. Further, they suffered from low membership. Table 6.2 shows that in 1983, nearly 45 percent of all the groups reported a total membership of less than 50 in a nation of 800 million people.[35] Some groups, such as Mitiani Kehan (in Kerala) and the Institute of Himalayan Environment and Ecology (in Uttar Pradesh) had only 5 members. Established in 1977, the Population and Environment Centre reported having only 6 members, while its staff strength was 12, 2 full-time and 10 part-time employees. A further analysis reveals that more than a quarter of all the environmental groups had 25 or fewer members, while a total of 22 organizations had 10 members or less. However, groups such as the Kerala Sahitya Parishad had a membership of over 5,000. This membership data becomes more critical when one looks at the financial support base of the environmental interest groups. More than 70 percent of them depended, fully or partially, on the membership fees for financial support. Contrast this funding to the support base of the British environmental groups which, according to one survey[36], reported the government as one of their three important sources of funding. In addition, for the 23 percent of the British environmental groups, the government was either their first or second source of support. In India, with the membership figures being so low, environmental groups certainly did not have the economic support needed for effective functioning and lobbying. In brief, environmental interest groups lacked the two most crucial resources— membership and money—to influence governmental decisions. According to the available data, donations constituted the second largest source of income for the groups; however, except for the few well-known organizations, it was highly unlikely that the donations were adequate for their needs. No direct support from the government was received by any of the organizations.

The effectiveness of the environmental groups' lobbying efforts was also limited by the differences in their respective goals and functions. The groups varied significantly in their level of expertise—from purely emotional (Chipko Aandolan in Uttar Pradesh) to very technical (Society of Biological

Table 6.2
Membership Status of Environmental NGOs

Total Membership	Frequency	Cumulative Percentage
Less than 50	77	44.77
51 to 100	34	64.53
101 to 200	23	77.91
201 to 300	10	83.72
301 to 400	7	87.80
401 to 500	6	91.28
501 to 1000	5	94.19
1001 to 2000	4	96.51
2001 to 5000	6	99.99
5001 to 10000	1	100.00
Missing information	10 *	--
TOTAL	182	--

* missing cases have not been included in calculating the cumulative percentages.

Source: The table is based on the information provided in *The Directory of Non-governmental Organizations in Environment* (New Delhi: Government of India, Department of Environment, 1983).

Chemists in Karnataka). Some of the groups were informal in their structure (Hulgol Groups Villagers Service Cooperative Society in Karnataka), while others were formally structured (Wildlife Conservation Society in Gujarat). Similarly, their level of activism also ranged from ad hoc and narrow (Save Mahabaleshwar Panchagini Association in Maharashtra) to broad and even legally oriented (Bombay Environmental Action Group in Maharashtra).

In general, environmental groups were poorly structured, had low membership, lacked financial support, and were narrowly focused. Two patterns were clear: first, that the groups existed in a large number; and second, that they were not politicized. The question that now remains is why? Why is it that the groups emerged, and if they emerged, then why did they stay outside the political arena? What purpose did they serve by being "non-politicized"? Once again, the political culture of India offers an answer to it.

It can be argued that the democratic traditions of the nation encourage the establishment of environmental organizations; however, some inherent characteristics of the same traditions restrain these organizations from transforming themselves into influential political units. To begin with, democracy is a new concept for Indians. The nation was dominated by foreign powers for over 900 years. Despite the politicization of the masses, the people are still either fatalistic or apathetic toward their political surroundings. While the political consciousness forces them to "speak up" and join a group, the low level of trust in the political system and the element of fatalism in their thinking prevents them from being overly involved. There is a general apathetic feeling, which one can hear while talking to the people, that "things don't change."

Also, the one-party-dominance system hurts the strength of interest groups in general, and of environmental groups in particular. Environmental groups, more often than not, must raise their voices against the status quo and the establishment. The Congress(I), the governing party for all but two years, has a close alliance with the elite, especially the business sector; therefore, it is highly unlikely that environmental groups can gain political leverage. In the past, the groups tried to seek the support from the leftist parties; but, as the power base of these parties was limited at the national level, the groups did not find much benefit by aligning with them.

Furthermore, the parliamentary system also inhibits environmental groups from exerting influence on policymakers. Under the parliamentary system, voting in the parliament is strictly on party lines: individual members of the parliament, unlike the congressmen in the United States, have little or no say in determining their vote. Groups, therefore, do not find it worthwhile to lobby to individual members. For the same reason, members of the parliament also lack any desire to be sensitive to the individual needs of their constituencies; their candidacy is often linked with the overall performance of their party, and not with their individual performance. Thus, the former Minister of State for Environment, Digvijay Pratap Sinh, himself could afford to keep his constituency unhappy over environmental issues. According to an investigative report by *India Today*, farmers from Sinh's constituency complained that "effluent from the factory [the Dharangandhra Chemical Works] which are discharged into River Falku are pushing up the salinity of the soil and making it infertile."[37] To stage their protest, the farmers decided to abstain from voting in the 1980 parliamentary elections, but they were persuaded to vote by Sinh, who promised to take action against the factory. But as the report continues, "Ironically enough, Digvijay Sinh went to become the Union Environment Minister, but has not yet done anything about the grievances in his own constituency."[38]

Last, the general perception regarding governmental officials also discourages the public to treat organizations as effective tools of political communication. The public shows little trust for politicians and bureaucrats because of the prevailing practices of corruption, nepotism and favor-trading. Public officials are described as corrupt, dishonest and ineffectual. In a survey conducted in Delhi, almost 60 percent of the respondents said that they believed that at least half of all public officials were corrupt.[39] The negative perception, needless to say, discourages the people from forming organizations and appealing to officials.

In brief, environmental groups in India function more as philanthropies than as pressure groups. Some scholars even argue that the environmental concern in India is not environmentalism, but it is at best a manifestation of new awareness of economic and social impacts of environmental issues. However, in recent years, environmental groups have taken a more militant role by staging strikes, street demonstrations and anti-regime protests. Obviously, their existence itself has given them their power base. Their strategy to appeal to the public directly, rather than to fight the power of the elite in the policy-making arena, has created a favorable atmosphere for group activity. However, the group activity has also created political tensions. For instance, environmental awareness among the people and the government is now being cited as a major factor in making India a less appealing place for foreign investors.[40] The government of India is accused of reaching a settlement of $470 million for the Bhopal victims simply to attract foreign companies which are concerned over environmental and liability regulations. Considering the fact that India has only $600 million investment from the United States (especially compared to the $3 billion figure in China) and is in search for more investments, it is unlikely that the nation will actually succeed in implementing environmental standards. In fact, Union Carbide itself is planning to seek approval on three other plants to be built in India in the near future.

Political Parties and the Environmental Issue

Political parties, another significant medium for transforming public demands into policy inputs, were also silent on the environmental issue until

1980. No political party included environmental issues in its political platform prior to the 1980 general elections. The Congress(I) Party focused its resources on economic growth under its slogan of "Remove Poverty," and the Janata Party—the only other party to ever form a government in Delhi—gave priority to political and individual freedom with its slogan of "Remove Indira." In 1980, in the wake of a number of environmental controversies, both major parties, as well as several other parties, included environmental protection in their election campaigns for the first time. However, their party campaigns and speeches during the 1980 and the 1984 general elections never emphasized the environmental issue as a priority issue. It should be remembered, though, that the 1984 elections were fought under unusual circumstances following Indira Gandhi's assassination just two months previously. Therefore, sentiments, rather than actions, were the issues in the election.

The main reason for this political apathy rested with the parties' moral perception of the issue. All parties in general agreed on the moral appeal of protecting the environment; therefore, no party received any particular political benefit by aligning with the environmental issue. If there was any political potential in the issue, it was at the local level. However, even at that level, political parties shied away from taking a specific stand. The local elite constantly identified the environmental issue as an anti-growth issue, where any expenditure on environmental treatment facilities meant a loss of employment for the poor and an adverse effect on the growth of the local economy. There were few cases where local and regional political parties took interest in environmental projects. Even then, their interest was dominated more by their desire to embarrass the government in New Delhi rather than to achieve environmental miracles.

An analysis of various party manifestos from the 1980 and 1984 general elections indicates that parties did not take the issue of environment seriously. The problem was accepted by party leaders; however, they were never clear about the desired course of action. Goals were not specified and options were not selected. Other than the Congress(I), parties did not express any desire to create an administrative unit in charge of environmental protection or to institutionalize the environmental aspect in policy making. The following extracts from the leading parties' manifestoes during the 1980 general elections prove this point[41].

Congress (I)   [It] feels deep concern at the indiscriminate and reckless felling of trees and the depletion of our forests and wildlife, which upsets the ecological balance with recurring misery to the people and disastrous consequences for the country's future. Projects which bring economic benefits must be so planned as to preserve and enhance our natural wealth, our flora and fauna. In response to the economic and social necessity for ecological planning, the Congress (I) will take effective steps--including setting up in the Government a specialised machinery with adequate powers—to ensure the prudent use of our land and marine resources by formulating clear policies in this regard for strict implementation.

Janata Party [It] realises that the country's natural resources, both living and finite, on which all human economic activities depend are being depleted at a pace that can only spell ecological and economic disaster within a foreseeable future. Therefore, the Party believes that drastic remedial action must be taken without delay. There is need to arrest ecological degradation and to reverse and prevent desertification, deforestation and soil erosion. There is similar need to arrest ecological damage of all aspects of India's cultural heritage, especially national monuments.

Indian National Congress (U) In villages, the lack of protected drinking water sources and poor sanitation results in disease and squalor. Demand for fodder and fuel leads to the denudation of forests. In many urban areas, industrial pollution is reaching serious proportions and sanitation is still very inadequate in the poorer neighbourhoods. Our wealth in forests and wildlife have not only to be protected but much more investment will have to be made in afforestation.

Any specific commitment for environmental protection from over two dozen regional parties was non-existent for the same time period. The environmental issue was rarely mentioned in their party manifestoes. This lukewarm response from political parties stemmed from the two distinct features of the Indian party system. The Indian party system, among other things, is characterized by federalism (one-party-center, multiple-party-state phenomenon) and unpredictability (of support base).[42] The history of political parties and of elections in India indicates that two separate images of parties exist in voters' minds: they are able to separate the role of parties at national and at state levels. Voters interpret party ideologies and manifestoes differently depending on the scope of the elections. In search of political stability and national interests, for example, voters support the Congress (I) at the national level, but at the same time, they vote for non-Congress (often even regional or leftist) parties at the state level to assert their political interests and policy preferences. With the exception of the 1977 post-emergency elections, Congress (I) has won between 41 and 49 percent of the popular votes and between 54 and 79 percent of the total seats in every parliamentary election. With such a strong hold at the center, it is surprising that every single state in India has been ruled at one point in time or another by a non-Congress party. In brief, voters display a dual voting behavior. The implications of this dualism are significant for the development of the party system. During the 1960s and the 1970s, this dual behavior produced a unique arrangement of one-party-center-and-multi-party-state. The arrangement helped in retaining the democratic spirit of the nation; nevertheless, it also crippled the responsiveness of the party system. It made national parties immune to local issues. Since environment was viewed as a local issue, national parties did not feel the need to rally around the issue. Regional parties were equally limited in their role. Moreover, regional parties' support came because they treated the environmental issue more as a vehicle to embarrass the Congress (I) rather than to devise any localized environmental protection strategy. In addition, even in the states where Congress (I) itself maintained the majority, the role of state governments in the environmental area was reduced to being simply a defender of national governmental policies.

In addition to dualism, the unpredictable nature of the support base also undermines the role of political parties. While the electoral support base for Congress (I) is broad and non-committal, the base for other parties remains fragile and unpredictable. With over 230 million voters participating and over 5,000 candidates contesting, the Indian parliamentary elections are the largest elections held in the world. Moreover, voter swings are often drastic and unrelated to the changes in voters' political attitudes or ideology. Indira Gandhi, for example, faced a crushing defeat in the 1977 parliamentary elections; but just after 33 months, she was brought back to power with an equally over-whelming enthusiasm. The election history reveals that the Congress (I) has lost several times in those states where its victory was predicted to be certain. On the other hand, the Congress (I) has also won several times in weak-Congress states. In brief, there has not been a consistent pattern of the Congress's support. Its support base is general and broad. It has always been an umbrella party: it attracts voters from all religions, regions, castes and classes. The level of the Congress's tolerance as a political party is often credited for this remarkable image. However, in order to be tolerant of various sectors, and in order to be appealing to different interests, the Congress (I) party has to stay away from establishing clear-cut agendas. The ability of the Congress (I) to make a serious policy commitment is thereby severely limited. Since it draws its financial support from businesses and industrialists, and since it finds its electoral support from the blue-collar workers and farmers, the party is in no position to give real support to controversial issues. It, therefore, opts to be a "balancer" and a majority-builder. Its role in the environmental policy area was also non-committal and idealistic. It opted for policies that were all-inclusive.

While the support base of the Congress (I) was too broad to have allowed it to rally behind the environmental issue, the support base of the non-Congress parties was too narrow to have permitted them to afford to the issue. Two factors in the development of the non-Congress parties are worth considering. The first is the rate of defections and the second is their campaigning strength. Regional and non-Congress parties in India are constantly challenged by the overwhelming mass appeal of the Congress (I). Even ethnically oriented parties, such as Akali Dal, AIADMK, and Telugu Desam, have to fight hard to keep their supporters from aligning with the Congress (I). In the past (prior to the passage of the anti-defection bill by the Rajiv Gandhi administration), the system allowed leaders and active members of a party to defect from one party and join another without having to pay a political cost. Therefore, defections were a weapon in the hands of the Congress (I) to break opposition and regional parties. According to estimates, over 2,700 defections took place between 1967 and 1987, and over 70 percent of these were from non-Congress parties to the Congress (I).[43] Thus, the support base of the non-Congress parties was not only unpredictable; it was constantly under threat. Members failed to make policy commitments and were distracted by the promises of political rewards (especially ministership in new ministries). The anti-defection bill, passed by the Rajiv Gandhi government, helped the tension somewhat; nevertheless, its impact is yet to be felt.

Other than defections, the near monopoly of the Congress (I) over campaign spendings also distorts the image of other political parties among voters. A great disparity exists between the expenditure figures of various political parties. For instance, over one billion rupees was spent by Congress(I) in the 1984 parliamentary elections; the amount spent by all the opposition parties together totalled less than ten percent of this amount.[44] Faced by defections and the tough financial situation, non-Congress parties, including the two communists parties, are forced to expand their support base and to undercut their ideological focus. In their attempt to appeal to the electorate, the non-Congress parties try to stay away from controversial issues. This vagueness of the support base adversely affects the building of party support for controversial issues, the environmental issue being one of them. In other countries, the support for the environmental issue has come from the parties of the left; but in India, as this study reveals, the left-oriented parties failed to provide such support. Like the Congress(I), they also found "limited-attention" to be their safest political strategy. By championing the environmental cause, the parties ran the risk of being labelled as "anti-development." As long as the support for environmental protection was moral and philosophical, the parties stayed in the safe zone, but once they started to design strategies (which included not just the need for action, but also obtaining resources to support those actions) the parties faced challenge from their support base itself. Ironically, the level of mass political awareness and the intensity of election competitions themselves forced political parties to be cautious in the environmental policy area.

The role of political parties, however, changed significantly in the post-1980 years. The level of their activism increased and the scope of their influence also widened. Various environmental controversies and tragedies aroused the interest of the public and tilted the cost-benefit ratio of the environmental issue in favor of political parties, particularly the local and regional parties. Consequently, during the 1989 general elections, all parties stressed the environmental issue as one of their planning priorities.

Public Participation and Its Implications

The role of the people in the environmental policy area, whether direct or indirect, has interesting implications. The role greatly contrasts from the role established in industrialized countries. Although it is similar to the public's role in other developing countries, yet, at least in some respects, it appears to be more aggressive, vocal and politicized. The analysis of public protests reveals that the public played neither a fully cooperative nor a totally disruptive role. In fact, its role was mixed in the sense that the direct response from the masses was confrontational, displaying very little faith in the ability of the government to bring results, while at the same time, the response from the elite (the organized sector or environmentalists) was mostly cooperative, at least in the initial stages.

Throughout the 1970s, the national and state governments sought cooperation from various scientists and environmentalists by appointing them on parliamentary committees and even nominating them on leading positions in governmental agencies. Input from other affected groups, such as industry and business, was also sought with equal enthusiasm. The policy process was nearly friction-free and non-political. A two-tier strategy was adopted by the government: while at the local level, the public's sporadic demands were met by providing emergency resources to affected areas; at the national level, an active cooperation was sought from the "experts" and from the organized interests. The strategy was to find a politically optimum solution, rather than an ecologically sound one. The result was the building up of a quick consensus regarding the environmental priorities at the national level, but a growing disillusionment at the local level. Consequently, when the nationally designed consensual environmental policy came to the local level for implementation, it faced severe opposition from the people, who continued to be suspicious of the government.

While the cooperative and consultative role of the elite (both environmentalists and developmentalists) helped evolve a consensual policy, it actually crippled the public's surveillant strength. To begin with, the process excluded those who were being most severely affected by environmental deterioration. Very little, if any, attention was paid to the dependency of the people on natural resources, such as fodder, wood and coal. Secondly, a more drastic after-effect came in the later years as the process continued to undermine the power of the environmental elite to play the role of a pressure group. Environmental groups soon found themselves caught in the captivity trap. While the consultative policy process promoted the notion of consensual decision-making, it also limited the scope of those groups which were being consulted. Since the groups were part of the process, they were expected to be "obedient" to the government. Additionally, the groups also lost the basis on which to oppose the government if the policy eventually failed to meet its goal. Lowe and Goyder have also found this to be true in their study of the British environmental groups. They explained this limitation as following:

The exercise of influence is of course a two-way process. Groups drawn into elaborate consultative procedures with government are induced to moderate their demands and tactics. Much time can be spent responding to a flow of consultative documents from government, sitting on official committees and providing information for policy making. Group leaders become enveloped in the consensual atmosphere of Whitehall with civil servants attempting to explain the constraints on government action and the rival claims which have to be balanced. Consultive status is gained and maintained by adhering to an unwritten code of moderate and responsible behaviors. It may be forfeited if a group is too outspoken in its criticisms or fails to show the necessary tact and discretion...Some 30% of leaders of environmental groups agreed to the statement that 'Involvement in governmental or parliamentary discussion often precludes keeping the membership informed'.[45]

Despite limitations, consultative groups played an important role in the development of the environmental policy process. Their participation provided legitimacy to the policy. They also fostered the implementation of the policy. The consultative role of the environmental groups in India was very similar to the role played by the Swedish and British environmental groups. The Indian government, similar to its British and Swedish counterparts, used the consultative groups to build national consensus. In India, however, there are indications that the consultative groups are turning into confrontational groups. The sense of frustration is prevalent among environmentalists who are increasingly getting disillusioned of their consultative role.

Based on this analysis, some general conclusions on the role of public participation can also be drawn. The analysis indicates that despite public support, an issue may remain outside of the domain of the social agenda simply because it lacks the support of social and political agents. The process also identifies indigenous ways in which the public expresses its policy priorities. Popular methods of participation, such as organized demonstrations, picket lines, leaflet distribution and signature drives, are not commonly found in developing countries. Nevertheless, their absence does not equate with the absence of public participation. At the same time, their presence does not indicate the existence of a political issue. The scope and nature of public participation is a complex issue and more fitting attention needs to be devoted to it.

Notes

1. The claim has been made by nearly all of the studies done in developing countries. Still, for a stronger argument, reference can be made to Y. Yishai, "Environment and Development: The Case of Israel," *International Journal of Environmental Studies*, 14: 205-16; H.J. Leonard and D. Morell, "Emergence of Environmental Concern in Developing Countries: A Political Perspective," *Stanford Journal of Environmental Law*, 17: 281-313.

2. Steven Reed acknowledged the role of the public along with the strong initiative role played by the local governments in his two important works: "Environmental Politics: Some Reflections based on the Japanese case," *Comparative Politics*, 13: 253-70; and *Japanese Prefectures and Policymaking* (Pittsburgh, University of Pittsburgh Press, 1986).

3. Cynthia Enloe, *The Politics of Pollution in a Comparative Perspective* (New York: David McKay, 1975).

4. J.O. Field, *Consolidating Democracy: Politicization and Participation in India* (New Delhi: Manohar, 1981).

5. Samuel P. Huntington, *Political Order in Changing Societies* (New Haven: Yale University Press, 1968).

6. Samuel J. Eldersveld and Bashiruddin Ahmed, *Citizen and Politics: Mass Political Behavior in India* (Chicago: University of Chicago Press, 1978).

7. Field, *Consolidating Democracy*.

8. Eldersveld, *Citizen and Politics*, 45.

9. Robert Hardgrave and Stanley Kochanek, *India: Government and Politics in a Developing Nation* (San Diego: Harcourt Brace Jovanovich, 1986), 299.

10. The argument was strongly made in James Manor's writing, "India: Awakening or Decay," *Current History*, March 1986, 101-104.

11. Charles Lewis Taylor and David A. Jodice (New Haven: Yale University Press, 1983).

12. These case studies are taken from media reports and from books written by environmentalists, and their "other side" has not been verified by me. The purpose behind citing these examples is to reveal the nature

of public support, and not to present technical information on the cases per se.

13. Anil Agarwal, Ravi Chopra and Kalpana Sharma, *The State of India's Environment, 1982* (New Delhi: Centre for Science and Environment, 1982), 26.

14. Ibid, 27.

15. *Annual Report* (Trivendrum: Government of Kerala, Kerala Water Pollution Control Board, 1983), 5.

16. Agarwal, Chopra and Sharma, *State of India's Environment*, 26.

17. "Volcano in the Valley," *India Today*, 15 August 1986, 57.

18. Ibid, 57.

19. A report titled "The Bhopal Bonanza" in *India Today* (30 September 1987, 80) reports that lawyers and private medical practitioners have significantly benefitted from the tragedy. "Many of the estimated 69,000 methyl isocyanide (MIC) patients have turned to the private doctors rather than stand in queues in governmental hospitals." In addition, when the state government announced it would provide a subsistence grant of Rs 1,500 to gas-affected families, fictitious identity papers were used to claim the money. Fraud was eventually detected in a total of 551 cases involving Rs 8.26 crores. Under the Welfare of Gas Victims, it is reported that the government initiated to build a new airport and a new electric trolley system for the city.

20. Segments of this section have appeared as "Research Communication" in *Journal of Developing Societies*, 5.

21. Agarwal, Chopra and Sharma, *State of India's Environment*, 42-43.

22. These are based on my personal correspondence with Mr. Bhatt during 1986-87.

23. Sunderlal Bahuguna, *Chipko Message* (Sylyara, India: Chipko Information Centre, 1984); also by the same author "People's Response to Ecological Crises in the Hill Areas," in J. Bandyopadhyay (et al.) *India's Environment: Crises and Responses*, (Dehra Dun: Natraj, 1985).

24. *A Directory of Non-Governmental Organizations in Environment,* (New Delhi: Government of India, Department of Environment, 1984), 39.

In 1989, the Department of Environment, through its Environmental Information System (ENVIS) has published a new directory.

25. "Ganga Fisherfolk: Between Ancient Oppression and Modern Destruction," in *The State of India's Environment: 1984-85*, ed. by Anil Agarwal and Sunita Narain (New Delhi: Centre for Science and Environment, 1985), 47.

26. "A Town Goes on Strike," in *State of India's Environment* by Agarwal, 35.

27. Quoted in Agarwal, ibid, 302.

28. These interviews were conducted during my field trip from December 1985 through January 1986.

29. Thomas Mathew, "Interview: Environment for Survival" (an interview with B.B. Vohra, the then chairman of National Committee on Environmental Planning and Coordination) in *Indian International Centre Journal* (December, 1982), 361.

30. A. Bhargava & M. Bhargava, "Public Awareness About Air Pollution: An Opinion Survey for Jaipur City," *Scavenger*, 6-11.

31. T. Sekar, "Role of Newspapers in Creating Mass Concern with Environmental Issues in India," *International Journal of Environmental Studies*, 17: 115-120.

32. The Centre for Science and Environment is located in New Delhi and brings out several important journals and reports on environment, including the *The Status of Environment in India*.

33. F. Sandbach, "A Further Look at the Environment as a Political Issue," *International Journal of Environmental Studies*, 12: 99-110.

34. Enloe, *Politics of Pollution*.

35. Data on environmental NGOs has been compiled from *A Directory of Non-Governmental Organizations in Environment* (note #24).

36. Philip Lowe and Jane Goyder, *Environmental Groups in Politics* (London: Allen & Urwin, 1983), 42-45.

37. Ramesh Menon, "Dhrangadhra: Dangerous Discharge," *India To-*

day, 15 May 1984, 88.

38. Ibid.

39. Samuel J. Eldersveld, et al., *The Citizen and the Administrator in a Developing Country* (Chicago: Scott, Foresman, 1968), 133-134.

40. "Soviet Losing Interest in Tehri Dam," *India Abroad*, February 17, 1989; "Can India Woo Foreign Business?" *The Christian Science Monitor*, 23 February 1989, 9.

41. Taken from *The Report of the Committee for Recommending Legislative Measures and Administrative Machinery for Ensuring Environmental Protection* (New Delhi: Government of India, Department of Environment, 1980), 37.

42. A voluminous literature exists on Indian political parties and on the Indian electorate. For political parties, see Horst Hartmann, *Political Parties in India* (New Delhi: Meenakshi, 1982); S.N. Sadasivan, *Party and Democracy in India* (New Delhi: Tata McGraw-Hill, 1977); and V.M. Sirsikar and L. Fernandes, *Indian Political Parties* (Meerut: Meenakshi, 1984). On elections, some useful studies are David Butler, et al., *A Compendium of Indian Elections* (New Delhi: Arnold-Heinemann, 1984); V.B. Singh and S. Bose, *Elections in India: Data Handbook on Lok Sabha Elections, 1952-80* (New Delhi: Sage, 1984); and John O. Field, *Consolidating Democracy: Politicization and Partisanship in India* (New Delhi: Manohar, 1980).

43. Hardgrave, *Government and Politics in a Developing Nation*, 234.

44. Ibid, 268.

45. Lowe, *Environmental Groups in Politics*, 66.

CHAPTER 7

Environmental Politics
in a Broader Perspective

T he major argument raised in this study relates to the nature of environmental politics and policy-making in India. It is argued that the environmental issue can best be understood as a reconciliatory issue and that environmental politics, at best, is the politics of reconciliation between the real goals of development and the desired goals of environmental preservation. Further, the political perspective model based on an understanding of political calculations is forwarded as an appropriate model for comprehending environmental policy developments in India. The analysis of the environmental policy process highlights several policy patterns which are valuable not only in understanding the "politicalness" of the environmental issue or in acknowledging the predominant role of politics in India, but also in gaining important insights to several basic political concepts. While summarizing the findings of the analysis, the purpose of this chapter is to relate these findings to more fundamental debates in the literature, especially the unfolding debate on the autonomy of the state as an institution.

The environmental record of India is one of the most impressive ones in the Third World, and based on the high level of governmental activity, it may even compete with industrialized nations. Since 1974, there has been a surge of governmental activity in the environmental policy area: major national laws have been passed; a centralized environmental bureaucracy has been created; and the government's share of environmental expenditures has been increased tremendously. Interestingly, this governmental fervor is also matched by an equally visible show of public enthusiasm: non-governmental environmental groups have mushroomed; anti-regime protests focusing specifically on environmental issues have mounted; and more importantly, the media coverage of environmental issues has also matured. In brief, the last two decades have witnessed the arrival of the environmental movement in the nation. Due to the increased environmental awareness, the environmental issue has slowly gained political saliency and has come to the forefront of the nation's policy agenda.

Despite an accelerated pace of activity, the environmental movement has made only a limited impact on the quality of the environment. The rhetoric has failed to break the patterns of environmental destruction in any significant way: forests continue to disappear; the level of pollution in major rivers remains well over the acceptable limits; and the concentration of atmospheric pollution in most urban areas stays beyond dangerous limits. Although it is difficult to argue whether the levels of pollution and defor- estation would have remained the same even without any governmental interference, nevertheless, it is apparent that the intensity of the govern- mental effort did not result in a similarly intense level of performance. Often, programs have proven to be totally ineffectual. The obvious example is the forest policy objective set forth in 1952. According to the objective, the   forest cover of the nation was to be increased from 20 percent (in 1952) to 33 percent of the total land area. Ironically, the forest cover in 1987--after 25 years of policy implementation--was only 14 percent of the land area.   Clearly, the Indian environmental policy is faced with an implementation deficit.

Most countries, regardless of their level of economic prosperity and political openness, confront the problem of environmental policy deficit, i.e., the gap between policy objectives and policy performance. As early as the 1950s, the inadequacies of Western democracies were exposed by researchers. Following the failure of these governments in curbing the rate of environmental degradation, some scholars argued that political openness was not conducive to environmental management.[1] They hypothesized that compared to an open political system (that of Western countries), a closed system was better able to protect its environment.[2] Political "openness" invited unnecessary delays by transforming environmental issues into po- litical issues. A closed political system, it was assumed, was able to find the best solution because it was equipped to tackle the problem from a scientific and technological stand point, whereas an open system was necessarily forced to search for a "politically feasible" solution, because it had to balance various conflicting interests. Nevertheless, the futility of this argument was quickly exposed by subsequent case studies undertaken in "closed" systems, particularly in China and the Soviet Union.[3] The studies revealed that despite being unchallenged during policy formulation, the closed governments were highly vulnerable to political challenges during policy implementation. Lester Ross, in his study of the China's environmental policy, concluded that local bureaucrats possessed substantial autonomy and discretion in their implementation exercises, even when clear-cut central directives for their actions existed.[4] Needless to say, even in cases where the decisions taken at the top were adequate from an environmental stand point, severe implementation flaws persisted. Consequently, the environmentally sound decisions of the Beijing government almost always faced resistance from the local bureaucrats who were more concerned with immediate economic rewards rather than with far-fetched environmental gains.

According to Sovietologists, the Soviet environmental policy also suffers from the same tragic fate where local officials readily sacrifice the long-term environmental gains in order to fulfill their current production quotas.[5] In brief, the Chinese and the Soviet policies fail to incorporate the appraisal of the environment-related performance of their local units into the overall evaluation criteria of performance. In the end, the failure of the closed systems in managing their environmental crises emerges from the same set of political variables that also render the efforts of the open systems largely ineffectual.[6] Despite their monopoly over decision-making, the closed systems also fail to "internalize" the environmental concern.

Environmental policy deficits are common in the decentralized societies of the West. Research work in this area has focused on two separate dimensions—policy implementation and policy impact. Assuming that policy deficit emerges from the lack of implementation, the first group of scholars targets its efforts toward identifying the factors that motivate a government to try harder than others.[7] Their research, after testing several conventional factors for their influence on the implementation of environmental policies across nations, establishes the explanatory power of political competitiveness, resource availability, public pressure and the severity of the crisis itself.[8] On the other hand, the second group of scholars focusing its attention on the actual impact of policies, rather than the implementation per se, is puzzled to find that even when processes diverge across nations, the outcomes emerging from them, in fact, converge. In other words, most developed countries confront a roughly similar deficit problem, despite their level of implementation efforts. In his attempt to explain this paradox, Badaracco examined the nature of scientific knowledge.[9] For him, not only was the technology available to every government similar, but it was also limited in its application to contain environmental deterioration to the desirable limits. Hence, most governments had no alternative but to rely on the same limited global knowledge to solve their environmental problems. This limitation, according to Badaracco, led to similar policy performances in the countries of Europe and North America.

The experiences of developing countries in environmental management are even less promising. Their environmental policy deficits are well-documented in several case studies, which expose a large number of independent variables responsible for this poor performance.[10] Economic hardships, political uncertainty and administrative incompetence are the three broad categories that can accommodate various specific factors, such as the lack of leadership, corruption, poverty, ethnic conflicts and cultural beliefs. Being a developing country, India is not free from any of the above-mentioned systemic weaknesses. In addition, it faces several additional challenges emerging particularly from its large population base and a rapidly politicizing citizenry.

The environmental policy deficit in India emerges from a host of political, administrative, economic and cultural sources. Moreover, political processes in the nation are not geared toward reducing the deficit; they are instead tuned to find an equilibrium where the environmental issue can be made non-threatening. The environmental process, therefore, emphasizes non-scientific, politically feasible, and reconciliatory objectives. It is apparent that the issue is being coerced into adapting to the prevailing social ideology and culture, and not vice versa. Despite the governmental rhetoric on the importance of physical environment, the last two decades have not seen any change in either the formal planning style of the government or the informal behavior of the society. A strong desire to reconcile, rather than to confront, has been prevalent throughout the policy process. In the following section, I attempt to summarize the findings of the study and draw some broader conclusions based on this case study.

Two major policy patterns bearing significant political meaning for the policy process in India can be identified here. The first policy pattern refers to the pre-formulation (issue-creation and agenda-setting) stage of the policy process. Contrary to the experiences of the industrialized nations where public opinion has played a leading role in the environmental issue-creation process, the impetus for environmental movement in India came from the government itself. While the contribution of international and local forces cannot be altogether dismissed, it is safe to argue that it was the national government's rhetoric that in fact provided legitimacy to the environmental issue. The second policy pattern refers to the post-formulation (strategy selection and the implementation) stage of the policy process. In this case, the government clearly chose regulation as the primary policy tool for environmental protection, despite the fact that it had neither the ability, nor the resources to shoulder this responsibility. The two policy patterns are discussed in greater detail in the following two sections on agenda-setting and administrative capabilities.

Environmental Politics and Agenda-Setting

Agenda-setting is a process through which issues are brought to the agenda for political consideration. Two types of agendas have been identified in the literature: (1) social or informal agenda and (2) institutional or formal agenda.[11] In a normal democratic setting, issues emerge on the social agenda because of their relevance to the public, or at least a part of the public. At any given time, several issues must exist on the social agenda for the simple fact that the needs and demands of the members of society are independent, and often even contradictory, of each other. In the next stage, certain issues—issues that are able to command substantial attention from the political community—are elevated to the status of political issues and are placed on the institutional agenda. While the social agenda is unstructured and fragmented, the institutional agenda by no means is always well-manifested and structured. In fact, several institutional agendas may exist simultaneously and may create jurisdictional confusion and rivalry. Even the most centralized societies are not free from this multiplicity of agendas. Lester Ross's study has revealed the existence of multiple sub-institutional agendas existing within one legitimate institutional agenda in China. At least visibly, there are usually as many institutional agendas as there are sources of political power. Thus, the executive, legislature and judiciary at national, state and local levels are all legitimate institutional agendas. Often, the bureaucracy and army also possess the ability to have their independent agendas or to shape institutional agendas in a decisive way.

India, unlike the centrally directed societies, offers a wide range of legitimate and competing institutional agendas to its citizens. The citizens also exploit a great range of methods, including street demonstrations and protests, to influence the institutional agendas at every level. A comparative look at the cross-national statistics reveals that the Indian public takes full advantage of these agenda-influencing tools: India ranks nearly at the top on most indicators of protest activity. Yet, the analysis of the environmental agenda-setting indicates that (1) social agendas are unable to provide guidance to institutional agendas; (2) there is a lack of cooperation between national institutional agendas and sub-national institutional agendas; (3) the executive controls and shapes the legislative agenda; and finally (4) personalities, and not issues, are paramount in giving political saliency to issues.

Environmental issues, such as deforestation, pollution and soil erosion, have been on local agendas, both social and institutional, since the 1920s. Even in the early 1900s, complaints and protests were lodged in several pockets of the nation. However, there was a considerable lack of political support for the issue. The central government remained silent up until the 1970s. Although several environment-related areas were constitutionally beyond the jurisdictional scope of the central government, but even where such a limitation did not exist, the government restricted itself to an unusually passive role. Contextual factors played a major role in diverting the attention of the national government. The major reason identified in this study is the composition of the institutional agenda itself. Being a British colony for two hundred years and, prior to that, being under foreign domination of Moguls for several centuries, India entrusted its leaders with the paramount task of nation-building. Moreover, the nation did not enjoy a secluded and safe international milieu; from the cradle itself it had to face a hostile relationship with its neighbors, resulting in several wars throughout its childhood. The wars robbed the Indian leaders of their opportunity to direct the nation's economy and to nourish its cultural heritage. Consequently, leaders faced serious social and economic challenges involving ethnic conflicts, mass poverty, public safety and social corruption. Fortunately, the nation did not suffer the crisis of political instability--so commonly experienced by other newly decolonized countries. Yet, the stress arising from international insecurity and social turbulence crippled the nation's economy. Consequently, the institutional agendas remained filled with other pressing issues. The environmental issue, thus, was forced either to take a back seat or to piggy-back ride on other seemingly similar issues.

It was not until the early 1970s that the national government was able to treat environmental protection as an independent issue. How did this change in priorities occur? Did natural catastrophes claim the attention of the government? Or did the society display a significant change in its attitudes?[12] Or was it merely an act of imitation influenced by the post-materialism of the West?

Previous studies reveal that agendas can be altered by a number of factors. First, calamities and catastrophes may augment the need for action and may consolidate political support for a long-standing issue. Japan's experience with the pollution issue related to the breakout of Itai Itai, which gave its local governments an unprecedented power to interfere in the activities of the private sector.[13] Similarly, the London Fog became the impetus for environmental action in Great Britain. In India, no single catastrophe can be readily identified, although several areas were suffering from serious pollution and erosion problems. The problems, however, were seen as localized in nature. The policy strategy was to compensate the victim, rather than to prevent the problem. Consequently, the issue was handled by health departments rather than by planning bodies. It must be pointed out that the social awareness of environmental problems was not totally lacking; nevertheless, it was not ripe enough to have given the environmental issue an aura of political urgency. Paradoxically, once the issue was taken over by the government, the public awareness started to mature and manifest itself through nationwide protests and demonstrations. Thus, the sudden rise in the public's environmental activism, which had surprised observers in the late 1970s, was in fact only the culmination of the long-standing environmental awareness in the society.

Second, as discussed in the electoral political model, internal pressures emerging from public activism may also invite governmental action and, thus, may alter the agenda. Several studies, after focusing on this particular aspect, conclude that public opinion plays a decisive role, albeit reasons for public participation vary from country to country. For Ronald Inglehart, the public's interest in the quality of environment results from a change in their overall values from materialism to post-materialism.[14] For Sears et al., public opinion reacts only to self-threatening situations.[15] Based on this assumption, the perception of the people regarding the severity of the problem, and not necessarily the problem itself, is the root cause of public activism. Yet, for other observers, the concern for the environment is genuine and it results from the increased understanding of the implications of environmental degradation.[16]

While public participation in other policy areas is quite common in India, it is only reactive and indirect in the environmental policy area. Until 1980, the environmental issue did not even appear on the platforms of major political parties. During the 1980 general elections, the three national parties—the Congress (I), the Janata Party, and the Congress (O)—had only made passing remarks in favor of environmental protection. At the same time, the support from organized political groups was also negligible. Being unaware of the extent of destruction and the feasibility of solutions, existing interest groups treated the environmental issue only as an issue of secondary importance. Moreover, the voice of the scientific community was muffled and obscure, while the environmental news reporting was almost frivolous. Media interest, which Cynthia Enloe cites as one of the crucial independent variables affecting the emergence of the environmental issue, did not culminate until after the government had already taken the initiative. Despite the localized nature of the environmental awareness, it is surprising that even local newspapers did not allow environmental reporting until a decade after the government's acceptance of the environmental issue. Therefore, the "electoral political" and the "organizational initiative" models of issue emergence, supported by the scholars of North America and Western Europe, do not hold true in India.

Third, it is believed that agendas are frequently altered because of the diffusion of issues from one agenda to another. Indeed, developing countries are vulnerable to diffusions. Particularly in the environmental policy area, the universality of the problem demands a worldwide approach to solve the crisis. Furthermore, since environmental solutions require sophisticated technology, most developing nations look toward developed nations for assistance. However, this borrowing is not limited to only technological tools, but is stretched further toward political directions as well. The evidence suggest that policymakers in India consulted several arrangements throughout the world before selecting their policy strategy.[17] It is not surprising, then, that what emerged from the process was a hybrid of several traditions in environmental management, especially the British and the American. Unfortunately, as this study indicates, these traditions are not necessarily compatible with each other, nor are they agreeable with the Indian traditions in general. The incompatibility has ensued much jurisdictional overlapping and confusion.

The Indian government embraced the environmental issue in the early 1970s at a time when the issue was of paramount interest to the leading Western nations as well as to the international community. The 1972 United Nation's Conference on Human Environment provided the needed motivation to the Indian government to establish its first national level environmental committee. The committee, though only exploratory in nature, allowed the institutionalization of the environmental issue within the realms of the rigid governmental structure. It also provided a platform for the scientific community to raise its concerns. In addition, it worked as the link station for international cooperation and information exchange for several years.

Thus, the formulation of the Indian environmental policy reflected not only policy diffusion but also issue diffusion. International forces clearly played a significant role in the legitimization of the environmental issue. Nevertheless, this role should not be over-emphasized. I argue that the Indian soil was already fertile for the issue. The potential of the issue was clearly visible to its leaders, who so willingly embraced it. Given that there was no mounting public pressure, it is incomprehensible why the government should have fostered such a difficult issue and, thus, should have placed itself in a trying situation. Therefore, the model of "issue diffusion," in terms of international pressures, which has been most often accepted by the scholars analyzing the environmental politics of developing countries, is valid, albeit its validity should not be mistaken for its being the solitary explanation.

The Indian environmental agenda, as I argue in this study, was primarily shaped by the political calculations of the leaders of the nation. The motives for support (by leaders and the system) stretched beyond electoral victory. Leaders, especially Mrs. Indira Gandhi, took personal interest in the issue and championed it for its moral and political appeal. It is interesting to note that despite a system of decentralized agendas and a culture of regional assertiveness, Mrs. Gandhi was able to mold the national political agenda in a decisive way. The influence of personalities on agenda-setting is a little studied area, yet it holds promise for the further understanding of the environmental politics in the Third World.

This study highlights the reasons behind Mrs. Gandhi's unquestionable interest in the environment. With the help of Mrs. Gandhi's personality traits, several factors can be pointed out. The first and the foremost was her motherly concern for the nation and her perception of India being her personal responsibility. It was Mrs. Gandhi's genuine concern for the welfare of the people that justified her support for the environmental cause. However, there were several other political reasons which pointed to the reconciliatory aspect of the environmental issue. The environmental issue related well with the overall populist philosophy of the ruling party. The early 1970s were the experimental years for Mrs. Gandhi, when she tried to assert her style in national policies. Any issue area that would bring the administration closer to the people and away from the image of the corporate ruler was welcomed by her. Environmental issues, especially pollution control and land utilization, offered two-sided benefits to the administration. On one hand, the rhetoric helped Mrs. Gandhi in building a positive rapport with the public; and at the same time, new regulatory mechanisms provided her with the tools to control the powerful industrial community. In essence, regulations served as additional means of obtaining patronage.

How Mrs. Gandhi could shape the political agenda and legitimize the environmental issue despite a powerful development lobby in India is another intriguing question. Some factors that helped her assert her preferences are obvious. First, as a prime minister in a parliamentary system she was legally and constitutionally permitted to control the national agenda. Nevertheless, this characteristic of the parliamentary system can not be generalized. Studies indicate that prime ministers are often controlled by the preferences of their cabinet members, party members and even constituents. Mrs. Gandhi, however, was able to display a considerable amount of autonomy in outlining national priorities.

Second, Mrs. Gandhi's position was unique in the sense that she not only secured an unprecedented majority in the national parliament, but she also enjoyed an instant credibility from the people for being the daughter of Jawahar Lal Nehru.

Third, none of the political parties formed any sound opposition to the ruling party. Its closest rival, the Congress(O), had already suffered a major defeat in the 1971 elections.

Fourth, Mrs. Gandhi had won a major national war against Pakistan and was viewed as *Durga*, the goddess of bravery and courage.

Fifth, due to the colonial legacy, the style of administration in India was still paternalistic, giving enormous powers to the leader of the nation.

Sixth, India's emphasis on socialism had traditionally allowed the government to intervene in new areas of social welfare. The issue of environmental protection was undoubtedly viewed as a governmental responsibility.

And the last but not the least important factor was the "patronage system" that had gradually turned into a national political characteristic. Even though the feudal structures of the past had disappeared due to the growing awareness of democratic values and individual rights, feudal attitudes still prevailed, especially in the countryside, giving rise to a unique political culture. Under Mrs. Gandhi's administration, loyalty was the most valuable qualification for political offices. Such a system had a natural reactionary impact on political processes in the sense that the processes became intolerant even to inside challenges. Mrs. Gandhi surrounded herself with loyalists; therefore, any open discussion on issues and policies within the realm of the established norms was nearly impossible. Once Mrs. Gandhi showed her personal commitment to the environmental issue, the issue instantly gained political credibility. This partly explains why major environmental legislation, such as the Water Act of 1974 and the Air Act of 1981, were passed nearly unopposed in India.

One may infer from the experience of India that personalities exert significant influence on political agendas. Of the three models of issue-creation identified earlier in the introductory chapter, none plays close attention to the "personality" dimension. In fact, I argued earlier that none of the models treats politics as a substantial influencing variable. While politics plays a paramount role in the electoral politics model, its role is reduced to being merely a motive for electoral victory. Consequently, the emergence of the environmental issue in an electorally non-competitive society cannot be explained with the help of the electoral politics model. However, the political perspective model (based on a broader study of political calculations) relies on political factors and takes into consideration a wide range of political calculations other than electoral victory. It may, therefore, explain the emergence of the environmental issue in those societies where public is quiescent and bureaucracy is non-innovative. It may also explain why issue diffusion affects different societies in different ways.

Table 7.1 highlights the basic differences in the policy processes based on the electoral politics model and the political perspective model. The policy formation process under the electoral politics model is identified as an open process that quickly results in an over-ambitious and non-comprehensive policy. The pressure of electoral politics leaves very little room for the development of a comprehensive policy. Conversely, the policy formation process is relatively closed and consultative under the political perspective model. The resulting policy, thus, is comprehensive albeit vague,

Table 7.1
Policy Process Under Electoral-Political and Political-Perspective Models of Issue-Creation

Policy Characteristics	Electoral-Political	Political-Perspective
Policy Formation	Open/Quick	Closed/Consultative
Policy Strategy	Over-ambitious/Non-comprehensive	Comprehensive/Vague
Implementation	Hasty/Uneven	Unwilling/Inconsistent
Role of Public	Active/Surveillant	Quiescent/Indirect

giving policy makers enough flexibility to interpret it according to their political needs. Similarly, policy implementation also differs significantly under the two models. Public scrutiny, under the electoral politics model, puts an unnecessary pressure on policy implementors to show substantial results in a short time span. Consequently, the process of implementation is hasty and unpredictable. In addition, it appears to be inadequate because of the over-ambitious choices made during the policy formation process. On the other hand, implementation, under the political perspective model, depends heavily on the political calculations of policy actors. It is often unwilling and inconsistent. The role of the public is also quite different in the two models. While an active and aware public is a pre-requisite for the electoral politics model, the political perspective model assumes a quiescent role of the public.

Environmental Politics and Administrative Capabilities

Since the nucleus of the Indian environmental policy is state regulation, the question of the administrative capability of the Indian government becomes crucial. The analysis of the environmental policy process highlights several paradoxes related to the scope and power of public administrators in India. The Indian bureaucracy has a unique love-hate relationship with the public. Whereas its organizational strength is a source of continuity and stability to the society, its rigidity is a cause for major concern. So far, at least 20 different commissions and committees have been set up to consider the issue of administrative rigidity and incompetence with little or no real success.

The administrative capability of the environmental bureaucracy has always been questionable. The capability of the proposed environmental bureaucracy was debated even during the enactment of the environmental laws against water and air pollution. Why then, did the Indian government choose the policy strategy that depended primarily on its administrative capability? Once again, we turn to the issue-creation process, discussed in the previous section, for initial explanations. Since the interest in the environment was generated by international sources and since the impetus was provided by the upper echelon of the government itself, it was inevitable that the government would adopt the "state-regulated environmental management" as its primary policy strategy. Moreover, since the government lacked the support of the public, its best strategy was to opt for the least controversial option available.

Roughly, a government has three major policy strategies to chose from. First is the "hands out" strategy or the strategy of no action. In this context, environmental resources are treated as merit goods, whose supply and demand are directed by society's culture. Government, thus, is free of any formal obligation to act. Needless to say, most governments followed this strategy until recently.

Second is the policy of "guided market mechanisms," in which environmental goods are treated as property goods for which ownership rights do not exist. In this context, the role of a government is limited to establishing the property rights and providing the coordination whenever necessary. It is assumed that once property rights are established, the cost of the environment is automatically internalized. Its use, like that of other raw materials, is afforded in the market. Market forces, thus, allow for an equilibrium to emerge--an equilibrium where the optimum use of environmental resources is possible. The strategy of "guided market mechanisms," however, has only limited application. Several environmental goods, such as wildlife, simply do not have any market utility; therefore, their market price cannot be established. In addition, the strategy requires an established capitalistic economic base, which is available only in a handful of nations. Socialist governments find such strategy incompatible with their basic political philosophy, while most developing societies suffer from feudalistic practices. In a feudalistic economy, the fair price of goods cannot be established because goods can be bought or sold for other intangible benefits, such as status, loyalty or ethnic identities.

The third and the most widely accepted strategy is the strategy of "state activism," where environmental goods are viewed as scarce common goods. Their "commonness" makes it inevitable that the goods must suffer from the "tragedy of the commons" and their scarcity makes it necessary that their demand and supply be controlled. Since individuals are motivated by their own self-interest, the responsibility of controlling the environment falls upon the shoulders of the government, which is a selfless body motivated by the welfare of the people, or at least the majority of the people. This assumption allows the government to act as a guardian in the management of the environment; thus, it invites state activism. Most governments rely on regulations, albeit to a varying degree and for different reasons. Socialist governments opt for the strategy because this suits their political ideology; democratic governments choose the strategy because it allows them to establish a policy direction; and the governments of the Third World select it because it invites the least amount of challenge and controversy.

Nonetheless, the regulatory strategy offers some unique political benefits. It gives the pretense of urgency, a sense of governmental activeness,
and also a means of reconciliation. The regulatory approach in India, for
instance, allows the two conflicting policies—of economic growth and of
environmental preservation—to coexist. The changing needs of the society
continue to find and modify the equilibrium between the two. Even though
"eco-development" remains as the overall planning objective of the government, the emphasis within planning bodies dwindles between economic
growth and environmental protection from year to year. The government,
thus, enjoys a certain degree of flexibility with its regulatory strategy. Other
policy strategies, i.e. the strategies of "no-action" and "guided market
mechanisms," clearly do not provide this flexibility to the government.

Also, regulations are most cost-effective, because they involve the least
amount of political confrontation and controversy. They are also preferred
by state authorities because they require the least amount of state power
to be delegated. In most cases, regulations enhance, rather than diminish,
a government's control over society.

Considering Mrs. Gandhi's personal commitment for the issue and her
authoritative style of administration, it is not surprising that the Indian
government opted for the policy of "state-regulated environmental management." The performance record of the policy, however, is dismal, partly
because of the nature of the issue itself, but mostly because of the inherent
characteristics of the Indian bureaucracy in general.

There are three major caveats to the administrative capability of the
Indian government: structural, behavioral, and contextual. The analysis of
the environmental policy has brought all these challenges to the forefront;
and therefore, a brief look in to each of these categories is necessary.
Structural caveats emerge, to some extent, because of the nation's colonial
past, which shapes the organizational disposition of the Indian bureaucracy.
As established by the British, the Indian bureaucracy was structured to foster
compliance and loyalty. Legalism, proceduralism, formalism, and adherence
were some of the ground rules for the rational functioning of this Weberian
bureaucracy. The merit-based system of entrance was also introduced to
attract the best-talented people into the government. The same structure
was kept intact even after the nation's independence from the British in
1947, partly because the leaders of the nation recognized the importance
of the bureaucracy as an institution, and partly because no other alternate
method of organizing the bureaucracy was considered to be promising at
that time. Today, the role of the bureaucracy has changed considerably.

Bureaucrats are not only required to enforce political decisions; they are also expected to give advice, direction and guidance in the overall planning process. They are the development administrators. Nevertheless, bureaucrats under the current rigid system are neither socialized, nor are they equipped to carry on this task. They lack responsiveness and innovation in their administrative style.

The environmental bureaucracy not only inherits these structural short-comings, but it also suffers from some of its own organizational weaknesses. In the past, the responsibility of environmental management was dispersed in several departments. Now, even when most of these units have been brought under the umbrella of the Ministry for Environment and Forestry, the units maintain their sub-level autonomy. Additionally, being the late-comer, the environmental bureaucracy is considered to be an outsider; therefore, it faces hostility from other horizontally situated ministries and departments. The nature of the task, which requires coordination and supervision over other areas, such as health, urban planning, energy, transport, etc., makes the environmental bureaucracy the prime target of resistance and animosity. The middle-level and street-level environmental units face multiple pressures—from horizontal as well as from vertical sources. In order to avoid this pressure, they engage in procedural activities and adhere to rules and regulations.

Another source of challenge for the administrative performance comes from behavioral factors. The Indian Civil Service, under the British, had enjoyed a considerable degree of social and financial status. Today, due to the opening up of several other equally rewarding professional areas, the status of the civil service jobs is reduced considerably. According to surveys, the morale of civil servants is affected by this trend. Also, the public's faith and trust in the bureaucracy has eroded over the last few decades. Bureaucrats are viewed as corrupt, lazy and incompetent. These perceptions have demoralized the civil services and have given birth to a paradoxical behavior: bureaucrats are becoming increasingly aloof of their responsibilities on one hand, and they are being more aware of their authority on the other hand. To compensate for the loss in their status, they keep a tight control over state resources, often using them as tools to buy social and financial rewards. The position of civil servants becomes crucial in a political system that revolves around patronage and loyalty. Studies indicate that this paradox of having "less status yet more power" is a prime working force behind the Indian bureaucratic behavior.

The behavioral traits have a direct effect on the workings of the environmental bureaucracy. The strength of the environmental bureaucracy depends, to a great extent, on the support that it gets from the public. However, the environmental bureaucracy of India suffers from a very low level of public trust. In fact, the majority of public complaints and media criticism is directed toward environmental agencies. Forest departments are viewed with suspicion and water boards are dismissed as feeble. Based on my personal observations and interviews, I may argue that the environmental bureaucracy is seen as a nuisance in the system. Industrialists view it as an additional hand in the list of many to whom the "grease money" has to be given in order to get governmental approval. Environmentalists, on the other hand, see it as incompetent and insensitive to the public cause. In addition, the position of the street-level bureaucrats is open to even harsher criticism. Their discretionary powers are viewed with suspicion by nearly everyone.

The third source of challenge to the effective public administration stems from contextual variables. The context in which public officials in the nation operate is not conducive to effective policy implementation. At the top management level, bureaucrats face pressures from the political and economic elite. Since the party structure is unpredictable, most interest groups direct their lobbying efforts more toward public officials than toward politicians per se. Public agencies alone can provide them with long-lasting commitments. Thus, public agencies are often forced to perform the task of interest aggregation by accommodating and balancing diverse interests. Whereas public agencies benefit from this politicization because it gives them an important political clout, public policies necessarily suffer from the practice. This double role puts an unnecessary stress on the performance of individual public administrators.

Contextual variables also limit the administrative capability of the government at the local level. It is the street-level bureaucrats who must, in the end, interpret and enforce policy objectives. According to several studies in the West, street-level bureaucrats possess considerable discretionary powers in their interpretation of the details of regulations.[18] However, this study of the environmental administration in India reveals that local level bureaucrats are greatly constrained in the exercise of their discretionary power because of the prevailing political and social culture, which I have referred to as the "local policy culture" (LPC).

The LPC of India is shaped by three predominant forces: social heterogeneity, semi-capitalism and a highly competitive electoral system. Social heterogeneity impedes the emergence of a true Weberian-style bureaucracy. Bureaucrats fail to be rational in a society that places heavy emphasis on ethnic identities. Individual identities in such a society are manifested through their ties to a particular class, caste, religion, region and social circle. Consequently, what is viewed as a rational behavior from the Weberian standpoint may very well be an irrational behavior from the ethnic viewpoint. The reverse is also true. Civil servants, for instance, may show favoritism based on their loyalties to their family, class, caste or religion, which are clearly more real to them than their political obligations.

Similarly, the semi-capitalistic system, existing especially in the countryside, also hampers the implementing ability of public administrators. In the environmental policy area, where most policy actions must challenge the status quo, bureaucrats often find it difficult to undermine the power of the elite whose interests are best served in maintaining the status quo. In situations where confrontation is necessary, bureaucrats are left with two choices: either they may conform with the local elite and enjoy the fruits of being in the elite circle, or they may confront the elite and bear the brunt of political wrath from their own superiors. I may add that more often than not, the local elite are well-connected with regional or even national level bureaucrats and politicians. Therefore, a confrontation brings an embarrassing situation for the local bureaucrat who has to face vertical pressures coming from his/her own administrative unit.

Social forestry in Gujarat is a good example of the elite power, where most of the governmental assistance and subsidies were exploited by big farmers. Surveys indicate that only 15 percent of the beneficiary farmers fell in the category of "marginal farmers." In addition, it was also found that more than 60 percent of the trees were planted on the land that was already being used for either cash or food crops.[19] The planting of eucalyptus trees under the farm forestry program also indicated that, beyond adhering to written rules, the local bureaucrats were limited in the exercise of their power. Eucalyptus was hazardous to soil and it also failed to meet the basic objectives of farm forestry. Similarly, the experience of state water boards suggested that the administrative capability of local bureaucrats was restricted because they lacked the political support from their higher-up authorities on one hand, and the moral support from the public on the other hand. Industrialists viewed them as a mere annoyance and were willing to pay the cost of passing through legal loopholes rather than be meaningfully involved in the making of decisions.

A high level of competition in elections further aggravates the problems arising from the existence of semi-capitalism and ethnicism. Since elections are unpredictable, politicians often search for predictable means of securing loyalty from voters. And, since issue-based loyalties are unreliable, politicians opt for the loyalties based on ethnic identities. The highly competitive nature of elections also strengthens the power of the local feudal[20] lords, whose support is essential for electoral victory. Politicians, thus, engage in a corporate-style alliance with feudal lords and continuously trade patronage and favors with them. In the case study of social forestry, this dependence was clearly revealed. The local career officials bore the burden of this arrangement. They joined the alliance by adhering to the procedures while ignoring the goals.

The local policy culture of India, in general, limits the administrative capability of public administrators. The context in which public officials operate is neither conducive for change, nor does it offer any incentives to public administrators to be innovative and objective. Despite their enormous responsibilities, public officials lack any jurisdictional and legal rights to carry out their task. They lack the support of a constituency enjoyed by their American counterparts; and at the same time, they also do not possess the cultural protection granted to their British counterparts.

Environmental Politics: State-centered or Society-centered?

The question of state autonomy has drawn considerable scholarly attention since the publication of *Bringing the State Back In* by Peter Evans, Dietrich Rueschemeyer and Theda Skocpol.[21] Although it was not my intention to use India's environmental policy as a testing ground for the debate between state-centrist and society-centrist, nevertheless, I feel that several findings of this study bear significant implications for the debate. Based on the state-centrist argument, the role of the state as an institution is critical in the understanding of political processes, and it should not be dismissed by viewing the state either as an arbitrator or as an impotent actor.[22] Even though there is no consensus regarding the definition of the term "state"[23] it is agreed that "state" very much exists in the form of the collectivity of those who use its powers on its behalf. James N. Rosenau defines the concept of state as:

> consisting of the norms of governing relationships, the habits of voluntary and coerced compliance, and the practices of cooperation through which large numbers of people form and sustain a collectivity that possesses sovereign authority with respect to them....

The state finds expression in those individuals who act on its behalf, employing its force and applying its laws so as to preserve and enhance the norms, habits, and practices of the collectivity in its entirety.[24]

The state-centrist school has offered three insights to the workings of the state. First, the state has an autonomous and explicit preference; therefore, its actions are often independent, or may even be conflicting, of the majority or the dominant class. Second, the state is constrained by its surroundings. In other words, social and economic forces shape and define the sphere within which the state may reflect its autonomy. Third and final, the state is persistent: while its activities are influenced by individual personalities, there are some patterns of state activity that persist beyond individuals and time. The three hypothetical statements, since then, have been well tested by a number of case studies in developed as well as in developing countries.[25] Most studies, however, failed to give any conclusive explanations regarding the degree of state autonomy or the causes of state constraints. Nevertheless, the argument of some degree of state autonomy was accepted in most studies.

Based on the analysis of the environmental policy process, it is my contention that the assumption of one "collectivity" on the part of state actors is inaccurate. In the context of India, for example, at least two state collectivities seem to coexist, one at the local level and one at the national level. These two collectivities do not share a single objective; neither do they possess a single behavioral motive. In fact, in the environmental area, both often work not only independent of each other, but also in conflict with each other. Yet both collectivities accept and adapt to the idea of the other's existence.

Most case studies attempting to support either state-centerism or society-centerism have taken their policy area under investigation as a single entity. Consequently, they have reached conclusions that are one-sided, either accepting or rejecting the idea of state autonomy. I argue that the idea of state autonomy can be better examined by identifying various levels of state collectivity. Below, I endeavor to test the three assumptions of the statist debate, i.e., autonomy, restraint and persistence, in the context of the Indian environmental policy.

Undoubtedly, the state has displayed a preference of its own in identifying and fostering the environmental issue in India. The establishment of the first governmental committee was neither in response to the voice of the majority, nor was it a reaction to any particular interest in the society. The government took the initiative in the policy area and played a paternalistic role. In fact, the action of the government was in direct conflict with the established elite interest. Governmental actions were meant to challenge the status quo, even if superficially, and were undoubtedly aimed at restricting the economic freedom enjoyed by the elite, namely the industrial and business community. Despite a close corporate-style alliance with this community, the government was able to enact important legislation against the discharge of water and air pollutants. It is interesting to note that no significant public pressure existed at that time. Governmental actions, however, have increased the level of public awareness since then.

The state has clearly not been a pawn in the hands of the bourgeoisie class, as suggested by the neo-Marxists; nor has it been a mere arbitrator between various conflicting interests, as conceded by the pluralists. The activities of the Indian state in the environmental policy area seem to support the argument forwarded by Nordlinger that "the democratic state is not only frequently autonomous insofar as it regularly acts upon its preferences, but also markedly autonomous in doing so even when its preferences diverge from the demands of the most powerful groups in civil society."[26] The state in the present context of the environmental policy worked against the interests of the industrial/developmentalist class. Nevertheless, being aware of the possibility of confrontation, the state generated its own defense by seeking the support of the scientific community through consultative mechanisms. Since no strong support was to be expected from the public, the role of the scientific community became critical in justifying the state's bold actions against the dominant economic interests. In the initial stages of the policy formulation process, the state opted for a closed process, where outside consultants played a significant role, but the affected parties, i.e., the industrial and development oriented communities, were not invited to participate. This helped the government to keep the environmental issue outside of the realm of political negotiations. The government, in fact, emphasized the morality of the environmental issue; and by doing so, it managed to undermine the political fervor of the dominant classes.

The high degree of state autonomy in this particular case should not, however, be generalized. The environmental issue was unique in the sense that the international community had already accepted its global legitimacy. Moreover, the issue had an unfailing sense of urgency and morality. The position of the issue was further secured by the personal attention given to it by Mrs. Gandhi. It is not clear whether the issue would have attained a similar level of status were it not for Mrs. Gandhi's personal crusade. Subsequently, the question of state autonomy, in this case, has depended on the personal charisma of the leader. Whether a state can assert its preferences in conditions of weak leadership is still open for debate.

Whereas the state played an autonomous role at the top level of political activity, its autonomy was greatly restrained at the lower levels of activity. In fact, the incongruity between state officials and their surroundings is found to be the major reason behind the ineffectual implementation of the environmental policy. I find that the environment-related state activities at the street level are almost fully controlled by the dominant interests in the society.

Environmental officials are forced to use their discretionary powers to perpetuate the interests of the elite, while elected officials are persuaded to conform to the rules of the existing feudalistic system. State officials, whether elected or appointed, are indeed allowed to use their state authority to gain personal benefits, but they are not permitted to use the same authority to obtain policy compliance. For instance, significant tangible and non-tangible benefits are available to site inspectors for ignoring emission standards. These benefits are available to them because of their discretionary powers; but at the same time, the officials are unable to use their power position to seek compliance from polluting industries. Industries almost always have their "connections" with the higher-up authorities that they can use to undermine the power of site-inspectors.

The assumption of congruity between the state and its surroundings is relevant at the national level, but the assumption does not hold true at the local level. The "local state" is restrained not only from using its discretionary power, but it is also barred from using its legitimate authority.

Based on the study of the environmental policy process, I argue that the two different contexts in which national and local state officials operate have produced two separate state collectivities in the nation. The national state collectivity (NSC) is assertive, explicit, and innovative. Due to its control over patronage, it can demand conformity, compliance and loyalty from the dominant classes. Its autonomy is preserved due to a close competition for its patronage between various contenders. On the other hand, the local state collectivity (LSC) is submissive, subordinated and reactionary. Its autonomy is restricted by social and economic forces that are able to isolate it from the main power source. Inactivity, thus, becomes the strategy of self-preservation for local state actors.

Despite having conflicting goals and strategies, the two state collectivities coexist and cooperate. In the environmental policy area, they openly accept the existence of each other and use it to justify their actions. The top level environmental officials, for instance, hide their inefficiency behind their complaints of local officials' incompetency and unwillingness. Local officials, on the other hand, pass the blame of policy failure to the insensitivity of their national counterparts. In fact, the local level environmental officials often find more in common with other horizontally located officials than with their higher-up environmental officials. To make the situation even worse, elected officials at both levels point their fingers at career officials. Since all parties benefit, the situation continues and separate state collectivities persist.

In brief, the analysis of the Indian environmental policy process suggests that the identities of national and local state officials are not necessarily the same. Two, or perhaps more, collectivities exist under the banner of one abstract state collectivity.   In this case, the Indian state enjoys a considerable degree of autonomy at the national level, whereas its ability to seek congruence from its environment at the local level is severely limited.

Future Trends

The Indian environmental policy continues to be in a transitional and experimental stage. The government has taken a paternalistic role in which it enjoys the exclusive right of directing the future course of action. State regulation continues to be the major policy strategy and bureaucratic administration stands as the primary implementing tool. The government continues to play a critical role in the molding of the environmental culture of the nation.

The politicalness of the environmental issue is on rise. Several recent developments signal the dawn of a new "environmental era" in the Indian politics. Mr. V.P. Singh's government, which took its charge after the 1989 elections, showed its solid commitment for environmental preservation by appointing Maneka Gandhi, a staunch environmentalist and an extremely outspoken politician, to the Ministry of Environment and Forests. Within a few months, Maneka Gandhi, because of her directness and her aggresive style of operation, unknowingly succeeded in annoying several top officials and businessmen. However, her step-on-others'-toe style certainly benefitted the environmental issue. Her controversial stand on more than one occasion attracted the media attention. Her commitment gave the Ministry a political platform of its own.

However, the government, because of its weak political base, found this new form of environmental issue unpalatable. The government faced pressure not only from the industrialists but also from its own civil servants. The Singh government surrendered to the mounting pressures and created a new administrative barrier between the political power center and Maneka Gandhi. The barrier came in the form of a newly created position of the Union Minister of Environment. The appointment of Nilamani Routray, a 77-year old political veteran, to this position was also significant. Routray had a reputation of being modest. In addition, Routray and Maneka had never been on friendly terms. The Union Minister was to assume the ultimate responsibility in the Ministry, which until this point was symbolically vested with the Prime Minister, but was practically enjoyed by Maneka Gandhi, the Minister of State for Environment. Immediately after the appointment, Routray issued an executive order divesting Maneka Gandhi of her powers. She was left in-charge of 17 defined tasks, which, according to the critics, were nothing more than the managment of "Delhi Zoo."[27]

The ministry, under Maneka Gandhi's supervision, took several major steps to strengthen its power base. The most innovative idea was to establish separate environmental courts for speedy justice in cases relating to violation of environmental acts. The proposal failed to win government's approval in the first round, but Maneka Gandhi shows her commitment to continue the fight.[28] The rift between the two ministers, which continues to intensify, clearly indicates that the environmental issue is beginning to mature.

The last 15 years of governmental activism in the environmental policy area have generated several social and political changes that warrant a more serious environmental battle in the future. Considering the political and social forces surrounding the issue, it is unlikely that the issue will remain symbolic for long. First, the level of environmental literacy in the nation has increased, making it mandatory, and not only optional, for the government to produce visible results. Second, as a result of the environmental movement, several new groups have entered the political power game: rural women have found their interests manifested through the Chipko Aandolan; village workers have identified environmental concerns to be an important vehicle for them to raise their voices against industries. These groups are likely to continue their fight because, for them, the environment issue is not only an end, but it is also a means to fight against social injustice. Third, the environmental bureaucracy has already carved its niche in the enormous public sector, and its interests are best served by strengthening the environmental issue.

In the future, the Indian government is likely to face a more real pressure to remain active in the management of the environment. Yet, considering the economic and political resource base, its options will continue to be limited. In fact, the reconciliatory approach of the government is most likely to come under attack from the developmentalists and environmentalists alike. Nevertheless, any major shift in the government's strategy to manage the environment will depend on its ability to restructure the local policy culture. In addition, political and economic factors will also shape the strength of the environmental issue. Since the government lacks the ability to generate its own resources to provide for environmental protection, it will continue to emphasize campaign and cooperation as its important policy mechanisms and will continue to engage more heavily in regulations. At least as long as the developmental challenge exists in its present intensity, reconciliation, rather than resolution, is likely to remain as the primary goal of environmental politics.

Notes

1. The most notable work in this direction is of Robert J. McIntyre and James B. Thornton, "On the Environmental Efficiency of Economic Systems," *Soviet Studies*, 30 (1978).

2. The adjective "open" is used to describe a system in which political processes, especially the decision making process, is open to the public for its input and surveillance. The "closed" system, thus, is a system in which political processes are blocked from outside influences.

3. Lester Ross, *Environmental Policy in China* (Bloomington: Indiana University Press, 1988); T. Gustafson, *Reform in Soviet Politics: Lessons of Recent Policies on Land and Water* (Cambridge: Cambridge University Press, 1981); M.I. Goldman, *The Spoils of Progress: Environmental Policy in Soviet Union* (Cambridge: Cambridge University Press, 1972).

4. Ross, ibid.

5. Charles E. Ziegler, "Soviet Environmental Policy and Soviet Central Planning: A Reply to McIntyre and Thornton," *Soviet Studies*, 32 (January 1980): 124-134.

6. Lennart Lundqvist's comparative study of the American and Swedish environmental policy is particularly illustrative of this point. In his book, *The Hare and the Tortoise: Clean Air Policies in the United States and Sweden* (Ann Arbor: University of Michigan, 1980), he argues that the Swedish policy is more effectual than the American policy due to the nature of decision-making in Sweden, which is relatively more closed than the American.

7. James P. Lester, "Partisanship and Environmental Control: The Mediating Influence of State Organizational Structures," *Environment and Behavior*, 12: 101-131; Paul B. Downing & Kenneth Hanf, eds., *International Comparisons in Implementing Pollution Control* Boston: Kluwer-Nijhoff, 1983; Kingsley W. Game, "Controlling Air Pollution: Why Some States Try Harder?" *Policy Studies Journal*, 7: 728-738.

8. Paul A. Sabatier, "State and Local Environmental Policy," *Policy Studies Journal,"* 1 (1980): 217-225; James P. Lester, "Partisanship and Environmental Policy: The Mediating Influence of State Organizational Structures," *Environment and Behavior*, 12 (1980); Mathew A. Crenson, *The Unpolitics of Air Pollution: A Study of Non-Decision-making in Cities* (Baltimore: John Hopkins, 1971).

9. Joseph L. Badaracco, Jr., *Loading the Dice: A Five-country Study of Vinyl Chloride Regulation* (Cambridge: Harvard Business School Press, 1985). The thesis is also supported by Ronald Brickman, Sheila Jasanoff and Thomas Ilgen, *Controlling Chemicals: The Politics of Regulation in Europe and the United States* (Ithaca: Cornell University Press, 1985).

10. Jeffrey Leonard and David Morell, "Emergence of Environmental Concern in Developing Countries: a Political Perspective," *Stanford Journal of International Law*, 17 (1981): 281-313; Lester Ross, "The Implementation of Environmental Policy in China: A Comparative Perspective," *Administration and Society*, 15 (1984): 489-516; Renu Khator and Lester Ross, "Water Pollution Policy in India," *International Journal of Environmental Studies*, 33 (1989): 79-91; R. M. Lasacca, "Pollution Control Legislation and Experience in a Developing Country: The Philippines," *Journal of Developing Areas*, 8 (1974): 537-556.

11. R.W. Cobb, J.K. Ross, and M.H. Ross, "Agenda-building as a comparative political process," *American political Science Review*, 76 (1976): 126-138.

12. William M. Chandler and Alan Siaroff, "Postindustrial Politics in Germany and the Origins of the Greens," *Comparative Politics*, 18 (1986): 303-326.

13. Steven Reed, *Japanese Prefectures and Policy-making* (Pittsburgh: University of Pittsburgh Press, 1986).

14. Ronald Inglehart, "Postmaterialism in an Environment of Uncertainty," *American Political Science Review*, 75 (1981): 880-900.

15. D. Sears et. al., "Self-interest vs. Symbolic Politics in Policy Attitudes and Presidential Voting," *American Political Science Review*, 74 (1980): 670-684.

16. D. Kinder and R. Kiewit, "Sociotropic Politics: The American Case," *British Journal of Political Science*, 11 (1981): 129-161.

17. Digvijay Pratap Sinh, *The Eco-vote: People's Representatives and Global Environment* (New Delhi: Prentice-Hall, 1985).

18. Michael Lipsky, *Street-Level Bureaucracy: Dilemmas of the Individual in Public Services* (New York: Russell Sage, 1980).

19. Statistics provided by Gujarat Forest Department and quoted in Sevanti Ninan, "Gujarat: Many Trees, Little Firewood," in *The State of India's Environment, 1984-85: The Second Citizen's Report*, ed. by Anil Agarwal and Sunita Narain (New Delhi: Centre for Science and Environment, 1985), pp. 53-54.

20. The word "feudal" is used to denote to those powerful land-holders who are not feudal in the literal sense, but whose power base is still feudalistic.

21. *Bringing the State Back In* (Cambridge: Cambridge University Press, 1985).

22. The "Statism" grew primarily in response to the behavioralists on one side, and the Neo-marxists on the other hand, "who together considered the state as primarily an arena or political market for contending societal forces, thus denigrating the institutions of government," said Forrest D. Colburn in "Statism, Rationality, and State Centerism-A Review Article," *Comparative Politics*, 20 (July 1988): 485-494.

23. Stephen D. Krasner, "Approaches to the State: Alternative Conceptions and Historical Dynamics-A Review Article," *Comparative Politics*,

16 (January 1984): 223-246. According to Krasner, the "state" as applied in state-centrist studies could mean (1) government (2) bureaucracy or administrative apparatus (3) ruling class, and even (4) a normative order. G.L. Clark and M. Dear in *State Apparatus: Structures and Language of Legitimacy* (Boston: Allen & Unwin, 1984) have identified 18 possible theories of "state."

24. "The State in An Era of Cascading Politics," *Comparative Politics*, 21 (April 1988): 15.

25. Among the most illustrative and insightful studies are Leonard Binder, *In a Moment of Enthusiasm: Political Power and the Second Stratum in Egypt* (Chicago: University of Chicago Press, 1978); Clement H. Moore, *Images of Development: Egyptian Engineers in Search of Industry* (Cambridge: MIT Press, 1980); Alfred Stephen, *State and Society: Peru in Comparative Perspective* (Princeton: Princeton University Press, 1978); Peter Hall, *Governing the Economy: The Politics of State Intervention in Britain and France* (New York: Oxford University Press, 1986); and Eric Nordlinger, *On the Autonomy of the Democratic State* (Cambridge: Harvard University Press, 1981).

26. Nordlinger, Ibid, 1.

27. "Routray, Maneka Rift Comes to the Fore," *Indian Express*, 2 June 1990.

28. Based upon my informal interview with Maneka Gandhi, 3 August 1990 at her New Delhi office.

Bibliography

Agarwal, Anil & Sunita Narain (1985). *The State of India's Environment, 1984-85: The Second Citizen's Report*. New Delhi: Centre for Science and Environment.

Agarwal, Anil, Ravi Chopra & Kalpana Sharma (1982). *The State of India's Environment, 1982: A Citizen's Report*. New Delhi: Centre for Science and Environment.

Anderson, Fredrick R., et al. (1977). *Environmental Improvement Through Economic Incentives*. Baltimore: John Hopkins University Press.

Anderson, Robert S. and Walter Huber (1988). *The Hour of the Fox*. New Delhi: Vistaar.

Arya, O.P. (1976). "Forest Policy," *The Administrator*. 21: 425-427.

Arya, V.P. (1981). *A Guide to Industrial Licensing in India*. New Delhi: Iyengar Consultancy.

Bachleti, N. (1987). *Social Forestry in India: Problems and Prospects*. New York: Advent.

Badaracco, Joseph L., Jr. (1985). *Loading the Dice: A Five-country Study of Vinyl Chloride Regulation*. Cambridge: Harvard University Press.

Baden, John & Richard L. Stroup (1981) *Bureaucracy vs. Environment*. Ann Arbor: University of Michigan Press.

Bahuguna, Sunder Lal (1984). *Chipko Message*. Sylyara, India: Chipko Information Centre.

Baker, Randall (1989). "Institutional Innovation, Development and Environmental Management: An 'Administrative Trap' Revisited," *Public Administration and Development*, 9: 29-47 and 9: 159-168.

Bandopadhyay, J., N.D. Jayal, U. Schoettli & Chhatrapati Singh (1985). *India's Environment: Crises and Responses*. Dehradun: Natraj.

Bansal, P.L. (1974). *Administrative Development in India*. New Delhi.

Barrett, Richard N. (1982). *International Dimensions of the Environmental Crisis*. Boulder: Westview.

Bassow, W. (1979). "The Third World: Changing Attitudes Toward Environmental Planning," *ANNALS*, 444: 112-114.

Basu, R.K., D.P. Panchal & S.V. Mandke (1980). "Industrial Noise," *Institute of Engineers Journal*, 60: 58-60.

Baumol, William and Wallace Oates (1979). *Economics, Environmental Policy and the Quality of Life*. Englewood Cliffs: Prentice-Hall.

Bharadwaj, R.K. (1980). *Democracy in India*. New Delhi: Asia Books.

Bhargava, A. & M. Bhargava (1982). "Public Awareness About Air Pollution: An Opinion Survey for Jaipur City," *Scanvenger*, 6-11.

Bhat, H.R. (1981). *Problems of the Management of Bamboo Resource in Tamilnadu*. Bangalore: Indian Institute of Management.

Bhatia, J. (1986). "India Finds Green Gold in its Social Forests," *Far Eastern Economic Review*, 133: 38-45.

Bhatt, Anil (1979). "Colonial Bureaucratic Culture and Development Administration: Portrait of an Old-fashioned Indian Bureaucrat,' *Journal of Commonwealth and Comparative Politics*, 17: 159-175.

Bhatt, S. (1986). *Environmental Laws and Water Resources Management*. New Delhi: Radiant.

Bhattacharya, A.Q. (1978). "Irrigation and Water Management by the Damodar Valley Corporation," *Journal of Developing Studies*, 15: 34-58.

Boehmer-Christiansen, S. (1988). "Black Mist and Acid Rain - Science as Fig Leaf of Policy," *Political Quarterly*, 59: 145-160.

Boserup, Ester (1976). "Environment, Population and Technology in Primitive Societies," *Population and Development Review*, 2: 21-36.

Bouton, Marshall M. & Philip Oldenburg, eds. (1988). *India Briefing: 1988*. Boulder: Westview.

Brickman, Ronald, Sheila Jasanoff & Thomas Ilgen (1985). *Controlling Chemicals: The Politics of Regulation in Europe and the United States*. Ithaca: Cornell University Press.

British Government of India (1865). *The Forest Act, 1865*. New Delhi.

Brookes, S.K. (1976). "The Growth of the Environment as a Political Issue in Britain," *British Journal of Political Science*, 6: 245-255.

Brown, Lester (1981). *Building a Sustainable Society*. New York: W.W. Norton.

Burley, J. (1983). *Ostalles to Tree Planting in Arid and Semi-arid Lands: Comparative Case Studies from India and Kenya*. Lanham: Berman-UNIPUB.

Butler, David et al. (1984). *A Compendium of Indian Elections*. New Delhi: Arnold-Heinemann.

Caldwell, Lynton (1972). *In Defense of the Earth: International Protection of the Biosphere*. Bloomington, In: Indiana University Press.

Carras, Mary C. (1979). *Indira Gandhi in the Crucible of Leadership: A Political Biography*. Boston: Beacon Press.

Center for International Environmental Information (1980). *Government Agencies with Environmental Responsibilities in Developing Countries*. Washington, DC (April 15).

Central Board for Prevention and Control of Water Pollution (1982-1989). *Annual Report*. New Delhi: Government of India.

Chandler, William M. & Alan Siaroff (1986). "Post-industrial Politics in Germany and the Origins of the Greens," *Comparative Politics*, 18: 303-326.

Chandran, V.N. (1981). "Kerala's Vanishing Greenery," *Indian Express* (October 2), 17.

Chatterji, Manas (1981). *Energy and Environment in the Developing Countries*. New York: Wiley.

Chaturvedi, A.N. (1976). "Eucalyptus in India," *Indian Forester*, 102: 57-63.

Chaturvedi, H.R. (1977). *Bureaucracy and Local Community: Dynamics of Rural Development*. Delhi: Allied.

Chengappa, Raj (1989). "Seeking Radical Solutions," *India Today* (January 31), 62-64.

Cigler, B.A. (1987). "Environmental Policy and Management: A New Era," *Policy Studies Journal*, 16: 162-170.

Cobb, R., J.K. Ross & M.H. Ross (1976). "Agenda-building as a Comparative Political Process," *American Political Science Review*, 76: 126-138.

Colburn, Forrest D. (1988). "Statism, Rationality and State-centerism-A Review Article," *Comparative Politics*, 20: 485-494.

Cooper, C.M. & R. Otto (1977). *Social and Economic Evaluation of Environmental Impacts in Third World Countries-A Methodical Discussion*. Sussex: Institute of Development Studies.

Cooper, Charles (1980). *Policy Intervention for Technological Innovation in Developing Countries*. Washington, DC :World Bank.

Crenson, Mathew A. (1971). *The Un-politics of Air Pollution: A Study of Non-Decision-making in the Cities*. Baltimore: John Hopkins.

Crotty, P.M. (1988). "Assessing the Role of Federal Administration Regions: An Analysis," *Public Administration Review*, 48: 642-648.

D'Abreo, Desmond (1982). *People and Forests: The Forest bill and a New Forest Policy*. New Delhi: Indian Social Institute.

Dasgupta, B. (1978). "The Environment Debate: Some Issues and Trends," *Economic and Political Weekly*, February, 384-387.

Davies, K. (1988). "What is Eco-feminism," *Women Environment*, 10: 4-6.

Department of Environment (1984). *Directory of Non-Governmental Organizations in Environment*. New Delhi: Government of India.

-------- (1985). *An Action Plan for Prevention of Pollution of the Ganga*. New Delhi: Government of India.

-------- (1989). *Environmental NGOs In India: A Directory*. New Delhi, Government Of India.

Department of Science and Technology (1981). *A Profile*. New Delhi: Government of India.

-------- (1980). *Report of the Committee for Recommending Legislative Measures and Administrative Machinery for Ensuring Environmental Protection*. New Delhi: Government of India

-------- (1972). *National Committee on Environmental Planning and Coordination Terms of Reference*. New Delhi.

Dernberger, Robert F. & Richard S. Eckaus (1988). *Financing Asian Development 2: China and India*. Lanham: The Asia Society.

Desai, Arijana (1985). *Environmental Perception: The Human Factor in Urban Planning*. New Delhi: Ashish.

Dixit, D. (1981). "Deadly Pollution of Our Rivers," *Imprint*, August, 15-17.

Douglas, J. & R. Hart (1985). *Forest Farming: Towards A Solution to Problems of World Hunger and Conservation*. Boulder: Westview.

Douglas, James (1984). "How Actual Governments Cope with the Paradoxes of Social Choice: Some Anglo-American Comparisons," *Comparative Politics*, 17: 67-84.

Downing, Paul B. & Kenneth Hanf, eds. (1983). *International Comparisons in Implementing Pollution Control*. Boston: Kluwer-Nijhoff.

Downs, Anthony (1972). "Up and Down with Ecology: The Issue-attention cycle," *Public Interest*, 28: 28-50

Dudley, Nigel (1985). *The Death of Trees*. London: Pluto.

Dunlap, Riley E. & K.D. Van Liere (1977). "Further Evidence of Declining Public Concern with Environmental Problems: A Research Note," *Western sociological Quarterly*, 8,

Dunlap, Riley E. "The Impact of Political Orientation and Environmental Attitudes and Actions," *Environment and Behavior*, 7.

Dwivedi, O.P. & B.N. Tiwari (1987). *Environmental Crisis and Hinduism*. New Delhi: Gitanjali.

Dwivedi, O.P. & R.B. Jain (1985). *India's Administrative State*. New Delhi: Gitanjali.

Dwivedi, O.P. & Brij Kishore (1982). "Protecting the Environment from Pollution: A Review of India's Legal and Institutional Mechanism," *Asian Survey*, 22: 894-911.

Dwivedi, O.P. (1977). "Pollution Control Policy and Programmes," *International Review of Administrative Science*, 43: 123-133.

Eckholm, Eric (1979). *Planting for the Future: Forestry for Human Needs*. Washington: Worldwatch Institute, No. 26.

------- (1979). *Planting for the Future: Forestry for Human Needs*. Washington, DC: Worldwatch Institute.

Edelman, Murray (1952). "Governmental Organization and Public Policy," *Public Administration Review*, 12: 276-283.

Elder, C.D. & R.W. Cobb (1983). *The Political Uses of Symbols*. New York: Longman.

Eldersveld, Samuel J. & B. Ahmed (1978). *Citizen and Politics: Mass Political Behavior in India*. Chicago: University of Chicago Press.

Eldersveld, Samuel J. et. al. (1968). *The Citizen and the Administrator in a Developing Democracy: An Empirical Study in Delhi State*. Chicago: Scott Forseman.

Emmel, Thomas C. (1977). *Global Perspectives on Ecology*. Palo Alto, CA: Mayfield Publishing.

Enloe, Cynthia (1975). *The Politics of Pollution in a Comparative Perspective: Ecology and Power in Four Nations*. New York: David Mckay.

Evans, Peter, Dietrich Rueschemeyer & Theda Skocpol (1985). *Bringing the State Back In*. Cambridge: Cambridge University Press.

Fenno, Richard F. (1966). *The Power of the Purse*. Boston: Little, Brown & Co

Fernandes, Walter & Sharad Kulkarni (1983). *Toward A New Forest Policy: People's Rights and Environmental Needs*. New Delhi: Indian Social Institute.

Field, John O. (1981). *Consolidating Democracy: Politicization and Participation in India*. New Delhi: Manohar.

------- (1980). *Consolidating Democracy: Politicization and Partisanship in India*. New Delhi: Manohar.

Fisher, Anthony (1981). *Resource and Environmental Economics*. Cambridge: Cambridge University Press.

Fowler, Linda L. & Ronald G. Shaiko (1987). "The Grassroots Connection: Environmental Activists and Senate Roll Calls," *Amercian Journal of Political Science*, 31: 484-510.

Frankel, F.R. (1978). *India's Political Economy: 1947-1977*. Princeton: Princeton University Press.

Frederick, Buttel & William Flinn (1978). "The Politics of Environmental Concern," *Environment and Behavior*, 10: 17-36.

Futehally, Z. (1975) "Conservation in a World of Rising Expectations," *Ekistics*, 37: 50-52.

Gadgil, M., S. Narendra Prasad & Rauf Ali (1982). *Forest Management in India: A Critical Review*. Bangalore: Indian Institute of Science.

Galper, Jeffry H. (1975). *The Politics of Social Services*. Englewood Cliffs: Prentice-Hall.

Game, Kingsley W. (1979). "Controlling Air Pollution: Why Some States Try Harder?" *Policy Studies Journal*, 7: 728-38.

Gandhi, Indira (1972). "Man and His Environment," Washington: Proceedings of the *United Nations Conference on Human Environment*.

Ganapathy, R.S., S.R. Ganesh, R.M. Maru, Samuel Paul & Ram Mohan Rao, ed. (1985). *Public Policy and Policy Analysis in India*. New Delhi: Sage.

Gant, G.F. (1966). "A Note Application of Development Administration," *Public Policy*, 15: 199-211.

Ghose, S. (1975). *Indira Gandhi, the Resurgent Congress and Socialism*. New Delhi: Asia Books.

Ghosh, A. (1970). *The Split in the Indian National Congress*. Calcutta: Vaibahv.

Gill, Raj (1980). "Waste Water Hazard to Urbanization," *The Hindustan Times*, (April 23), 1 & 8.

Glaeser, Bernhard, ed. (1984). *Ecodevelopment: Concepts, Projects, Strategies*. New York: Pergamon Press.

Goldman, M.I. (1972). *The Spoils of Progress: Environmental Policy in Soviet Union*. Cambridge: Harvard University Press.

Gray, Virginia (1973). "Innovation in the States: A Diffusion Study," *American Political Science Review*, 67: 1174-1185.

Gupta, Ranjit, Prava Banerji & Amar Guleria (1981). *Tribal Unrest and Forestry Management in Bihar*. Ahmedabad: Indian Institute of Management.

Gupta: S.D. (1988). "Development Dilemma: Debate over Project Delays by Environmental Bureaucracy," *India Today* (November 30), 60-61.

Gustafson, T. (1981). *Reform in Soviet Politics: Lessons of Recent Policies on Land and Water*. Cambridge: Cambridge University Press.

Hardgrave, Robert L., Jr. (1984). *India Under Pressure: Prospects for Stability and Change*. Boulder: Westview Press.

Hardgrave, Robert L., Jr. & Stanley A. Kochanek (1986) *India: Government and Politics in a Developing Nation*. San Diego: Harcourt Brace Jovanovich.

Hardgrave, Robert, L., Jr. (1970). "The Congress in India: Crisis and Split," *Asian Survey*, 10: 256-262.

Hart, Henry C. (1976). *Indira Gandhi's India: A Political System Reaprraised*. Boulder: Westview.

Hartman, Horst (1982). *Political Parties in India*. New Delhi: Meenakshi.

Hasan, Zoya, S.N. Jha & Rasheeduddin, ed. (1989). *The State, Political Processes and Identity*. New Delhi: Sage.

Hirsch, Fred (1976). *Social Limits to Growth*. Cambridge: Harvard University Press.

Hoberg, George, Jr. (1986). "Technology, Political Structure and Social Regulation: Review Article," *Comparative Politics*, 18: 357-376.

Holdgate, Martin (1979). *A Perspective on Pollution*. Cambridge: Cambridge University Press.

Huntington, Samuel P. (1976). "Will More Countries Become Democratic?" *Political Science Quarterly*, 99: 193-218.

India (1971). *Some Aspects of Environmental Degradation and its Control in India*. A country report prepared for presentation at the UN Conference on Human Environment.

India, The Consitution of (1950). New Delhi: Government of India.

Inglehart, Ronald (1981). " Post-materialism in an Environment of Uncertainty," *American Political Science Review*, 75: 880-900.

Ippopolito, D.S., T.G. Walker and K.L. Kolson (1976). *Public Opinion and Responsible Democracy*. Englewood: Cliffs: Prentice-Hall.

Isaac, P. & W. Pescod (1982). "Water Pollution Research and Its Application in Developing Countries," *Water Supply & Management*, 14: 205-213.

Jain, L.C. (1985). *Grass Without Roots: Rural Development Under Government Auspicies*. New Delhi: Sage.

Jain, R.K. & B. Hutchings, eds. (1978). *Environment Impact Analysis: Emerging Issues in Planning*. Urbana: University of Illinois Press.

Jalees, K. & R. Vemuri (1980). "Pesticide Pollution in India," *International Journal of Environmental Studies*, 15: 49-53.

James, Jeffrey (1978). "Growth, Technology and the Environment in Less Developed Countries: A Survey," *World Development*, 6: 937-965.

Johnson, Basil & Leonard Clive (1979). *India: Resources and Development*. New York: Barnes & Noble Books.

Jones, Charles O. (1975). *Clean Air: The Policies and Politics of Pollution Control*. Pittsburgh: University of Pittsburgh Press.

Jones, Charles O. (1974). "Speculative Augmentation in Federal Air Pollution Policy-making," *Journal of Politics*, 36: 438-464.

Jordan, Carl, ed. (1987). *Amazonian Rain Forests: Eco-system Disturbance and Recovery*. New York: Springer-Verlag.

Joshi, Gopa (1983). "Forests and Forest Policy in India," *Social Scientist*, 11: 43-52.

Kannan, K.P. (1982). "Forests for Industry's Profit," *Economic and Political Weekly*, 17: 836-838.

Kaufman, Herbert (1970). *The Forest Ranger: A Study in Administrative Behavior*. Baltimore: John Hopkins University.

Kay, David A. & Harold K. Jacobson (1983). *Environmental Prtoection: The International Dimension*, Totowa, NJ: Allenheld, Osmun & Co.

Kelly, Donald R. (1976). "Environmental Policy-making in the USSR: The Role of Industrial and Environmental Interest Groups," *Soviet Studies*, 28: 570-589.

Kelly, Donald R., R.R. Wescott & K. Stunkel (1976). *The Economic Superpowers and the Environment: The United States, the Soviet Union and Japan*. San Francisco: W.H. Freeman & Co.

Kerala Water Pollution Control Board (1983). *Annual Report*. Trivendram: Kerala State Government.

Kerr, Alex (1981). *Resources and Development in the Indian Ocean Region*. Boulder: Westview Press.

Khan, R.N. (1980). "Managing the Physical Environment: An Empirical Approach," *Impact of Science on Society*, 30: 347-356.

Khanna, Gopesh Nath (1990). *Environment Problems and the United Nations*. New Delhi: Ashish.

Khator, Renu & Lester Ross (1989). "Water Pollution Policy in India," *International Journal of Environmental Studies*, 33: 79-91.

Khator, Renu (1984). "Environment as a Political Issue in Developing Countries: A Study of Envrionmental Pollution in India," *International Journal of Environmental Studies*, 23: 105-112.

------- (1987). "Determinants of Policy Performance: an Empirical Examination of the Impact of Environmental bureaucracy in India," *Indian Journal of Public Administration*, 33: 20-30.

------- (1989). *Forests: The People and the Government*. New Delhi: National Book Organization.

------- (1989). "Eco-development and Developing Countries: Chipko Aandolan in India," *Journal of Developing Societies*, 5: 58-63.

Khorev, B.S. (1987). "On Basic Directions of Environmental Policy in the USSR," *Soviet Geographer*, 28: 485-489.

Kinder, D. & R. Kiewit (1981). "Sociotropic Politics: the American Case," *British Journal of Political Science*, 11: 129-161.

Kitschelt, Herbert (1988). "Organization and Strategy of Belgian and West German Ecology Parties," *Comparative Politics*, 20: 127-154.

Kneese, Allen V. & Charles L. Schultze (1975). *Pollution, Prices and Public Policy*. Washington, DC: Brookings Institute.

Kneese, Allen V. (1977). *Economics and the Environment*. London: Penguin Books.

------- (1979). "Development and the Environment," *Washington, DC: Resources for the Future*.

Knoepfel, P. & N. Watts, eds. (1983). *Environmental Politics and Policies: An International Perspective*. Frankfurt: Campus Verlag.

Kochanek, Stanley A. (1974). *Business and Politics in India*. Berkeley: University of California Press.

Kohli, Atul ed. (1988). *India's Democracy*. Princeton: Princeton University Press.

Kothari, Rajni (1980). "Environment and Alternative Development," *Alternatives*, 5.

Krasner, Stephen D. (1984). "Approaches to the State: Alternative Conceptions and Historical Dynamics-A Review Article," *Comparative Politics*, 16: 223-246.

Kulkarni, Sharad (1982). "Encroachment on Forests: Government Versus the People," *Economic and Political Weekly*, 17: 55-59.

Kunwar, S.S., ed. (1982). *Hugging the Himalayas: The Chipko Experience*. gopeshwar, India: Dasholi Gram Swarajya Mandal.

Lasaca, R.M. (1974). "Pollution Control Legislation and Experience in a Developing Country: The Philippines," *Journal of Developing Areas*, 8: 537-556.

Lee, J. & R. Goodland (1986). "Economic Development and the Environment," *Finance Development*, 23: 36-39.

Leonard, J.H. & D. Morell (1981). "Emergence of Environemental Concern in Developing Countries: A Political Perspective," *Stanford Journal of International Law*, 17: 281-313.

Lester, James P. (1980). "Partisanship and Environmental Control: The Mediating Influence of State Organizational Structures," *Environment and Behavior*, 12: 101-131.

Lindblom, Charles (1977). *Politics and Markets: The World's Political-economic Systems*. New York: Basic.

Lipsky, Michael (1980). *Street-Level Bureaucracy: Dilemmas of the Individual in Public Services*. New York: russell Sage.

Lok Sabha Debates. New Delhi; Government of India.

Lowe, Philip & Jane Goyder (1983). *Environmental Groups in Politics*. London: Allen & Urwin.

Lundqvist, Lennart J. (1974). "Do Political Structures Matter in Environmental Politics?" *American Behavioral Scientist*, 17: 731-750.

Lundqvist, Lennart J. (1973). "The Comparative Study of Environmental Policy," *Policy Studies Journal*, 1.

------- (1980). *The Hare and Tortoise: Clean Air Policies in the United States and Sweden*. Ann Arbor: University of Minchigan Press.

------- (1974). *Environmental Policies in Canada, Sweden, and the United States: A Comparative Overview*. Beverly Hills: Sage.

Luttbeg, N.R. (1974). *Public Opinion and Public Policy: Models of Political Linkage*. Homewood, IL: Dorsey.

Maheshwari, S.R. (1985). *Rural Development in India*. New Delhi: Sage.

Mandelbaum, David G. (1973). "Social Components of Indian Fertility," *Economic and Political Weekly*, 8: 171-173.

Mann, Dean E., ed. (1981). *Environmental Policy Formation: The Impact of Values, Ideology and Standards*. Lexington: Lexington Books.

Manor, James (1986). "India: Awakening or Decay," *Current History*, (March), 101-104.

Mansingh, S. (1984). *India's Search for Power: Indira Gandhi's Foreign Policy 1966-82*. New Delhi: Sage.

Masani, Zarrer (1976). *Indira Gandhi: A Biography*. New York: Crowell.

Mathew, Thomas (1982). "Interveiw: Environment for Survival," *Indian International Centre Journal*, 356-370.

Mathew, Thomas (1982). "Government Response to Environmental Needs in India," *Indian International Centre Journal*, 238-248.

Mayur, Rashmi (1979). "Environmental Problems of Developing Countries," *American Acadamy of Political & Social Science Annals*, 444: 89-101.

McKean, Margaret A. (1981). *Environmental Protest and Citizen Politics in Japan*. Berkeley: University of California Press.

Mehta, Ashok (1978). *Report of the Committee on Panchayati Raj Institutions*. New Delhi: Government of India, Ministry of Agriculture and Irrigation.

Mehta, R.S. (1978). "Air Pollution Problem in India," *Asian Environment*, 1: 26-28.

Mellor, John A. (1976). *The New Economics of Growth: A Strategy for India and the Developing World*. Ithaca: Cornell University Press.

Mellos, K. (1988). "The Conception of "Reason" in Modern Ecological Theory," *Canadian Journal of Political Science*, 21: 715-727.

Milne, R.S. (1973). "Bureaucracy and Development Administration," *Public Administration*. 51.

Ministry of Science and Technology (1974). *The Water (Prevention and Control of Pollution) Act, 1974*. New Delhi: Government of India.

Ministry of Environment and Forests (1986). *The Environment (Protection) Act*. New Delhi: Government of India.

Ministry of Environment and Forests (1987). *Annual Report: 1986-87*. New Delhi: Government of India.

Ministry of Science and Technology (1981). *The Air (Prevention and Control of Pollution) Act, 1984*. New Delhi: Government of India.

Misra, B.B. (1986). *Government and Bureaucracy in India: 1974-1976*. New Delhi: Oxford University Press.

Mitchell, R.C. (1980). *Public Opinion on Environmental Issues*. Washington, DC: US Council on Environmental Quality.

Moore, Barrington, Jr. (1966). *Social Origin of Dictatorship and Democracy*. Boston: Beacon.

Morris-Jones, W.H. (1984). "India--More Questions than Answers," *Asian Survey*, 24: 809-816.

Myers, Norman (1975). "China's Approach to Environmental Conservation," *Environmental Affairs*, 5: 33-63.

Naik, J.P. (1973). *Equality, Quality and Quantity: The Elusive Triangle in Indian Education*. New Delhi: Allied.

Narayen, S. (1976). "The Forests in the Life of the Tribals," *The Administrator*, 21: 208-211.

National Commission on Agriculture (1976). *Report of the National Commission on Agriculture Part IX: Forestry*. New Delhi: Government of India.

Newsom, D.D. (1988/89) "The New Diplomatic Agenda: Are Governments Ready?" *International Affairs*, 65: 29-41.

Nijkamp, Peter (1980). *Environmental Policy Analysis: Operational Methods and Models*. New York: Wiley.

Obeng, Letita E. (1980). "Some Environmental Issues in Water for Development," *Water Supply and Management*, 4: 115-128.

OECD (1977). *Environmental Policy in Sweden*. Paris: OECD.

Pal, B.P. (1981). *Environmental Conservation and Development*. New Delhi: Indian Environmental Society.

Palmer, Norman D. (1967). "India's Fourth General Election," *Asian Survey*, 7: 275-291.

Pande, J. & S.M. Das (1980). "Metallic Contents in Water and Sediments of Lake Nainital, India," *Water, Air and Soil Pollution*, 13: 3-8.

Parikh, Jyoti K. (1977). "Environmental Problems of India and Their Possible Trends in Future," *Environmental Conservation*, 4: 189-199.

Passow, Shirley S. (?). "Stockholm's Planners Discover People Power," *Journal of the American Institute of Planners*, 39.

Pearce, D.W. (1977). *Environmental Economics*. London: Longmans.

Pierce, J.C., T. Tsurutani & N.P. Lovrich, Jr. (1986). "Vanguards and Rearguards in Environmental Politics: A Comparison of Activists in Japan and the United States," *Comparative Political Studies*, 18: 419-447.

Pierce, J.C. et. al. (1987). "Culture, Politics and Mass Publics: Traditional and Modern Supporters of the New Environmental Paradigm in Japan and the United States," *Journal of Politics*, 49: 54-79.

Pilat, J.F. (1980). *Ecological Politics: The Rise of the Green Movement*. Beverly Hills: Sage.

Planning Commission (1969). *The Fourth Five Year Plan: A Summary*. New Delhi: Government of India.

Planning Commission (1985). *The Seventh Five-Year Plan*. New Delhi: Government of India.

Planning Commission (1952). *The First Five Year Plan: A Summary*. New Delhi: Government of India.

Planning Commission (1978). *Report of the Working Group on block Level Planning*. New Delhi: Government of India.

Portney, Paul R. (1978). *The U.S. Environmental Policy*. Baltimore: John Hopkins.

Prasad, V.S. (1980). "Organics in Drinking Water," *Journal of the Institution of Engineers (India)*, 60: 38-41.

Prottas, Jeffrey (1979). *The Street-Level Bureaucrat in Public Service Bureaucracies*. Lexington: Lexington Books.

Quarles, John (1976). *Cleaning Up America. Boston: Houghton Mifflin Co.*

Rai, Hardwar & S. P. Singh (1973). "Indian Bureaucracy: A Case for Representativeness," *Indian Journal of Public Administration*, 19: 73-77.

Ram, Mohan (1988). "8th Plan Aims at 6% Growth Rate," *India Abroad*. (November 4) 16-18.

Rao, D.N. (1963). "Disparities of Representation Among the Direct Recruits to the IAS," *The Indian Journal of Public Administration*, 11: 88-89.

Rao, U.R. (1979). "Energy, Environment and Ethics," *Society and Science*, 2: 1-15.

Ray, S.D. (1980). "Pollution Spreads to India's Sacred Rivers," *Earthwatch*, 3.

Reed, Steven R. (1986). *Japanese Prefectures and Policymaking*. Pittsburgh: University of Pittsburgh Press.

------- (1981). "Environmental Politics: Some Reflections Based on the Japanese Case," *Comparative Politics*, 13: 253-270.

Reese, Craig (1983). *Deregulation and Environmental Quality: The Use of Tax Policy to Control Pollution in North America and Western Europe*. Westport: Quorum.

Reich, Michael R. (1984). "Mobilizing for Environmental Policy in Italy and Japan," *Comparative Politics*, 16: 379-402.

Reilly, Conor (1975). "Environmental Action in Zambia," *Environment*, 17: 31-35.

Riddel, Robert (1981). *Ecodevelopment*. London: Gower.

Riggs, F.W. (1964). *The Ecology of Development*. Bloomington: Indiana University Press.

Rohrschneider, Robert (1988). "Citizen's Attitudes Toward Environmental Issues: Selfish or Selfless?" *Comparative Political Studies*, 21: 347-367.

Roos, Leslie L., Jr., ed. (1971). *The Politics of Ecosuicide*. New York: Holt, Rinehart and Winston.

Rosenbaum, Walter A. (1973). *The Politics of Environmental Concern*. New York: Praeger.

Rosenthal, Donald B. (1977). *The Expansive Elite: District Politics and State Policy-making in India*. Berkeley: University of California Press.

Ross, Lester (1986). "Market Reform and Collective Action in China," *Comparative Political Studies*, 19: 217-232.

------- (1984). "The Implementation of Environmental Policy in China: A Comparative Perspective," *Administration and Society*, 15: 489-516.

------- (1988). *Environmental Policy in China*. Bloomington: Indiana University Press.

Rourke, Francis E. (1976). *Bureaucracy, Politics and Public Policy*. Boston: Little Brown.

Roy, R. (1975). *Bureaucracy and Development: The Case Study of Indian Agriculture*. New Delhi.

Sabatier, Paul & Geoffrey Wandesforde-Smith (1979). "Major Sources on Environmental Politics, 1974-1977: The Maturing of the Literature," *Policy Studies Journal*, 7: 592-604.

Sadasivan, S.N. (1977). *Party and Democracy in India*. New Delhi: Tata: McGraw-Hill.

Sahagal, N. (1978). *Indira Gandhi's Emergence and Style*. Durham: Carolina Academics.

Sahu, N. (1987). *Economics of Forest Resources Problems and Policies in a Regional Economy*. Delhi: B.R. Publishing.

Sandbach, F. (1980). *Environment, Ideology and Policy*. Oxford: Basil Blackwell.

------- (1978). "A Further Look at the Environment as a Political Issue," *International Journal of Environmental Studies*, 12: 99-110.

Sankhdher, M.M. (1983). *Framework of Indian Politics*. New Delhi: Gitanjali.

Sapru, R.K. (1987). *Environmental Management in India*. New Delhi: Ashish.

Sardana, Nandita (1987). "Foul Fumes," *India Today* (March 31), 55-56.

Schelling, Thomas C. ed. (1983). *Incentives for Environmental Protection*. Cambridge: MIT Press.

Schnaiberg, Allan (1980). *The Environment: From Surplus to Scarcity*. New York: Oxford University Press.

Schumacher, E.F. (1975). *Small is Beautiful: Economics As is People Mattered*. New York: Harper & Row.

Sears, D. et al. (1980). "Self-interest vs. Symbolic Politics in Policy Attitudes and Presidential Voting," *American Political Science Review*, 74: 670-684.

Sekar, T. (19 ?). "Role of Newspapers in Creating Mass Concern with Environmental Issues in India," *International Journal of Environmental Studies*, 17: 115-120.

Selya, Roger Mark (1975). "Water and Air Polluion in Taiwan," *Journal of Developing Areas*, 9: 177-202.

Sigurdson, Jon (1977). "Water Policies in India and China," *Ambio*, 6: 70-76.

Singh, Mahendra Prasad (1981). *Split in a Predominant Party: The Indian National Congress in 1969*. New Delhi: Abhinav.

Singh, V.B. & S. Bose (1984). *Elections in India: Data Handbook on Lok Sabha Elections, 1952-1980*. New Delhi: Sage.

Singhi, N.K. (1974). *Bureaucracy: Positions and persons: Role Structures, Interactions and Value Orientations of Bureaucracy in Rajasthan*. New Delhi: Abhinav.

Sinh, Digvijay Pratap (1985). *The Eco-vote: People's Representatives and Global Environment*. New Delhi: Prentice-Hall.

Sirsikar, V.M. & I. Fernandez (1984). *Indian Political Parties*. Meerut: Meenakshi.

Sivard, Ruth Legar (1988). *World Military and Social Expenditures 1987-88.* Washington, DC: World Priorities.

Smicock, B.L. (1972). 'Environmental Pollution and the Citizen's Movement: The Social Sciences are the significance of Anti-pollution Protest in Japan," *Area Development in Japan*, 5: 19-20.

Smith, V. Kerry (1985). "A Theoretical Analysis of the 'Green Lobby,' *American Political Science Review*, 79: 132-147.

Srinivasan, M.R. (1975). "India: Rubber tires for Bullock Carts," *Environment*, 17: 38-42.

Steel, B.S. & D.L. Soden (1989). "Acid Rain Policy in Canada and the United States: Attitudes of Citizens, Environmental Activists, and Legislators," *Social Science Journal*, 26: 27-44.

Stretton, Hugh (1976). *Capitalism, Socialism and the Environment.* New York: Cambridge University Press.

Taub, Richard, P. (1969). *Bureaucrats Under Stress.* Berkeley: University of California Press.

Tripathi Salil & N.K. Singh (1988). "A Flood of Controversies: Narmada Valley Project," *India Today* (October 31), 74-77.

Troisi, Joseph (1978). *Tribal Religion: Religious Beliefs and Practices Among the Santals.* New Delhi: Manohar.

Tucker, William (1978). "Environmentalism and the Leisure Class," *Harper's Magazine* (February), 49-80.

Tyner, Wallace E. (1978). *Energy Resources & Economic Development in India.* Netherlands: Martinus Nijhoff.

United Nations (1972). *Report of the Secretary General on the United Nations Conference on the Human Environment, Stockholm, Sweden, 5-16 June, 1972.* (UN Doc. A/CONF.48)

Venkatasubramanian, K. & B. Bowonder (1980). "Forest Resources in India," *Futures*, 12: 317-324.

Vogel, David (1986). *National Styles of Regulation: Environmental Policy in Great Britain and the United States*. Ithaca: Cornell University Press.

Vohra, B.B. (1981). "Needed-A Policy for Water," *The Hindustan Times* (June 2), 17 & 21.

Volgyes, Ivan, ed. (1974). *Environmental Deterioration in the Soviet Union and Eastern Europe*. New York: Praeger.

Walker, J. (1969). "The Diffusion of Innovation Among the American States," *American Political Science Review*, 63: 880-899.

Walker, K.J. (1989). "The State in Environmental Management: The Ecological Dimension," *Political Studies*, 37: 25-38.

Walter, Ingo (1975). *International Economics of Pollution*, New York: John Wiley.

Ward, Morris A. (1982). *The Clean Water Act: The Second Decade*. Washington, DC: E. Bruce Harrison.

Weber, T. (1987/88). "Is There Still A Chipko Aandolan?" *Pacific Affairs*, 60: 615-628.

Weidner, Edward W. (1970). *Development Administration in Asia*. Ann Arbor: Books in Demand.

Weiner, Myron (1978). *India at the Polls: The Parliamentary Elections of 1977*. Washington: American Enterprise Institute.

------- (1971). "The 1971 Elections and the Indian Party System," *Asian Survey*, 11: 1153-1166.

Wilson, James Q. (1980). *The Politics of Deregulation*. New York: Basic Books.

World Bank (1988). *World Development Report 1988*. Oxford: Oxford University Press.

Yishai, Y. (1979). "Environment and Development: The Case of Israel," *International Journal of Environmental Studies*, 14: 205-216.

Ziegler, Charles E. (1986). "Issue Creation and Interest Groups in Soviet Environmental Policy," *Comparative Politics*, 18: 171-192.

------- (1980). "Soviet Environmental Policy and Soviet Central Planning: A Reply to McIntyre and Thornton," *Soviet Studies*, 32: 124-134.

Index

About the Author

Renu Khator is assistant professor of Political Science at the University of South Florida. She earned her doctorate at Purdue University in 1985. Having made several research visits to India, Dr. Khator has published several journal articles and also a book entitled *Forests: The People and the Government.*